TYPES OF THINKING

including

A SURVEY OF GREEK PHILOSOPHY

—Photo by Joseph Breitenbach

TYPES OF THINKING

including

A SURVEY OF GREEK PHILOSOPHY

by

John Dewey

TRANSLATED FROM THE CHINESE AND EDITED BY

Robert W. Clopton / Tsuin-Chen Ou

With an Introduction by

Samuel Meyer

PHILOSOPHICAL LIBRARY
NEW YORK

Library of Congress Cataloging in Publication Data

Dewey, John, 1859-1952.
Types of thinking including A survey of Greek
Philosophy.

Includes bibliographical references.
1. Philosophy—History—Addresses, essays, lectures.
I. Title.
B73.D48   1983   109   83-13245
ISBN 0-8022-2404-0

"Philosophy recovers itself when it ceases to be a device for dealing with the problems of philosophers and becomes a method cultivated by philosophers for dealing with the problems of men."

John Dewey
(*The Need for a Recovery of Philosophy*, 1917, reprinted in *On Experience, Nature and Freedom*, pp. 66-67.)

In memory of my brothers Abe and Sol
who gave me courage to think and love.

CONTENTS

A Survey of Greek Philosophy

TYPES OF THINKING

INTRODUCTION

The publication of a history of philosophy by John Dewey is an event for celebration. The lectures had hitherto been available only in Chinese and these suppressed for over thirty years of totalitarian rule.[1]

"In his lectures on 'Types of Thinking', Dewey states and criticizes several schools of philosophic method. Four schools are involved. They are: 1) The Systematizing or Classifying School represented by Aristotle, 2) The Rationalistic or Deductive School represented by Descartes, 3) The Empirical or Sensationalistic School represented by Locke, and 4) The Experimental School represented by Dewey. (Dewey has not mentioned his own name in this connection.)

"Judging by the contents of this series of lectures, it is to be noted that this is his first systematic treatment of the subject. As we know, in his previously published works like the articles in *Studies in Logical Theory* and *Essays in Experimental Logic, How We Think*, and Chapter 25 on 'Theories of Knowledge' in *Democracy and Education*, Dewey had already criticized the traditional methods of philosophy and had advanced his own position as an experimentalist. But the former cases lack systematic, comparative presentation of the schools concerned. One may say that it is in China that Dewey first developed this subject matter into a systematic form. It is also to be remarked that shortly after returning to Columbia University from his visit to China, Dewey offered in 1922-23 a course, the syllabus of which is entitled 'Types of Philosophic Thought.' This syllabus must have been based on his lectures on Types of Thinking. In 1938 Dewey published *Logic: The Theory of Inquiry*. In this epoch-making book Dewey writes another chapter on 'The Logic of Inquiry and Philosophies of Knowledge' similar to Types of Thinking and the chapter mentioned from *Democracy and Education*. In view of these facts, it can be said without much risk that although in terms of content Types of Thinking contains no more material than what appears in Dewey's works concerning the theories of knowledge, it is historically significant because it constitutes an important stage of the development of Dewey's logical thought."[2]

"The major contribution one can make in any field of endeavor is to prepare the way for his successor.... In his early *Essays in Experimental Logic*, written at or before the turn of the century, he indicated the new ways of thinking which are making possible new and promising approaches to contemporary problems...."[3]

Even so acute a critic as John Herman Randall, Jr. notes: "John Dewey has written no volume dealing primarily with the history of philosophic thought. Nor, unless in some now long-forgotten youthful indiscretion, did he ever elect to set before a class the simple record of objective and impartial knowledge of the past."[4]

Far from being a "youthful indiscretion" we have in this volume an opportunity to read Dewey at the height of his powers in lean, almost journalistic prose[5]. He gives the kernal of his mature thoughts in a matrix suitable to students as well as to advanced thinkers of an ancient civilization at a crucial juncture of its history. We are grateful to the publishers and all who have made it possible to have these vitally important lectures finally put in continuous permanent form available to the public and to Dewey scholars alike.

An overseas student attending Dewey's graduate seminar at Columbia University complained: "I did not come to America to hear Dewey lecture on Locke, Hobbes, and Plato. I came to hear Dewey lecture on Dewey." However, the point is that Dewey's thought on Locke, Hobbes, and Plato is the best road to Dewey on Dewey. If you were to assemble your thought on Malthus, Keynes and Darwin, it would approach a closer definition of you than if you attempted a systematic exposition of your formal philosophy.

Many of Dewey's students claim they learned more from Dewey's books than his lectures. Let us eavesdrop on a "Dialogue on Dewey":

Lamont: ...There was no single book that sort of pulled his whole work or system—if he had a system—together. And I understand that toward the end of his life he did start to work on such a book and had finished about three-quarters of it.

Now the story is that that was lost. He and Mrs. Dewey came back one summer from Nova Scotia—they drove—and pulled up in front of their apartment house at Fifth Avenue and 97th Street. They left their bags with the doorman to bring up, and went upstairs in the elevator. When the doorman had brought up the baggage Dewey looked around and said to Roberta, "My heavens, my briefcase isn't here." Mrs. Dewey immediately rushed downstairs. The briefcase *had* been taken out of the car, they knew; but it had disappeared. And in that briefcase was the manuscript of Dewey's almost completed book summarizing his whole philosophy. There was no carbon copy. Perhaps some little boy came in off the street and ran away with the briefcase. I think it was a tragedy.

Farrell: I would say that *Experience and Nature* is a fairly complete account of his views.

Kallen: I would hold it's not a tragedy.

Lamont: Oh! Why, Horace!

Kallen: I think, Corliss, that if you wanted Dewey to state a system, he'd have to contradict himself. He'd have to set up a number of fixed points and a structured order of the universe, and deny practically all the fundamental concepts with which he's identified. He thinks the functional thoughts, and he writes the functional thoughts. And it doesn't matter what field you enter into, his quarrel with the psychologists, and his quarrel with Russell, his quarrel with the neo-realists, all turn on the fact that they want to use rigidities and to deny process.

You remember in *Human Nature and Conduct* the meaning that he gives to habit, which is a key concept there, is such that its bound to allow for variation and to discard the repetitive rigidities we usually identify with habit. And habit is a foundation of human nature; habit as varying indefinitely, from act to act, is the foundation of practically all interpretations of human nature that Dewey makes, as I see it.

Lamont: I would still insist that it was a tragedy, Horace, because this book—unlike *Experience and Nature* which was really quite a technical job and couldn't be understood by the average man, let us say—this outline was going to be in more simple language, something like *Reconstruction in Philosophy*, which is a very readable book. And sure, there may have been inconsistencies that would have come out in it, but I think that it was really a great loss.[6]

In reading *The Later Lectures of Dewey in China 1919-1921* (from which the present volume was extracted) one gets the impression that this book is close to the precious manuscript that Dewey had reconstructed and which was so tragically lost.

It becomes necessary to speak of Dewey's "style" since it came to occupy so much attention in the writings of his critics and made Dewey's consciousness rise at this supposed lack, perhaps unduly so. Style may be a gift. It may also be a matter of growth.

Writing of his earliest specimens of philosophic thought published in 1882:

The articles sent (to the Journal of Speculative Philosophy) were, as I recall them, highly schematic and formal; they were couched in the language of intuitionalism; of Hegel I was then ignorant. My deeper interests had not as yet been met, and in the absence of subject matter that would correspond to them, the only topics at my command were such as were capable of a merely formal treatment. I imagine that my development has been controlled largely by a struggle between a native inclination toward the schematic and formally logical and those incidents of personal experience that compelled me to take account of actual material. Probably there is in the consciously articulated ideas of every thinker an overweighting of just those things that are contrary to his natural tendencies, an emphasis upon those things that are contrary to his intrinsic bent, and which, therefore, he has to struggle to bring to expression, while the native bent, on the other hand, can take care of itself. Anyway, a case might be made out for the proposition that the emphasis upon the concrete, empirical, and "practical" in my later writings is partly due to considerations of this nature. It was a reaction against what was more natural, and it served as a protest and protection against something in myself which, in the pressure of the weight of actual experience, I knew to be a weakness. It is, I suppose, becoming a commonplace that when anyone is unduly concerned with controversy, the remarks that seem to be directed against others are really concerned with a struggle that is going on inside himself. The marks, the stigmata, of the struggle to weld together the characteristics of a formal, theoretic interest and the material of a maturing experience of contacts with reality also showed themselves, naturally, in style of writing and manner of presentation. During the time when the schematic interest predominated, writing was comparatively easy; there were even compliments upon the clearness of my style. Since then thinking and writing have been hard work. It is easy to give way to the dialectical development of a theme; the pressure of concrete experiences was, however, sufficiently heavy, so that a sense of intellectual honesty prevented a surrender to that course. But, on the other hand, the formal interest persisted, so that there was an inner demand for an intellectual technique that would be consistent and yet capable of flexible adaptation to the concrete diversity of experienced things. It is hardly necessary to say that I have not been among those to whom the union of abilities to satisfy these two opposed requirements, the formal and the material, came easily. For that very reason I have been acutely aware, too much so, doubtless, of a tendency of other thinkers and writers to achieve a specious lucidity and simplicity by the mere process of ignoring considerations which a greater respect for concrete materials of experience would have forced upon them.[7]

In reviewing Russell's book *Religion and Science* Dewey writes: "The detailed contents of Mr. Russell's book are accessible to all; his lucidity and felicity of expression are ever the despair of lesser writers, and in this volume he has almost surpassed himself."[8]

Professor Richard J. Bernstein in his introduction to his Dewey anthology writes:

> For the contemporary reader who is unacquainted with the context in which the *Studies* [*in Logical Theory—1904*] were written, the book presents difficulties. It is like a geological specimen in which three strata corresponding to the various plateaus in Dewey's thinking during the twenty years prior to its publication are intermixed. The language of Hegel and idealism is expressive of the oldest and deepest substratum. The theory of organic coordination of "The Reflex Arc Concept" forms the next stratum. The psychological doctrine described there is reflected in his analysis of thinking as an instrumental response to a specific stimulus. And lastly, the most recent stratum consists of the new pragmatic elements in which the testing and verifying of hypotheses by experimental consequences is emphasized. It is because these various strata are not clearly distinguished that the *Studies* is at first confusing to the reader. And when this book appeared, it immediately evoked a great deal of discussion and criticism.[9] Dewey was forced to clarify, explicate, and defend his position, a task which occupied him for the rest of his life.[10]

In the throes of transition during the period of growth from one mode of thinking to another, the immediate consequences make a tendency for obscurity, qualification, starts and withdrawals and a sense of re-orientation which the reader must share with the author. For those with a fixed point of view, such difficulties are nonexistent. It just, however, may be worth while to make the effort.

Despite Dewey's gracious appreciation of the qualities of Oliver Wendell Holmes,[11] Holmes writes "—he is a bad writer and I found him very hard reading."[12] A year later Holmes wrote:

> "But although Dewey's book [*Experience and Nature*] is incredibly ill written, it seemed to me after several rereadings to have a feeling

of intimacy with the inside of the cosmos that I found unequaled. So methought God would have spoken had He been inarticulate but keenly desirous to tell you how it was."[13]

According to the Book of Exodus the speech of God was inarticulate when He chose His spokesman Moses, the stammerer.[14]

Holmes finally managed unqualified praise of Dewey's *Art As Experience*.[15] "His insights into the movements of the universe as it shows itself to men goes to as high a point as has ever been reached by articulate speech".[16]

I find the prose of Dewey resembles the American landscape. There are arid flat stretches and periods of breathtaking beauty, all pervaded by an epic grandeur that overwhelms the spirit.

I

For Aristotle knowledge is knowledge of a cause or reason. All change is rational and has a cause. Cause is the answer to all questions which can be asked of being and becoming. Aristotle's theory of cause is four-fold:

1. The formal cause is that specific form which the object will embody when it reaches maturity. A child can only be defined in terms of an adult. It is revealed at its climax not its origin.

2. It is form that gives to the developing thing what reality it has. Only form can set in motion the development towards the thing's actual nature. This form becomes the *efficient* cause. It acts upon the thing in a separate external manner.

3. The perfection for the sake of which it is developing, the unreached goal, conforms as its final cause.

4. The fourth factor is the *material* cause. It is the passive condition of development out of which a thing develops and that into which it dissolves. It is a substratum of form persisting throughout change.

Matter is capacity or potency, the unrealized promise of actuality.

The purpose of matter is to subserve form as material unites for higher levels of complexity.

The State (Polis), including slavery, private property, the family, is a natural institution for that moral perfection of man to which his whole nature moves. For both Plato and Aristotle the end of moral perfection can only be attained in the *polis*—and that end is the measure of all things. They refuse to recognize an antithesis between political society and the individual. The state exists for the moral development and perfection of its individual members. The perfection of the individual means the perfection of the state. Political philosophy becomes a sort of moral theology.

That Dewey was not unaffected by this theory of the state is indicated in his "Lectures in China":

> ...the state as an organization should safeguard not only the material welfare of the people, but also their spiritual life, with the promotion of culture and education being major governmental enterprises.[17] Hegelian political doctrine (directly derived from Aristotle) has prevailed and will continue to prevail in the future: the responsibility of the state must not be limited to the protection of private property and the enforcement of contracts, but that it must also be responsible for the development of spiritual values.[18]

Such a state is not unlike a church—it exercises a holy discipline. Plato in the *Laws* develops a Sinatic creation of the canons of true religion, and advocates religious persecution. That there should be a limit to state interference is never suggested.

Dewey's notions were subject to change and growth. Writing in 1939:

> My contribution to the first series of essays in *Living Philosophies*[19] put forward the idea of faith in the possibilities of experience as the heart of my own philosophy. In the course of that contribution I said, "Individuals will always be the center and the consummation of experience, but what the individual actually *is* in his life experience depends upon the nature and movement of associated life." I have not changed my faith in experience nor my belief that individuality is its center and consummation. But there

has been a change in emphasis. I should now wish to emphasize more than I formerly did that individuals are the finally decisive factors of the nature and movement of associated life.

The cause of this shift of emphasis is the events of the intervening years. The rise of dictatorships and totalitarian states and the decline of democracy have been accompanied with loud proclamation of the idea that only the state, the political organization of society, can give security to individuals. In return for the security thus obtained—that individuals owe everything to the state....

As a friend of mine put it, the last thing the lord of the feudal castle would have imagined was that the future of society was with the forces that were represented by the humble trader who set up his post under the walls of his castle.[20]

This does not indicate that Dewey supported any form of "laissez-faire" economics.

The negative and empty character of this individualism had consequences which produced a reaction toward an equally arbitrary and one-sided collectivism.

The alternative is that individuals who prize their own liberties and who prize the liberties of other individuals, individuals who are democratic in thought and action, are the sole final warrant for the existence and endurance of democratic institutions.[21]

II

Descartes broke the back of Aristotelian final causes and bodies in motion coming to rest. The universe of Descartes is made of material things governed by no other laws than those of matter in motion. The heavens are a machine, the human brain and body are machines.

Descartes is searching for the first causes of nature—truth in science is to be obtained only by the use of mathematics. In the Middle Ages, under the influence of Aristotle, the dominant thought was away from quantitative analysis; events were understood through specific qualities or forms. It was thus assumed that everything sought its proper place, a state of rest in infinite quietude. A rock would lie on the earth because that was its final end, just as a flame would rise, for its nature was to mount upwards.

Descartes burst on the scene with mathematics that exposed the heart of physical relationships: the motion of the planets, the descent of falling bodies, the pendulum—all stated in quantitative terms. Order and measurement replaced qualities and became the foundation of science. Joined with painstaking observation, science made enormous progress. In physiology as well as mechanics Man was a machine: the human organism, automatic, and the solar system were mechanisms to be explained on the same principles.

The appeal and lasting value of Cartesianism lies in its simplicity. His philosophy rests on analytical geometry. The basic notion is substance. Substance is an entity with attributes. It is thus possible to represent a function of two variable quantities in analytic geometry. This is effected by drawing coordinates at right angles to one another, on which various quantities can be measured from the point of intersection. Geometry thus becomes the key to the existential material world. The material world is extension and motion in space.

Thinking is an activity; therefore there is a substance which is displayed in that activity. Extension is the property of the physical world and thinking the property of the mental world, and underlying these worlds is substance—two diverse realms.

There are times when the power a concept wields over human life is proportioned to the degree of error it contains. The successors of Descartes—Leibnitz, Berkeley, Hume, Spinoza—soon took the notion of substance to pieces. But what Descartes did provide in great measure was a general setting for the mechanical view of nature as well as subjective dualism. "I think, therefore I am," the *Cogito*, placed the self in the center of the universe and set new problems for philosophy. The idealists, Berkeley, Kant, Fichte and Hegel followed the emphasis on self.

It became once more necessary to discover and to recover the common world from the point of view of the individual mind rather than the communal mind of Aristotle. Spinoza attempted to bridge the problem of thinking mind and mechanical world by conceiving thought and extension as parallel attributes of one substance, God. God is the unity of the two.

During his lifetime Descartes was very cautious in his relations with the Church. He provided a proof of the existence of God and the philosophical justification of the sacrament of the Eucharist. Yet shortly after his death, the writings of Descartes were placed on the *Index librorum prohibitorum* of the Catholic Church. The Church correctly sensed an enemy in Cartesian philosophy. He opened the gates to the new physical science which was to overflow and inundate the medieval synthesis.

Dewey giving the instrumental viewpoint indicates that mathematical conceptions are instruments of interpretation of existential data.[22] Verification is not a matter of finding *an* existence—but a matter of ordering data by means of a theory as an instrumentality.[23] Universal propositions are in themselves neither true nor false. They state modes of *procedure* in inquiry. Like mathematical axioms, their meaning, or force, is determined and tested by what follows from their operative use.[24]

In reviewing Dewey's *Essays in Experimental Logic*, Russell writes:

> The writings of Hume, I know are inconvenient. There are two recognized methods of dealing with what he has to say on Cause: one is to maintain that Kant answered him, the other is to preserve silence on the matter.—The second is the one adopted by Professor Dewey.[25]

The problem of cause in Hume is one of the most complex questions in philosophy. Yet Russell is not altogether fair to Dewey.[26] Dewey noted: "The first thinker who proclaimed that every event is the effect of something and cause of something else, that every particular existence is both conditioned and condition, merely put into words the procedure of the workman...."[27]

> Extraordinary and subtle reasons have been assigned for belief in the principle of causation. Labor and the use of tools seem, however, to be a sufficient empirical reason: indeed, to be the only empirical events that can be specifically pointed to in this connec-

tion.[28] Analytic reflection shows that the ordinary conception of causation as a trait belonging to some one thing is the idea of responsibility read backward. The idea that some one thing, or any two or three things, are *the* cause of an occurrence is in effect an application of the idea of credit or blame—as in the Greek *aita* (cause or being the cause). There is nothing in nature that *belongs* absolutely and exclusively to anything else; belonging is always a matter of reference and distributive assignment, justified in any particular case as far as it works out well. Greek metaphysics and logic are dominated by the idea of inherent belonging and exclusion; another instance of naively reading the story of nature in language appropriate to human association. Modern science has liberated physical events from the domination of the notions of intrinsic belonging and exclusion....[29]

The qualities which Descartes and Hume banished from science to psychology, Dewey restores through the front door of moral goods and ends. It is just possible that the scientific withdrawal of values from objects in Descartes' sense, that quantity is the essence of matter, which created a violent dualism between thinking mind and extended matter, has been rectified to the extent that any existential data is a problem for thought to solve rather than a subject of dogmatic and inflexible rules. Science becomes an instrument and develops as any other instrument to bring natural forces to the service of human purposes and valuations.

Moral goods and ends exist only when something has to be done. The fact that something has to be done proves that there are deficiencies, evils in the existent situation. Morals is not a catalogue of acts nor a set of rules to be applied like drugstore prescriptions or cook-book recipes. The need in morals is for specific methods of inquiry and of contrivance. Methods of inquiry to locate difficulties and evils; methods of contrivance to form plans to be used as working hypotheses in dealing with them.[30]

Divorcing intrinsic religious, esthetic good from interests of daily life leads to "much of the obnoxious materialism and brutality of our economic life." When economic ends are recognized as intrinsic, "then it will be seen that they are capable of idealization, and that if life is to be worthwhile, they must acquire ideal and intrinsic value."[31]

He calls for "doing away once and for all with the traditional distinction between moral goods like virtues, and natural goods like health, economic security, art, science and the like."[32]

> If the need and deficiencies of a specific situation indicate improvement of health as the end and good, then for that situation health is the ultimate and supreme good. It is no means to something else. It is a final intrinsic value.[33]

When the consciousness of science is fully impregnated with the consciousness of human value, the greatest dualism which now weighs humanity down, the split between the material and mechanical, the scientific and the moral and ideal will be destroyed.[34]

III

In Great Britain industry and commerce centered in the production of wealth rather than its possession. Locke stressed that among the "natural" rights is that of property originating in the fact that an individual has "mixed" himself through his labor with some object. The concept of labor as the source of right in property was employed to justify freedom in the investment of capital and the right of laborers to move about and seek new modes of employment. Locke taught that labor and not land was the source of wealth.

According to Dewey, these new claims of laborers were "denied by the common law that came down from semi-feudal conditions. The enemy was no longer the arbitrary special action of rulers. It was the whole system of common law and judicial practice in its adverse bearing upon freedom of labor, investment and exchange."[35]

The question is an eternally recurring one: what is law, and more particularly, what is the common law? If we ask not "what is law?" but rather "what is the purpose of law?" we may hold it as the form of the security for the conditions of civilization and a social life. We speak not merely of the conditions of physical existence, but those goods which make life distinctly human. Law thus defined is not an absolute, not an end in itself, but a means to the shared enjoyment of the wider community of civilized discourse.[36]

Holmes in his treatise published 1881 remarks: "The life of the law has not been logic: it has been experience." The common law of England was a flexible device developed to meet every contingency and combination of circumstances from trade and war to the most intimate domestic matters. Though flexible, it yet remains peculiarly the province of judicial interpretation of established precedent. It is the glory of Anglo-American freedom, of tolerance, liberty and security from tyranny; the wonder and achievement of civilization.

It was not the common law that prevented the free movement of labor, but the guild system fostered and encouraged by the church. The Reformation in England dealt a fatal blow to the power of the guilds. The property and money of guilds acquired for religious purposes were entirely confiscated. In Europe the Reformation (16th Cent.) affected the continental guilds adversely. Pope Pius XII proclaimed his preference for guilds over trade unions as a safeguard for the church and a bulwark against socialism. The organic theory of society differentiates between the individual and the collective organism. They do away with the juristic person. If no true persons exist except individuals, the state can only be a fictitious person. Social bodies are independent wholes. They are real persons with a will and nature of their own, following Fichte and Hegel.[37]

The magna carta of labor was not any enactment of law, but the plague of the Black Death which devastated medieval Europe to the point where labor was a scarce commodity and in such demand that all restrictions on movement and organization were removed and the laborer worthy of his hire was welcomed wherever he chose to locate.[38] It was not until the Industrial Revolution that a surplus of labor appeared, and, following the great Enclosure Acts, made possible the abuses by some of the mill and mining interests. But to speak of the common law as an enemy of labor is to misread history.

To quote Holmes again:

The felt necessities of the time, the prevalent moral and political theories, institutions of public policy, avowed or unconscious, even the prejudices which judges share with their fellow-men, have a good deal more to do than the syllogism in determining the rules by which men should be governed.[39]

One of the most striking phrases Dewey uses in assessing the status of Locke is: "Locke's analysis was useful in destroying the old; it was inadequate for building the new" (infra p. 109). It was adequate enough for Jefferson to build his Declaration of Independence on, and for the Constitution of the United States and the State constitutions to use Locke's conception as ruling law guiding basic precepts.

Dewey had adequately treated Locke's theory of knowledge in his first published volume, "Leibnitz's New Essay Concerning The Human Understanding."[40] It was Locke as a philosopher of revolution and freedom that interested the later Dewey.

In his political writing Locke did not use the term "sovereignty" or "right of revolution." No government possessed sovereignty in the sense of ultimate power or authority. A government is always limited to the powers delegated to it in the social contract. "The liberty of man in society is to be under no other legislative power but that established by consent in the commmonwealth." The community retains always the supreme power. While the people have no right to revolt, they have a duty to defend themselves against a usurpation of illegitimate power. Locke wished to discourage tyranny, not encourage revolt.

The spirit of Locke is reflected in a Supreme Court decision written by Justice Brandeis:

The makers of our Constitution undertook to secure conditions favorable to the pursuit of happiness. They recognized the significance of man's spiritual nature, of his feelings and of his intellect. They knew that only a part of the pain, pleasure and satisfaction of life are to be found in material things. They sought to protect Americans in their beliefs, their thoughts, their emotions and their sensations. They conferred, as against the Government, the right to be let alone—the most comprehensive of rights and the right most valued by civilized men. To protect that right, every unjustifiable invasion of the privacy of the individual, whatever the means employed, must be deemed a violation of the Fourth Amendment.

And the use as evidence in a criminal proceeding of facts ascertained by such intrusion must be deemed a violation of the Fifth.[41]

Justice Field in the Slaughterhouse Cases:

...the fourteenth amendment secures the like protection to all citizens in that State against any abridgment of their common rights, as in other States. That amendment was intended to give practical effect to the declaration of 1776 of inalienable rights, rights which are the gift of the Creator, which the law does not confer, but only recognizes.[42]

Justice Field in Butchers' Union Slaughterhouse & Livestock Landing Co. v. Crescent City Co.:

As in our intercourse with our fellow-men certain principles of morality are assumed to exist, without which society would be impossible, so certain inherent rights lie at the foundation of all action, and upon a recognition of them alone can free institutions be maintained. These inherent rights have never been more happily expressed than in the Declaration of Independence, that new evangel of liberty to the people: "We hold these truths to be self-evident"—that is so plain that their truth is recognized upon their mere statement—"that all men are endowed"—not by edicts of Emperors, or decrees of Parliament, or acts of Congress, but "by their Creator with certain inalienable rights"—that is, rights which cannot be bartered away, or given away, or taken away—"and that among these are life, liberty, and the pursuit of happiness, and to secure these"—not grant them but secure them—"governments are instituted among men, deriving their just powers from the consent of the governed.[43]

John Locke defending the English Revolution of 1688 in his "Two Treatises of Government" declared that in the state of nature men have perfect freedom and complete equality. No man "can be put out of this estate and subjected to the political power of another without his own consent." This is the "consent of the governed" which Jefferson proclaimed in the Declaration of Independence.

The Constitution finally adopted by the United States established the principle that men have rights which are not the gift of the government but rights that are constitutionally protected which existed before government. The doctrine of individual liberty is combined with the freedom of association into a new whole.

Thus a group of men having inalienable rights by nature may by compact establish a sovereign state; and once they have done so, it endures at their will and may be altered or abolished entirely. This is the assertion of the original individual right, and that the people are the source of power—the theory of derivative government.

The European idea of freedom is a liberalism in which the beast is to be aired, fed, looked after, but always under the scrutiny of a landed, armed or educated elite. Lawyers, bishops, generals decree the nature, the bounds and metes, but he is never to make decisions. The common man is a suspect, somewhat ridiculous, but necessary evil, something to be endured, not celebrated. To Edmund Burke's vindication of the validity of traditional privilege and established order against the challenge of the French Revolution, Thomas Paine in his "Common Sense" replied: "Law cannot legitimate an ancient wrong; the past grants neither rights nor privilege with regard to the present; no dead hand shall hold back living men; to each generation its own destiny; man hath no property in man."

The classic conception of the modern state appears in the work of Jean Bodin, *Six Books of the Commonwealth* (1576).[44] The legists and canonists of medieval Europe were struggling with questions of authority in the state and church. The need for a theory of the state became acute with the break-up of the papal authority. A universal church could require princes to act as the sword of the church, but when princes had to consider which church to obey, confusion and conflict resulted. Another form of obligation had to be formulated.

Bodin began in the modern manner by asking what is a state and how is it constructed? The very question recognizes a new order had arisen and a new center of gravity had evolved superseding the scholastic debates over the boundaries of temporal and spiritual powers.

His preoccupation was the authority of the ruler. But the ruler to be legitimate is one who respects and guarantees the liberty and property of his subjects, and the distinguishing mark of a sovereign is power, perpetual and absolute. The origin of legitimate authority is derived of God. The commonwealth should be modeled on the natural society of the family.

Sovereignty was marked in terms of power, the unqualified right to command. The mark of the citizen was the virtue of obedience. The political authority was postulated of divine institution.

In 1562 the long series of wars of religion started. Bodin denied the right of resistance to absolute monarchy in the name of religion. Civil war, rebellion and anarchy inspired him with horror and the only remedy was the recognition of the absolute authority of the state. The condition of human well-being required that this power must in all circumstances be preserved.

While Bodin never spoke of "inherent" or "natural" rights and denied that consent plays any part in the obligation to obey, both the prince and the law are subject to divine and natural law and this is the ultimate guarantee of individual liberty.

A check on the arbitrary exercise of absolute power was the obligation of the sovereign to keep his 'covenants' with his subjects. This is deduced from the prince's subjection to divine and natural law. That the prince could not tax without consent, is an example of covenant.

Hobbes alone denies that the sovereign is bound by any contract made with individual subjects or with the whole body of subjects. They cannot, therefore, do injustice to their subjects either as individuals or as a whole. The people receiving the promise (reserved rights) disappears as a person with the institution of the sovereign. There is no contract between ruler and subject, only agreement among subjects to place or leave all power in his hands. They give up all natural rights to the ruler.

Even in Hobbes there are limits, or liberties of subjects. These consist of those powers or rights which the individual cannot surrender by any covenant. No man can be bound to kill himself, to abstain from self-preservation, or accuse himself. The obligation of subjects to the sovereign lasts no longer than he has power to protect them.

The right of self-preservation is absolute even against monarchs. This is logical since self-preservation is the motive for instituting government. On this ground Hobbes holds that a man has a right to refuse to fight when called upon by the government to do so. Only self-defense is justified.

Spinoza and Hegel deified the state. There is no right whatever of rebellion. Political authority was of divine institution. The cruelest of tyrants and the most unjust of laws may not be resisted.

Now the state is an organization just like any other organization. It may be efficient, just democratic, or profligate, autocratic and discriminatory. If a group of men decided to form a society, say, for the care of children who would otherwise be unprovided for, they hire experts in these matters and secure the necessary funds and implements to establish and promote this worthwhile cause. Let us suppose that the founders of this movement discover they are in a nest of thieves who are misusing funds and depriving the children of the necessities of life. They would swiftly disassociate themselves from this group and act to bring the villains to justice as well as to rectify the faults uncovered. The purpose of this worthwhile cause was corrupted and brought to naught by the evil behavior of selfish men. We would have no hesitation at a swift and complete re-organization.

Yet we act otherwise about the state. When politicians are discovered misusing their power, we throw the rascals out, but never associate this corrupt government with the state. As a matter of fact we may take pride in a state which can uncover villainy and inspire dedicated, loyal servants.

In one of Dewey's most important and least read books, *The Public and Its Problems*,[45] he makes the basic analysis of state, government and human rights. "The creation of adequate legal machinery to change political forms of the state has not yet been achieved so changes come only by revolt or conquest. Yet the need for reconstruction is constant."[46]

Conceptions of "*The State*" as something *per se*, something intrinsically manifesting a general will and reason, lend themselves to illusions. They make such a sharp distinction between *The State* and *a* government that, from the standpoint of the theories, a government may be corrupt and injurious and yet *The State* by the same idea retain its inherent dignity and nobility. Officials may be mean, obstinate, proud and stupid and yet the nature of *The State* which they serve remain essentially unimpaired. Since, however, a public is organized into a state through its government, *The State* is as its officials are.[47]

"One of the chief occupations of states has been the waging of war and the suppression of dissentient minorities."[48]

Dewey's interest in liberty was decidedly social rather than individual.[49] He deplored the pretext of liberalism as a cloak to trample the rights of those unable to take advantage of the new liberties that the emerging industrial revolution gave to manufacturers of goods.

Yet one of Locke's greatest interests was to uphold toleration in an age when intolerance was rife, persecution of dissenters in faith almost the rule, and when wars, civil and between nations, had a religious color. In serving the immediate needs of England—and then those of other countries in which it was desired to substitute representative for arbitrary government—it bequeathed to later social thought a rigid doctrine of natural rights inherent in individuals independent of social organization. It gave a directly practical import to the older semi-theological and semi-metaphysical conceptions of natural law as supreme over positive law and gave a new version of the old idea that natural law is the counterpart of reason, being disclosed by the natural light with which man is endowed.

The whole temper of this philosophy is individualistic in the sense in which individualism is opposed to organized social action. It held to the primacy of the individual over the state not only in time but in moral authority. It defined the individual in terms of liberties of thought and action already possessed by him in some mysterious ready-made fashion, and which it was the sole business of the state to safeguard.... It followed that the great enemy of individual liberty was thought to be government because of its tendency to encroach upon the innate liberties of individuals. Later liberalism inherited this conception of a natural antagonism between ruler and ruled, interpreted as a natural opposition between the individual and organized society.... Not until the second half of the nineteenth century did the idea arise that government might and should be an instrument for securing and extending the liberties of individuals.

Locke at times goes so far as to designate as property everything that is included in "life, liberties and estates"; the individual has property in himself and in his life and activities; property in this broad sense is that which political society should protect. The importance attached to the right within the political area was without doubt an influence in the later definitely economic formulation of liberalism. But Locke was interested in property already possessed.[50]

Dewey, reflecting on Jefferson, noted that he had no faith in the leadership of a small band of enlightened men, the illuminati, or French *philosophes*.[51] He found science, no matter how exalted, did not prevent wholesale misery and oppression if it was confined to a few. While ambassdor to France:

His deepest sympathies went to the downtrodden masses whose huts he visited and whose food he ate. His affection for the "people" whose welfare was the real and final object of all social institutions, and his faith in the "will of the people" as the basis of all legitimate political arrangements, made him increasingly sceptical of advances in knowledge and the arts that left the mass of the people in a state of misery and degradation.[52]

On the sources of the ideas Jefferson expressed in the Declaration of Independence, Dewey said:

I do not believe his remarks are intended in their denial of indebtedness to this and to that writer, to set up a claim for originality. On the contrary, I believe his statement is to be taken literally that his purpose was simply to be "an expression of the American mind." There was nothing that was novel in the idea that "governments derive their just powers from the consent of the governed," nor did it find its origin in Locke's writings.... Even the right of the people "to alter or abolish" a government when it becomes destructive of the inherent moral rights of the governed had behind it a tradition that long antedated the writings of even Locke.

There was, nevertheless, something distinctive, something original, in the Declaration.... What was new and significant was that these ideas were now set forth as an expression of the "American mind" that the American will was prepared to *act* upon.[53]

Jefferson's trust in the people was a faith in what he sometimes called their common sense and sometimes their reason.

I am not underestimating Jefferson's abilities as a practical politician when I say that this deep-seated faith in the people and their responsiveness to enlightenment properly presented was a most important factor in enabling him to effect, against great odds, "the revolution of 1800." It is the cardinal element bequeathed by Jefferson to the American tradition.[54]

This is the new, the distinctive American experience which has not touched European thought. It is the experience which we ourselves have ignored when our courts hold that the 14th Amendment to the Constitution was adopted in order to enhance corporate profits. It is a far more radical experiment than Lenin's Marxism or the utopian planners of Communist China. Surely in the entire history of ideas, of philosophy, of politics, there can have been few things more precious. It puts power where it belongs, at the base. Its only dogma is freedom to experiment, and freedom to think and act in accordance with the dictates of enlightened reason and conscience. It is the basic law in the organization of a political state.

In the break with the European tradition there appeared a new perception. Religion was a liberty, not an established hierarchy imposed from above. Theory and practice were the day to day vocations of natural behavior; the former was not the monopoly of a learned caste, nor was the latter a status to be born to.

IV

Professor Lewis E. Hahn has provided us with an excellent survey and introduction to Dewey's philosophic method.[55] Of particular relevance here is his section on "Instrumentalism and Reflective Inquiry."[56] The problem may be stated as to how thought functions in the experimental determination of future consequences. Dewey's work on this subject was expanded in "How We Think," "Essays in Experimental Logic" and "Democracy and Education." The growth of Dewey's philosophy from absolutism to empirical naturalism is indicated by his definition of experimental thought or inquiry in "Logic The Theory of Inquiry." Inquiry is "the directed or controlled transformation of an indeterminate situation into a determinately unified one."[57]

Morton White, about two genertions go, published a study entitled "The Origin of Dewey's Instrumentalism."[58] Thus began a lifelong antipathy to Dewey.[59] Dewey noted "that he thought White was good, but not tackling the 'fundament,' [60]although he admitted that he was under hospitalization when White's book came out and merely gave it "a hasty glance."[61]

White comments on Dewey's response to Thomas Huxley's lecture "Evolution and Ethics" given in 1893. Huxley stressed the difference between the "cosmic" and the ethical "processes." According to Huxley the law of cosmos was indifferent, cruel, and impartial; whereas ethical process was sympathy and cooperation. "Social progress," according to Huxley, meant the checking of the cosmic process at every step and the substitution for it of another which may be called the ethical process. White explores an essay by Dewey of the same title in 1898.[62]

Dewey's reply to Huxley pointed out that the ethical process is part of the cosmic process. As an example Dewey uses a farmer seeking to maintain his plot against the incursion of weeds and natural enemies. The methods of insight and reflection the farmer employs are those that have emerged within evolutionary development. Through *intelligent selection*, the farmer introduces conditions except for which the intended plot would fade into its original state. The employment of intelligence permits life conditions to be determined by one set of "natural" conditions as opposed to another.

It is critical to realize that with the advent of human life the environment itself is altered to accommodate the human-social dimension. What is judged "good" and "bad" is determined in view of the new conditions that have emerged as to whether it impedes or advances social life. Selection is found in the ethical process just as it is in the cosmic, but what was instinct in animal is intelligence or conscious foresight in man.

Dewey argued for the evolutionary method in morals which White attacks.[63] Morals evolve in man's social experience and his experience is instrumental for deepening and extending the ethical quality of life. What was good would be preserved and strengthened and what was not could be modified and altered. Indeed the school itself must be viewed as an integral part of the social life in which it functions.[64]

> The development of the experimental method as the method of getting knowledge and making sure it is knowledge and not mere opinion—the method of both discovery and proof is the remaining great force in bringing about a transformation in the theory of knowledge. The scientific experimental method is—a trial of ideas; hence even when practically—or immediately—unsuccessful, it is intellectual, fruitful; for we learn from our failures when our endeavors are seriously thoughtful.
>
> Men still want the crutch of dogma, of beliefs fixed by authority, to relieve them of the trouble of thinking and the responsibility of directing their activity by thought. They tend to confine their own thinking to a consideration of which one among the rival systems of dogma they will accept.[65]

When the Soviets launched their "Sputnik" missile in space an explosion of similar magnitude burst upon the education field. Admiral Hyman Rickover called for a complete revision of our educational system which would insure that our scientific and engineering capacity would overtake and forever surpass that of the Soviet Union. Dwight D. Eisenhower assailed our present educational lag as due directly to the educational theories of John Dewey.[66] Harold R.W. Benjamin responded:

> To those who have implied that the educational revolution of the last sixty years has been caused mainly by John Dewey's theories, I submit these two statements. The one describes clearly an institution that is an instrument of a settled power structure. It is the kind of school that every autocracy wants now and has always wanted. It is a school for the pouring into human heads of officially approved facts, and for the modification of human nervous systems to the requirements of officially needed skills. It is the laboratory for the development of faceless nonentities in the service of a corporation or a corporate state. It is a college for the preparation of willing workers who will never organize a union or man a picket line. It is the recruiting depot for the training of nameless weapons—users subsumed under the title of *well-drilled military personnel*.
>
> The second statement even more precisely defines a diametrically different school. It is a school in which the learnings are set by the needs and interests of the children themselves in relation to their communities. It is a school of no official doctrine. It is a school with a flexible timetable. Its pupils assist in the evaluation of their own efforts. Its model of the higher discipline is self-discipline. Such a school is preeminently the instrument of a free people who, while recognizing that their society needs enough uniformity of behavior for a minimum necessary security, are also persuaded that their society needs even more pressingly a development of individual capacities, not in spite of idiosyncracies but by their help. Such a school supports and develops a conviction among its people that society advances significantly only by the maximum cultivation of all the peculiar aspects of its original and creative minds and spirits.[67]

George E. Axtelle:

> Dewey's theory of education is the capstone of his philosophy; in education his ideas come to a focus and get their test. However, one who has read only his educational writings can have but a

slender grasp of his educational philosophy, for it is bound up with his whole thought. Moreover, if we identify education with all the agencies that shape and form character, it is clear that education is man's chief instrument for social and moral progress.

We should note that his great work on education was titled *Democracy and Education*—in other words, not just any education, but the particular education which would shape the understanding, dispositions and character necessary to a democracy.

To the genius of the civilization which he inherited, he contributed insights by means of which America might mobilize its human and democratic resources to bring all activities under the control of human ends.[68]

Dewey has the final word:

A democracy is more than a form of government; it is primarily a mode of associated living, of conjoint communicated experience. The extension in space of the number of individuals who participate in an interest so that each has to refer his own action to that of others, and to consider the action of others to give point and direction to his own, is equivalent to the breaking down of those barriers of class, race, and national territory, which kept men from perceiving the full impact of their activity. These more numerous and more varied points of contact denote a greater diversity of stimuli to which an individual has to respond; they consequently put a premium on variation in his action. They secure a liberation of powers which remain suppressed as long as the incitations to action are partial, as they must be in a group which in its exclusiveness shuts out many interests.[69]

"We are free not because of what we statically are, but in so far as we are becoming different from what we have been."[70]

V

The development of Dewey's philosophy is inseparable from the work of William James. Dewey called him "the most significant intellectual figure the United States has produced." The story of their interaction is well documented.[71] James thought of meaning in terms of the consequences of a statement—for meaning and truth are located in the future rather than the past. But James turned inward, toward the personal and private in the search for meaning rather than social and public. James left to Dewey the development of pragmatism. Dewey reformulated pragmatism into instrumentalism which dispensed with the separation of science and value, knowledge and morals.

"Meaning is wider in scope," points out Dewey, "as well as more precious in value than is truth, and philosophy is occupied with meaning rather than with truth—truths are but one class of meanings, namely, those in which a claim to verifiability by their consequences is an intrinsic part of their meaning. Beyond this island of meanings which in their own nature are true or false lies the ocean of meanings to which truth and falsity are irrelevant."[72]

In his autobiographical essay, "From Absolutism to Experimentalism," Dewey relates:

The great exception to what was said about no very fundamental vital influence issuing from books; it concerns the influence of William James. As far as I can discover, the one specifiable philosophic factor which entered into my thinking so as to give it a new direction and quality, is this one. To say that it proceeded from his *Psychology* rather than from the essays collected in the volume called *Will to Believe*, his *Pluralistic Universe*, or *Pragmatism*, is to say something that needs explanation. One is found in the adoption of the subjective tenor of prior psychological tradition; even when the special tenets of that tradition are radically criticized, an underlying subjectivism is retained, at least in vocabulary—and the difficulty in finding a vocabulary which will intelligibly convey a genuinely new idea is perhaps the obstacle that most retards the easy progress of philosophy. I may cite as an illustration the substitution of the "Stream of consciousness" for discrete elementary states: the advance made was enormous. Nevertheless the point of view remained that of a realm of consciousness set off by itself. The other strain is objective, having its roots in a return to the earlier biological conception of the *psyche*, but a return possessed of a new force and value due to the immense progress made by biology since the time of Aristotle. I doubt if we have as yet begun to realize all that is due to William James for the introduction and use of this idea; as I have already intimated. I do not think that he fully and consistently realized it himself. Anyway, it worked its way more and more into all my ideas and acted as a ferment to transform old beliefs.[73]

James was not entirely unaware of the "two unreconciled strains" in the *Psychology*. Consciousness with its "perchings and flights," a "great blooming buzzing confusion," was a disease. "It is a nonentity, and has no right to a place among first principles."[74] "Breath, which was ever the original of 'spirit,' breath moving outwards, between the glottis and the nostrils, is, I am persuaded, the essence out of which philosophers have constructed the entity known to them as consciousness. *That entity is fictitious....*"[75] "I mean only to deny that the word stands for an entity, but to insist most emphatically that it does stand for a function."[76] "Mental fire is what won't burn real sticks."[77]

So far as 'thoughts' and 'feelings' can be active, their activity terminates in the activity of the body. The body is the storm centre, the origin of co-ordinates, the constant place of stress in all that experience-train. Everything circles round it, and is felt from its point of view. The word 'I,' then, is primarily a noun of position, just like 'this' and 'here.'[78]

Dewey asks why James:

did not develop his treatment in the direction indicated by these considerations. We come back to the influence exercised by the surviving metaphysical dualism. For as long as this dualism is postulated, the connection the nervous system, including the brain, indubitably has with psychological phenomena is a "mystery," and the more detailed and complete the evidence for the connection the more the mystery deepens. The influence of the dualism is so strong that James does not follow out the implication of his hypothesis that the brain—and nervous system generally—functions as an organ in the behavior constituted by the inter-action of organism and environment [leading him] to express adherence to the most miraculous of all the theories about the "mystery" namely, the parallelism or pre-established harmony of physical and psychical.[79]

Dewey notes:

It was reserved for James to think of life in terms of life in action. This point and that about the objective biological factor in James' conception of thought (discrimination, abstraction, conception, generalization) is fundamental when the role of psychology in philosophy comes under consideration.[80]

Dewey's instrumentalism was a new conception arising from the biological approach of the *Psychology* of James. Dewey's formula-tion was the influential essay "The Reflex Arc Concept In Psychol-ogy"[81] which launched the behaviorist school of psychology. What he took from James with one hand, he returned as instrumentalism with the other. Dewey's emphasis, however, was distinctively social: "No organism is so isolated that it can be understood apart from the environment in which it lives."[82]

VI

An interior pain is privately suffered while architecture evokes a communal response. Direct apprehension is supplied by the French verb *connaître* as compared to *savoir*, to know about. The same distinction applied to the German *wissen* as compared to *kennen*. For Bergson ideas were the antithesis of matter, but one is not more "real" than the other. Ideas were anti-material, not material supplied by the outside world.

Bergson's theory of time was basic to his philosophy. Unlike the time of physical science, lived time was to be distinguished from physical time. The self alone is the apprehending subject. This *aperçu* is not far removed from Descartes' *cogito* and apprehending subject. This is not the sort of dualism we expect Dewey to take kindly to, yet he devotes many pages of patient analysis to this poetical mystic. Readers who desire a more technical analysis of the subject than is provided in Dewey's China lectures on Bergson are referred to his essay "Perception and Organic Action." "Bergson's whole theory of time, of memory, of mind and of life as things inherently sundered from organic action needs revision. With *this* revision, follows also that of "intuition" severed from practical knowledge."[83]

There is little doubt that Dewey was attracted to Bergson because of their common interest in Darwin's theory of evolution and the philosophical implications to be derived from this theory. He was sympathetic to the emphasis on process, culture and human experience. But to regard analysis as falsifying is to commit ourselves to a distrust of science as an organ of knowledge, to accept the products and not the method of science.[84]

> The pervasiveness of the tradition is shown in the fact that so vitally a contemporary thinker as Bergson, who finds a philosophic revolution involved in abandonment of the traditional identification of the truly real with the fixed (an identification inherited from Greek thought) does not find it in his heart to abandon the counterpart identification of philosophy with search for the truly Real; and hence he finds it necessary to substitute an ultimate and absolute flux for an ultimate permanence. Thus his great empirical services in calling attention to the fundamental importance of considerations of time for problems of life and mind get compromised with a mystic non-empirical "Intuition."[85]

"There are two profoundly different ways of knowing a thing. The first implies that we move round the object; the second that we enter into it. The first is the way of analysis; the second is the way of intuition."[86] Intuition "...is the kind of *intellectual sympathy* by which one places oneself within an object in order to coincide with what is unique in it and consequently inexpressible."[87]

Bergson and William James, animated by different motives and proceeding by different methods, installed change at the very heart of things. Bergson took his stand on the primacy of life and consciousness, which are notoriously in a state of flux. Fixed laws which govern change and fixed ends toward which changes tend are both the products of a backward look, one that ignores the forward movement of life. They apply only to that which life has produced and has then left behind in its ongoing vital creative course, a course whose behavior and outcome are unpredictable both mechanically and from the standpoint of ends.

The animating purpose of James was, on the other hand, primarily moral and artistic. It is expressed in his phrase "block universe," employed as a term of adverse criticism. Mechanism and idealism were abhorrent to him because they both hold to a closed universe in which there is no room for novelty and adventure. Only a philosophy of pluralism, of genuine indetermination, and of change which is real and intrinsic gives significance to individuality.

The nature of time and change has now become in its own right a philosophical problem of the first importance.[88]

"Science is concerned wholly with relations, not with individuals. Art, on the other hand, is not only the disclosure of the individuality of the artist but is also a manifestation of individuality as creative of the future."[89]

VII

The relations between Russell and Dewey were complex and of long duration. The interested reader is referred to the author's treatment of this subject in the book *Dewey and Russell: An Exchange.*[90] Nevertheless a few words may be said about the two outstanding figures in Twentieth Century philosophy. Though their personal contacts were cordial, their public encounters were abrasive. The pity is that no serious attempt was made by either to get to the heart of the opposing argument.

Russell's logic has an underlying presupposition that mathematical logic and the world of facts correspond as mirror images. Atomic facts are reflected by atomic propositions. How and why an atomic proposition corresponds to an atomic fact is not indicated. Underlying Russell's thought is the Leibnitzean optimism that nature is rational and will of necessity correspond to the laws of mathematics.

Dewey responds to this notion. "That moral-motivation is obvious in his metaphysics when he says that mathematics takes us 'into the region of absolute necessity to which not only the actual world but every possible world must conform.' "[91]

Russell and Whitehead collaborated on *Principia Mathematica* in which pure mathematics is supposedly derived from logical concepts. Dewey doubted "the existence of a faculty of pure reason independent of any and all experience."[92]

In the field of civil rights, academic freedom, the right of dissent, both men were in full accord, and collaborated on at least one occasion when Russell was denied a professorship at the College of the City of New York because of his views on marriage and "free" love.[93] The specific issues that divided these men may seem faded at this point, but their views provide us with the intelligent adaptation of our views to the new scientific age that is rapidly engulfing us and the preservation of moral values and the enhancement of individual personality.

Samuel Meyer
New York City, 1982

NOTES

[1] See John Dewey, *Lectures in China, 1919-1920*, tr. & ed. by Robert W. Clopton and Tsuin-Chen Ou (Honolulu: University Press of Hawaii, 1973).

[2] *Guide to the Works of John Dewey*, ed. Jo Ann Boydston (Carbondale: Southern Illinois University Press, 1970). "Dewey's Lectures and Influence in China, Ou Tsuin-Chen, pp. 348, 349.

[3] *John Dewey, Philosopher of Science and Freedom*, ed. Sidney Hook, (New York: The Dial Press, 1950) Lawrence K. Frank, p. 88.

[4] *The Philosophy of John Dewey*, ed. Paul Arthur Schilpp, (La Salle: Open Court, 1939) p. 77.

[5] For the near entry of Dewey into the world of philosophical journalism in 1892 see *Journal of the History of Ideas*, v. XX No. 4, Oct-Dec 1959, 545. This venture was realized a generation later by Dewey's contributions to the *New Republic*.

[6] *Dialogue on John Dewey*, ed. Corliss Lamont (New York: Horizon Press, 1959) pp. 50-52. See also Biographical Notes, pp. 143-155.

[7] *On Experience, Nature, and Freedom*, ed. Richard J. Bernstein (Indianapolis: The Bobbs-Merrill Company, Liberal Arts Press, Inc., 1960), pp. 7-9.

[8] John Dewey, *Problems of Men* (New York: Philosophical Library,

1946), pp. 169, 171.

9   In 1903 Dewey published a collection of essays of his colleagues
    and students entitled *Studies in Logical Theory*. Dewey's essays,
    together with some later studies were collected and published
    under the title *Essays in Experimental Logic* in 1916, University of
    Chicago Press. For a response to the later version by Bertrand
    Russell see *Dewey and his Critics*, ed. Sidney Morgenblesser (New
    York: The Journal of Philosophy, Inc. 1977), pp. 231 ff.

10   *On Experience, Nature, and Freedom*, pp. XXV, XXVI.

11   John Dewey, *Experience and Nature* (La Salle: Open Court
    Publishing Co., 1925), pp. 417-419. Frederick Pollock complains
    to Holmes that Dewey's quotations of Holmes "to my annoyance
    do not indicate exactly where they are to be found." For the benefit
    of Holmes scholars, the quotations Dewey uses come from Oliver
    Wendell Holmes, *Collected Legal Papers* (New York: Harcourt,
    Brace and Company, 1921), pp. 305, 314. *Holmes-Pollock Letters*,
    ed. Mark DeWolfe Howe (Cambridge: Harvard University Press),
    Vol. II p. 272.

12   *Holmes-Pollock Letters*, op. cit. p. 272.

13   *Ibid.* p. 287.

14   Martin Buber, *Moses, The Revelation and the Covenant* (New
    York: Harper and Row, 1958), p. 48.

15   John Dewey, *Art As Experience* (New York: Capricorn Books,
    1958).

16   *Ibid.* See back cover of volume.

17   John Dewey, *Lectures in China, 1919-1920*, op. cit. p. 139.

18   *Ibid.* p. 140.

19 *Living Philosophies, A Series of Intimate Credos* (New York: Simon and Schuster, 1931) p. 21.

20 *I Believe*, ed. Clifton Fadiman (New York: Simon and Schuster, 1939) p. 354.

21 *Ibid.* p. 348.

22 John Dewey, *Logic, The Theory of Inquiry,* (New York: Holt, Rinehart and Winston, 1938) p. 417.

23 *Ibid.* p. 418.

24 *Ibid.* p. 157.

25 *Dewey and his Critics*, p. 242.

26 See e.g., John Dewey, *Experience and Nature* (New York: Dover Publications, Inc. 1958), p. 234 and pp. 109, 110. "But in existence, or metaphysically, cause and effect are on the same level; they are portions of one and the same historic process, each having efficacy, or serial connection. Since existence is historic it can be known or understood only as each portion is distinguished and related. For knowledge "cause" and "effect" alike have a partial and truncated being. It is as much a part of the real being of atoms that they give rise in time, under increasing complication of relationships, to qualities of blue and sweet, pain and beauty, as that they have at a cross-section of time extension, mass, or weight."

27 *Ibid.* p. 84.

28 *Ibid.*

29 *Ibid.* p. 234.

30 John Dewey, *Reconstruction in Philosophy* (Boston: Beacon Press, 1957), p. 169.

[31] *Ibid.* p. 171.

[32] *Ibid.* p. 172.

[33] *Ibid.* p. 175.

[34] *Ibid.* p. 173.

[35] John Dewey, *Liberalism and Social Action* (New York: Capricorn Books, 1963), pp. 6-7.

[36] See *Readings in Jurisprudence*, ed. Jerome Hall (Indianapolis: The Bobbs-Merrill Company, 1938), pp. 189-190.

[37] See Samuel Meyer, *The Deacon and the Jewess: Adventures in Heresy* (New York: Philosophical Library, 1982), pp. 13-14.

[38] See Thorold Rogers, *Six Centuries of Work and Wages* (London: George Allen & Unwin Ltd., 1949), p. 240, "All at once, then, and as by a stroke, the labourer, both peasant and artisan, became the master of the situation in England."

[39] Oliver Wendell Holmes, Jr., *The Common Law* (Boston: Little, Brown & Co., 1946) p. 1.

[40] Hillary House Publishers, Ltd. (New York: 1961).

[41] Olmstead v. United States 277 U.S. 438, 470 (1928).

[42] Slaughterhouse Cases 83 U.S. 36, 105 (1872).

[43] 111 U.S. 746, 756, 757 (1883).

[44] Jean Bodin, *Six Books of the Commonwealth*, abridged & tr. M.J. Tooley (New York: Barnes & Noble, 1967).

[45] John Dewey, *The Public and its Problems—An Essay in Political*

Inquiry (Chicago: Gateway Books, 1946).

[46] *Ibid.* p. 31.

[47] *Ibid.* pp. 68, 69.

[48] *Ibid.* p. 73.

[49] Supra, note 19.

[50] *Liberalism and Social Action*, pp. 4, 5, 6.

[51] John Dewey, *Presents the Living Thoughts of Jefferson* (London: Cassell & Co., Ltd., 1941), p. 12.

[52] *Ibid.* p. 13.

[53] *Ibid.* p. 15.

[54] *Ibid.* pp. 17, 18.

[55] *Guide to the Works of John Dewey*, p. 15 ff.

[56] *Ibid.* pp. 25-38.

[57] John Dewey, *How We Think* (Boston: D.C. Heath & Co. 1910). Completely revised 1933; John Dewey, *Essays in Experimental Logic.* (Chicago: The University of Chicago Press, 1916); John Dewey, *Democracy and Education*, (New York: The Macmillan Company, 1916) Ch. XI, "Experience and Thinking", pp. 163-178; John Dewey, *Logic The Theory of Inquiry.* (New York: Holt, Rinehart and Winston, 1938).

[58] (New York: Columbia University Press, 1943).

[59] See *Social Thought in America*, (Boston: Beacon Press, 1957);

Foundations of Historical Knowledge (New York: Harper & Row, 1965).

[60] *John Dewey and Arthur F. Bentley, A Philosophical Correspondence*, ed. Sidney Ratner et al (New Brunswick: Rutgers University Press, 1964), p. 328.

[61] *Ibid. p. 439.*

[62] *Monist*, April, 1898, VIII 321-341.

[63] *Social Thought in America*, op. cit. pp. 52, 55 and *The Journal of Philosophy* vol. 42 #12, 328-331 (1945).

[64] For a vigorous defense of Dewey on this issue see *John Dewey: Philosopher of Science and Freedom*, ed. Sidney Hook (New York: The Dial Press, 1950) pp. 194-207 by Sidney Hook.

[65] *Democracy and Education*, pp. 393, 394.

[66] New York Times, 3/11/59; 19:6.

[67] *John Dewey and the World View*, ed. Douglas E. Lawson and Arthur E. Lean (Carbondale: Southern Illinois University Press, 1964), pp. 16, 17.

[68] *Ibid.* pp. 58, 63.

[69] *Democracy and Education*, op. cit. p. 101.

[70] John Dewey, *Philosophy and Civilization* (New York: Capricorn Books, 1963), p. 291.

[71] See Ralph Barton Perry, *The Thought and Character of William James*, (Boston: Little, Brown and Company, 1953) 2 Vol. See also Dewey's review of this book in John Dewey, *Problems of Men*, (New York: Philosophical Library, 1946) p. 379. See also *The Vanishing Subject in the Psychology of James* (ibid.) p. 396.

[72] John Dewey, *Philosophy and Civilization*, op. cit. pp. 4, 5.

[73] *On Experience, Nature and Freedom*, pp. 15, 16.

[74] *The Writings of William James*, ed. John J. McDermott (New York: Random House, 1967), p. 169.

[75] *Ibid.* p. 183.

[76] *Ibid.* p. 169.

[77] *Ibid.* p. 181.

[78] *Ibid.* p. 284.

[79] *Problems of Men*, pp. 402, 403.

[80] *On Experience, Nature and Freedom*, op. cit. p. 16.

[81] *The Psychological Review*, July (1896).

[82] *Philosophy and Civilization*, p. 251.

[83] *Ibid.* p. 202; 232.

[84] *Essays in Experimental Logic*, p. 37.

[85] John Dewey, "Need for Reconstruction of Philosophy," *On Experience, Nature and Freedom*, ed. Richard J. Bernstein, op. cit. p. 58. For conjecture on the relation of Bergson's thought to modern quantum physics, see Louis de Broglie, *Physics and Microphysics*, (New York: Grosset & Dunlop, 1966) pp. 186-194 and bibliography.

[86] Albert William Levi, *Philosophy and the Modern World*, (Bloomington: Indiana University Press, 1959) p. 65.

[87] *Ibid.* p. 66.

[88] *On Experience, Nature and Freedom*, pp. 228, 229.

[89] *Ibid.* p. 242.

[90] Samuel Meyer, *Dewey and Russell* (New York: Philosophical Library. Due 1984).

[91] *Experience and Nature*, p. 57.

[92] *Logic The Theory of Inquiry*, p. 156.

[93] See *The Bertrand Russell Case*, ed. John Dewey and Horace M. Kallen (New York: The Viking Press, 1941).

TYPES OF THINKING

TYPES OF THINKING

Aristotle's Concept of Species

As I begin this series of lectures I must confess that I had a great deal of trouble in selecting a title for it. For a while I considered "A Summary of the Method of Logic;" then I wondered about "A Summary of Thinking in the History of Philosophy;" but I discarded both titles, and have decided to call the series "Types of Thinking."* Ordinarily I should not be so much concerned with a title, but I recognized the need for a title which would call attention to the fact that these lectures deal with thinking not so much from the angle of psychology as from that of logic. Our subject matter is really the history of philosophy, and our purpose is to establish a historical perspective within which we can examine the major types of thinking which have characterized significant eras.

There will be a certain degree of specialization in this series, since we are dealing with logic, and logic is an established field of special-

* From John Dewey, Additional Lectures in China, 1919-1921. A series of lectures delivered in China retranslated into English and edited by Robert W. Clopton and Tsuin-chen Ou. A series of eight lectures at National Peking University; the first lecture delivered November 12, 1919.

ization. We must also pay attention to the historical context within which each type of thinking developed; some knowledge of the context is essential if we are to appreciate the full meaning of what we talk about. We can understand better if we can see developments against the background in which they occurred. We are interested in history not so much for itself as for what it can contribute to our understanding.

I hope not to be any more technical than is absolutely necessary; for a series of lectures such as this one I believe that specialization should be kept to an irreducible minimum. Also, I intend to be selective rather than to undertake to give a comprehensive coverage to my subject. It would, indeed, be presumptuous for me to undertake to deal with all major types of thinking that have developed throughout the history of philosophy within the few weeks available to us. I will make the historical treatment as brief as I can without sacrificing the purpose of the lectures; and our consideration of the types of thinking with which we do deal will be in great deal less detail than you will find in textbooks on the subject.

For this lecture series I have chosen four types of thinking for discussion. The first of these we might call the systematizing and classifying method, which emphasizes systematization, analysis, and classification. Aristotle is the exemplar of this type. The second is the rationalistic or deductive type of thinking which we see in the work of Descartes. The development of experimental science had much to do with the need for and development of this type of thinking, as it also did with the third type which we will consider, empirical or sensationalistic thinking. We associate this third type with the name of Francis Bacon, but it was taken to a more advanced stage of development by John Locke. The fourth type with which we will deal is the experimental method. Later on we will examine in some detail the ways in which this fourth type of thinking is to be distinguished from the second and third types.

The development of Western thinking has been discontinuous, and often in what appear to have been disconnected stages. Nevertheless, if we consider types of thinking within their historical contexts, we can discern threads which disclose more continuity of development than appears on the surface.

The first systems of organized thought of which we have record originated around 600 B.C. in Greece. When we look at European culture, we find that its religion derives largely from Judea, its politics from Rome, and its thought (which underlies both religion and politics) from Greece, a small peninsula in the Mediterranean in southeastern Europe.

Systematic and organized methods of thinking were first developed by the Greeks, who wrought so well that after the passage of twenty-five centuries textbooks in logic present material which is not very different from what the Greeks developed. It is true, of course, that sentences have been altered, and different examples are used; but it is also true that the essence of Greek logic still lives in modern logic. Naturally, then, when we talk about the first type of thinking, we have to start with the Greeks.

This first type of thinking had its origins in a period of social confusion and intellectual anarchy. The Sophists developed numerous approaches to organized thinking, but in many cases what one school advanced was totally incompatible with the teachings of another school. Some of them attacked and undermined existing institutions, and discredited moral codes, with resulting intensification of confusion to the point of anarchy. Then Socrates came on to the scene with a new method for thinking. Socrates taught that no matter how confused and confusing the situation might be, men could, by diligent searching, discern common elements among diversities, and by approaching problems systematically, bring order out of confusion.

Socrates attributed confusion about morals to ignorance; he said that men were unable to decide what they ought to do because they had failed to devise criteria which come as the result of knowledge. He made it his mission to discover a criterion by which men could distinguish right from wrong, truth from falsehood, good from evil. He believed that if knowledge could be organized and unified, man's behavior could become ordered by valid moral standards. The method he devised was designed to organize human thinking so that a discernible pattern of morals would govern man's behavior. His philosophy was primarily a search for unity. The problem was to enable men to recognize that which was common to the many things they argued about, and thus to make rational discussion possible. Even today we have to come to agreement about the common elements in the subjects we discuss, and work our discussion outward from this common core of understanding.

Our word "logic" derives from the Greek word "logos," or discourse. Originally the reference was to debate. Our term "dialectic" derives from the Greek word for dialogue. Both debate and dialogue are forms of social discourse, but formal logic developed primarily out of the need for rules to govern debate. Socrates' first rubric was that the parties to a debate must agree about the subject matter being debated. If, for example, A says "Mr. Smith is very tall," and B counters with "No, he is very short," there can not be any meaningful argument until A and B first agree that they are talking about the same Mr. Smith. If it turns out that A is referring to John Smith, and B to James Smith, there is nothing for them to argue about. The first condition of debate, therefore, is that it have a common object or topic.

Socrates' second rubric was that the subject being debated must possess the quality of permanence and not be subject to change. In philosophical terminology, the matter being debated must possess objective certainty. This means that debate is possible only when the object of the discussion has permanent existence. When Socrates debated with the Sophists about justice, they took different positions, but they did agree that justice conformed to the criterion of objective certainty. Without such agreement meaningful debate would have been impossible.

Aristotle's logic, or method of thinking, derived from that of Socrates. The two main points of his logical theory were (1) that it is possible to find a common characteristic shared by a group of phenomena, which is what Socrates had called the "form," and (2) that since this common characteristic is selected from the several dissimilar things, it can be used to fix a definition that will show clearly what that "form" is. Aristotle's various logical methods are all built on these two basic concepts. You should not consider them unimportant, or neglect them.

Aristotle's interests differed considerably from those of Socrates. Socrates emphasized politics, society, and human life, while Aristotle emphasized pure thinking. As a youth Aristotle had studied medicine, anatomy, and biology, and many of his theories were influenced by his early work in these fields. His concept of species resulted from his application of Socrates' methods to the subject matter of biology; he used the method of Socrates to create the concept of species which embraced numbers of individual objects and then he dealt with the individual object by referring it to the species within which it was embraced.

The concept of species was central to Aristotle's philosophy, and the starting point of the method of thinking which he developed. This development which occurred well over two thousand years ago, was an important milestone in the history of European philosophy. The Aristotelian concept of species has dominated European philosophy for more than two millennia. Its importance lies in the fact that it initiated a new era in the history of thought—and if I can make this point sufficiently clear in this lecture, I shall be happy.

Nature comprises more things than can be counted, but when natural objects are classified into species they come into manageable compass. As an example, there are innumerable kinds of trees— oaks, elms, mulberry, and so on; but when they are all embraced under the species of tree, we are provided with a concept with which we can easily deal. Since there are uncounted numbers of individual objects, each different in some degree from all the others, we have to search for common elements and group the objects into species, ignoring the differences among those grouped into any one species. We can say that all trees are the same with reference to the common characteristics which lead us to classify them as trees, or, in the same way, that all men are the same. Such classification enables us to deal intelligently with the phenomena of nature which, considered as individual objects, would overwhelm us with confusion.

Aristotle noted three characteristics of his concept of species. First, each species is a whole. It is comprehensive, representative of all the objects embraced within it, and any one of these objects may be used as an example of all others. The species tree, for example, embraces all trees, whether they are used for timber or for firewood; and any given tree may exemplify the species which includes all trees.

Second, any one species comprises objects which have common or identical elements or characteristics. Aristotle emphasized form. Each kind of thing is produced under its own form. All oaks have the same form, regardless of their location, whether they stand on the east side of the house or the west. Thus species is the representation of the common, typical, and standard form of the individual objects which it comprises.

Third, a species is permanent. In addition to being comprehensive and representative of the common form of its component parts, a species is permanent and unchanging. After an individual tree dies, for example, the species of tree continues to exist unimpaired. Similarly, one stone may crumble into dust, but the species of stone still exists. It does not matter that individual objects come into being and cease to be, either cyclically or otherwise, the species in which they are embraced has an unending existence.

The publication of Darwin's *Origin of the Species* sixty years ago wrought havoc in contemporary thought. Why? Because people were so completely under the influence of Aristotelian thought patterns. Aristotle had taught that every species is permanent and unchanging; but now Darwin was theorizing that each species had had its origin, and that it was subject to change—a challenge indeed to a two thousand year old traditional manner of thinking. It is not to be wondered at that Darwin's theory upset so many of his contemporaries. It ran exactly counter to the tradition which had dominated so many generations, and which had resulted in people taking for granted the unchanging nature of species.

The reason that this type of thinking constitutes such an important milestone in the history of philosophy is that the concept of species is essential to thought and the first step toward knowledge. When one is walking in the woods, for example, and asks the identity of a tree or a weed, and he is told that it belongs to such and such a species, he can place it right away, and recognize its relationship to other trees or weeds. The greatest single contribution of Aristotle was his invention of the concept of species, a concept which enables us to classify things under common headings in accordance with their common characteristics.

A precondition to knowledge is perception; but perception does not constitute knowledge. We can perceive without knowing what it is that we perceive. Not only is perception alone insufficient for pursuit of advanced knowledge, it is not even enough to provide us the rudimentary knowledge which we need to conduct our everyday affairs. It is not enough merely to perceive; we must understand what we perceive; we must know that this is a lamp, a sheet of paper, a watch, or a suit of clothes. But even when we recognize individual objects of perception, according to Aristotle, it is still necessary that we be able to think of them as representatives of the species to which they belong before we can rightfully speak of having knowledge of them.

The concept of species has been tremendously influential in the history of European thought. In politics and in other social arrangements Western Europeans have tended to emphasize the individual; but in their systems of thought, they have emphasized comprehensiveness, and have classified things according to the concept of species. The importance of this concept in the history of thought lies first in its comprehensiveness, and second in its independence and systematic nature. A genus is of a higher order than a species; a cow is a cow, and a horse is a horse, but both cow and horse belong to the species of beasts; and all beasts, together with birds, fishes, and so on, are embraced in the genus of animals. Using this concept, one may proceed step by step from the top to the bottom by inference; he can also move from bottom to top. Such systematic ordering has proved to be the most useful way of classifying objects.

The concept of species can be applied in mathematics as well as in biology. Angle is a species within which right angles, obtuse angles, and acute angles are embraced. And angles belong to the genus of plane, within which rectangles and circles are embraced. This is merely an example of the way in which the concept of species has made possible the systematization of knowledge and thought in all fields.

This concept of the species being embraced within the genus, and so on up to even more comprehensive classes, is not unlike the Chinese family register, with the great-grandfather at the top, then the grandfather, the father, and the son, so that each of you can trace his ancestry systematically and without confusion. Such knowledge is accurate because it is systematically organized. Aristotle's philosophy provides us with the means of getting this kind of knowledge. Indeed, it is not too much to say that Aristotelian logic, with its emphasis on systematization and classification, is the most important single development in the history of thought.

We have been talking in rather general terms about the first type of thinking with which these lectures will deal, systematizing and classifying. In our next lecture we will give closer examination to the method employed in such thinking. But here we must note two shortcomings in Aristotle's theory: the first is that it treats species as having unchanging permanence; and the second is that it does not provide for the function of invention. Metaphorically, everything is classified in the family register, but there is no means of getting knowledge that is not already recorded there, no provision for moving from the known to the unknown.

These shortcomings notwithstanding, we must recognize the inestimable value of Aristotle's concept of species in the history of thought. This value lies in the fact that the peoples of the West have become habituated to thinking in terms of species, and thus to the classification and systematization of knowledge. Without this all-important concept, contributed by the Greeks, western thinking could not have developed, and Europeans today might still be living in a state of barbarism.

Characteristics of Aristotle's Thought

In my first lecture I mentioned the four types of thinking with which this series will deal, and then discussed in somewhat general terms the first of these types, the taxonomic, which was developed in the Greek tradition, created by Socrates and brought to its full development by Aristotle.

This type of thinking originated in an age of intellectual anarchy, when both political and social situations were disordered and chaotic. Thoughtful men advanced the proposition that the chaos and confusion were the result of the absence of clearly defined criteria for valid knowledge. They thought that until such criteria could be provided, disorder and disorganization would continue to characterize the political and social scene. Hence, the most important task before them was to develop the criteria for knowledge which might then enable them to understand the nature of justice, of continence, and of virtue. They believed that if they could derive such criteria, a well-ordered and organized social and political state of affairs would naturally result.

The development of this type of thinking was thus a result of practical social motivation. The men who developed this system of thought did so for the purpose of bringing order out of confusion, system out of chaos, in the political and social affairs of their time.

Aristotle was a physician and scientist, so his orientation was considerably different from that of Socrates. But Socrates was a strong influence on Aristotle's passion for systematizing and classifying; and it was clearly Socrates' influence which prompted Aristotle's efforts to find common forms in confused situations, and to formulate his systematic approach to thinking.

Along with this brief summary of my first lecture, I must make reference to a factor of considerable importance to our understanding of Aristotle, namely the fact that Greek thinking was markedly influenced by the Greek fine arts. The Greeks had great appreciation of beauty, and their concept of the beautiful was one which emphasized proportion, equilibrium, and harmony. Both in architecture and in sculpture the Greeks strove for these objectives; Greek artists eschewed the peculiar and the ugly. Greek thinking reflects the concern with proportion and harmony in the arts. It was natural, then, for Aristotle to regard the universe as the headwaters of the fine arts; to speak of the creator of the universe as an artist, and to look upon natural phenomena as the prototype which embodied the proportionality which was such a dominant characteristic of the fine arts.

Let us go on from our general description into a more detailed examination of the characteristics of this type of thinking. The first requirement we note is that each individual object must be defined by assigning it to a species, and to a variety within the species. It is not enough, for example, to classify man as a member of the species, animal; we must also indicate what variety of animal man is, and assign him to the variety, tool-making animal. The first step of Aristotle's knowledge of reason is this sort of definition.

Definition thus has the function of describing the real nature of the object, and we first grasp this real nature through its definition. We must know to what species it belongs, as well as to what variety within the species. For example, a triangle is defined as "a plane figure formed by three lines each of which intersects the other two." Plane figure is the species within which the triangle is embraced; and three lines, each intersecting the other two, is the variety within the species of plane figure. Again, a right triangle is defined as "a triangle which contains one right angle." In this case, triangle is the species, and right triangle is the variety. This is the method by which Aristotle taught that we can grasp the real nature of an object.

We often make light of such truistic formal logic, but in actual fact it illustrates the very important concept of species. The individual object comes into being and then ceases to be, but the species is unchanging and eternal. Real knowledge of any object can be had only when we classify it into species and variety, grasp the nature of the eternal species, and discern its status and relationship in a systematized universe. There is no other way we can know the real nature of any object.

Quite obviously this concept of definition implies that human perception—seeing, hearing, smelling, touching—can grasp only the appearance of an object, not its species which constitutes its real nature. For this reason those who adopted this type of thinking disparaged sense perception, holding that real, or rational, knowledge of the object could be gained only by systematizing it, somewhat as a man's status is determined by the position of his name in the family register. In this view, the world was rational, or what Aristotle called the work of pure mind. The doctrine that the universe was rational had great appeal to theologians in the Middle Ages, and the Church cast its official dogma in the mold of Aristotelian theory.

The second essential characteristic of this type of thinking is its employment of the syllogism, a device which is based upon and which makes application of definition. The syllogism was regarded as a means of achieving complete rational knowledge, knowledge which is most accurately descriptive of the relationships among things, and particularly, the relationship between the individual object and the classifications under which it falls. The syllogism was not merely a convenience, but an expression of the rational universe; and for this reason Aristotle had profound respect for the syllogism as a method of arriving at truth.

Let us take a simple, everyday example. Someone tells us that "Socrates is mortal." We are not disposed to argue with this statement. It appears obvious on the face of it, but how can we demonstrate that it is true? The demonstration by means of a syllogism goes like this:

> The major premise: "All men are mortal."
> The minor premise: "Socrates is a man."
> The conclusion: "Therefore, Socrates is mortal."

The same argument can be presented diagramatically:

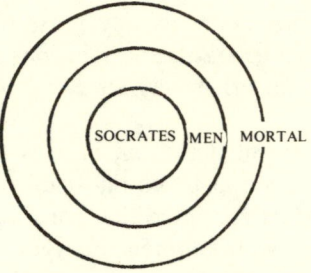

When the individual object and its species are incorporated into one systematic statement, the argument becomes of one rational form. To be sure, we need not think about everything in this form of argument, but Aristotle asserted that a rational proposition can be derived only through this kind of systematization, and not by any other means. Any thought which cannot be reduced to rational propositions he regarded as false, incomplete, or misleading.

In brief Aristotle taught that the syllogism is the most complete scientific form of knowledge, that is the one valid method of natural and rational systematization. Nowadays we are so familiar with the syllogism that we tend to make light of it, and to look upon it as hackneyed, or as a mere exercise. This is because the way of thinking to which we are accustomed is so vastly different from that which our ancestors used. Formerly people believed that the universe was rational and systematic, and that everything in it could be classified into species which were unchanging and eternal. Now that we have abandoned this belief and no longer look upon anything as being permanent and unchanging, we have virtually relegated the syllogism to the status of an intellectual exercise.

The two characteristics which we have been elaborating are predicated upon the assumption that the universe is static rather than dynamic. But Aristotle had to account in some way for the observable fact of change. When we observe external objects, we perceive changing phenomena on every hand—positional changes of high and low, growth and decay of trees and grasses, the aging of men, and innumerable others. But the change with which Aristotle dealt was not irregular or spasmodic variation, but was movement in the direction of fixed forms. Each separate tree grows toward its most complete form, the form that is typical of its species. A chick grows to be an adult chicken, which is the most complete form of the species, chicken. The oak also grows toward the most complete form of its species. Aristotle explained the upward movement of air, smoke and fire by positing heaven as the most complete form of their species. Thus, in order to understand change, we must know the complete form toward which, in each case, change is directed.

What is this form toward which changes in things are directed? It is cosmic purpose, or what Aristotle called final cause. This concept of final cause is an important aspect of Aristotle's philosophy. Aristotle taught that while we must be aware of what a thing changes into, and of the way in which it changes, these are much less important than knowing the purpose of the change. Even when Aristotle dealt with the concept of change, he persisted in his commitment to the concept of static, inflexible, and fixed purpose. This idea is summed up in the saying that "Nature does nothing in vain," which means that everything in nature is there to serve some purpose. This implies a rational universe in which all activity is directed toward the accomplishment of some purpose. This interpretation of nature had a marked and long-lasting impact on the history of philosophy. When we come, in a later lecture, to the second type of thinking, we will note that one of the reasons it was an advance over the one we are now discussing was that it was able to discredit the interpretation of nature as being purposive.

The fourth item for consideration is the fact that there are many cases of change which cannot be regarded as moving in the direction of a complete or perfect form. There is no complete form, for example, for the weather, which is unpredictable beyond the circumstance that it is usually warmer in the summer than in the winter. Similarly unpredictable and irregular changes occur in the human body. Our eyes and ears change with age; all we can be sure of is that they remain approximately the same in relation to the rest of the body. For Aristotle, such resistant form could not come within the scope of science. He admitted as scientific knowledge only that which was dead, inflexible, static, only that which was necessarily true, and not that which was only probably true.

Aristotle gave the name experience to change which is irregular, and differentiated this from scientific knowledge, or rational knowledge. The only changes that could come within the scope of science were those which moved in the direction of, and which were governed by, final cause—the chick and the oak, again. Typical of the things which Aristotle regarded as certain, and therefore admissible to the realm of science, were the stars of the heavens which could be counted and which moved in fixed orbits, and triangles, the angles of which invariably equalled two right angles. Because such things were fixed and invariable, he took them as rational knowledge, but the questions of a man's height or his rate of growth, or of the temperature in winter and in summer, referred at best to probabilities, and therefore were not proper subjects for scientific inquiry. The disparagement of experience, which is mutable, and the exaltation of rational knowledge, which is static and immutable, constituted Aristotle's most important legacy to western thought. This legacy resulted in a fundamental problem in the history of philosophy, the problem of the relative status of experience and reason in epistemology. This problem generated centuries of controversy.

This brings us to the fifth characteristic of Aristotle's type of thinking, the division of all knowledge into two levels—the higher, of which astronomy and arithmetic are examples, and the lower, which embraces such things as human behavior—morality, social change, ethics, sociology, philosophy of human life. Because these latter do not have a fixed direction of change, are unpredictable, have no complete form toward which to change, and are related to no final cause, they constitute a level of knowledge that is lower than that which deals with the eternal and the immutable. This relegation to inferior status of all human behaviors and practical actions, of politics and social philosophy, remained characteristic of western thought for nearly two thousand years.

A theory which denies the possibility of an ultimate criterion of human behavior and practical affairs renders impossible any perfect knowledge in this realm. The search for perfect knowledge must begin with that which is certain and immutable; it cannot be achieved by doing, which is inferior to knowing. The implication is that men can approach the most complete and highest form of their behaviors through knowledge, which must be sought within the mind. Doing involves others, and therefore can never be completely interior, as thought is. Philosophers seek knowledge through contemplation, and therefore live rational lives. This life of reason is the greatest happiness to which man may aspire.

To summmarize: in addition to the concepts of definition and classification, and the syllogism, Aristotle's thinking is characterized by three concepts which have had great influence on the development of western thought. The first of these is that only such changes as are regular and governed by a final cause are fit subjects for science, or rational knowledge, and that all other changes, those without regularity and purpose, are outside the scope of science. Science is the knowledge of fixed relationships. The second concept is that experience is inferior to reason, the latter being ultimate and formal. The third concept is that practice or doing is less important and less to be regarded than the life of reason. These three concepts have had a basic influence in the history of thought.

The next two types of thinking with which we will deal—the rationalistic and the empirical—both constituted reactions against Aristotelianism. Our purpose in these first two lectures which we have devoted to a general description of the first type of thinking has not been to repeat what textbooks say, but to draw attention to the methods employed, to make explicit its historical background, and to lay the basis for an examination of its influence upon and relationship to the second and third types of thinking.

Now that I have finished talking about the methods of Aristotle's thinking, I'd like to conclude my lecture by rendering a judgment. Westerners have typically regarded the people of the Orient as being extremely conservative, noting that the latter have been subjected to classical patterns of thought for some two thousand years or more. Westerners have thought that the old traditions persisted so long because of the innate conservatism of Orientals. But these people overlook the fact that Aristotle dominated western thinking for fully as long a time as classic thinking has prescribed the pattern for the Orient. It was only about three hundred years ago that revolutionary currents in western thought began to challenge the domination of Aristotle, and it was even more recently that Aristotle's fundamental concepts were superseded by others more appropriate to our time.

Descartes
Extension and Motion

At the beginning of this series of lectures I told you that we should be talking about four types and methods of thinking. Then we devoted the first two lectures to the first type, the systematizing and classifying thinking of the Greek traditon, which we might call the logic of systematization. In this evening's lecture and the one following it, we will address ourselves to the second type of thinking, which, as I have mentioned, is that of rationalistic logic.

Before we get into this subject, though, we should look at some of the changes and shifts in emphasis in Greek thinking over the centuries, and in particular to the application and utilization of Aristotelian logic by the Schoolmen of the Middle Ages. In the two thousand years between the time of Aristotle and the seventeenth century A.D., Aristotelianism, especially at the hands of the Schoolmen, underwent marked alterations and was ultimately transmuted into a system which Aristotle himself would have had difficulty in recognizing.

Aristotle had applied this first method of thinking both in the natural sciences and in the solution of human and social problems.

As a scientist—he was primarily a biologist—he used his method to deal wih natural phenomena. The Greeks did have a certain amount of interest in the natural sciences, although they were much more concerned with human life and the problems of society. But they did not apply their method to such questions as divine authority or other religious problems.

Some centuries later, however, the people of Europe adopted Christianity, which spread from southern Europe, then to the southwest, and finally to northern Europe until it embraced the entire subcontinent. At the time much of Europe was still semi-barbaric. Somewhat surprisingly the Greek method of thinking was adopted by Roman Christianity as a means of defending its religious dogmas, and as a pattern into which to cast its theology. We can be very sure that the idea that his method, derived from his concern with the natural sciences, would ever be appropriated and utilized for theological ends never even occurred to Aristotle.

Basically Aristotle's method assumes that each science has its own body of premises which are common, self-evident, and always true. For instance, the common truth of geometry is that "the whole is larger than any of its parts," something which is self-evident. Similarly biology, physics, and astronomy are based on common, self-evident truths. But Aristotle's rationality and truth are human rationality and human truth; they are not theological or mystical truth. Aristotelian truth is derived from human rationality; there is no theological or mystical element in it. We can say that Aristotelian logic is a natural logic, not a transcendental one.

But in the Middle Ages the Schoolmen appropriated the Aristotelian method and utilized it to deal with supernatural questions, with the existence of God, with the nature of angels, with life after death, and so on. They used the method which Aristotle had devised, but they had small interest in the subject matter to which he had applied it, such as geometry, physics, biology, and astronomy. They were more interested in the Bible, in papal encyclicals, and in the writings of the early Christian fathers. They accepted these as eternal truth, and using them as premises constructed a theology which dealt with every aspect of life.

The essentially liberal method of Aristotelian thinking was utilized by the Schoolmen chiefly between the eleventh and the thirteenth centuries. During these three hundred years the Schoolmen used the originally liberal method of Aristotle to bolster the authority of the Church; they applied a method which had been devised to deal with natural and social science to the sphere of religion and theology. Why, you may ask, do we insist on going into this matter? It is because we want to sketch in enough of the background to enable us to get a better understanding of the second of our types of thinking with which I am going to deal, and the third type. Both of them are indicative of an interest in going back to, and drawing upon the Greek concern with the natural sciences and with human problems.

Before the dominance of the first type of thinking was challenged by the rise of the second, philosophers were concentrating their attention on the supernatural, deprecating the problems of everyday living. The period during which these types of thinking were in competition was one in which preoccupation with otherworldliness was giving way to a growing interest in the here and now. A new interest in human life and its problems was being generated.

There are many reasons why this transformation took place. The first is that, by and large, the Schoolmen of the Middle Ages had little contact with, and consequently not much knowledge of, the literature and the arts of classic times; but in the Revival of Learning, sometimes referred to as the Renaissance, great enthusiasm developed for the study of the classics. Scholars discovered that the art, literature, and learning of ancient Greece and Rome constituted a vast resource for the improvement of life and for the extension of knowledge. The second reason was that the voyages of discovery and awareness of the existence of the Western Hemisphere extended people's vision and enlarged the range of their imagination and thinking. The third reason was that communication with Asia brought them into contact with the Arabs, who had developed science, mathematics, and medicine to a much higher level than the Europeans had known up to this time. In addition to these three reasons, contact between Europeans and the Turks in the course of the numerous Crusades was an important factor, but one which we do not have time to elaborate.

It is enough for us to say that the people of Europe, during this period, turned their attention to natural phenomena, and developed a vigorous interest in the world in which they were living. The development of this new interest was both cause and consequence of a new way of thinking which appeared on the scene at this time. Two sorts of demands called for the development of a new type of thinking. The first of these was the growing interest in the possibility of controlling the forces of nature and utilizing them to augment man's power and serve his welfare. The other was the desire to go further than the Schoolmen of the Middle Ages had gone in systematizing knowledge, and to devise a type of thinking which would, in addition to demonstrating and defending old truths, enable man to discover truths not previously known to him.

Francis Bacon is the most outstanding thinker associated with the first demand, that man learn to control the forces of nature to the end of increasing his own power. We cannot take time to elaborate on this phase at this time, but will return to Bacon when we discuss the third of our four ways of thinking. The French philosopher, René Descartes, is the foremost thinker among those who sought to meet the second demand, namely that we should employ old knowledge in the search for new truth.

There is quite a contrast between Bacon's bold purpose of conquering nature, and Descartes' more modest approach to a method for the discovery of new truth. This contrast is all the more interesting if we view the work of the two men in historical perspective. Bacon was an Englishman, and in England politics was more liberal and religion less restrictive, since religious revolution had occurred in England much earlier than it did in France. Thus when Bacon boldly proclaimed his purpose of subduing nature, he was, in a way, reflecting the greater freedom that was becoming characteristic of English political and intellectual life.

The situation was quite different on the Continent, and especially so in France, where the authority of the Church had not yet been successfully challenged. In fact, when the scientist Galileo, a contemporary of both Bacon and Descartes, propounded the theory that the earth, instead of being static as had been supposed, in reality revolved around the sun, he was condemned for heresy by the Inquisition because his theory contradicted the position of the religionists.

In the face of this sort of pressure, Descartes even burned his own books. When we consider these aspects of the time and situation in which Descartes worked, we must admire his claim that he had discovered a new method of arriving at truth, and can understand the reasons for his being more circumspect than Bacon was.

In talking about Descartes we will follow the same general plan that we followed in the first two lectures—that is to say, this evening we will discuss the basic concepts of his philosophy, and in our fourth lecture will deal in greater detail with the methods he employed.

In dealing with natural phenomena Descartes employed two basic concepts, extension and motion. The concept extension referred to volume, or the space occupied by a corporeal object, the length, breadth, and depth of the object. The positional change of the corporeal object was motion; that is, all change is to be explained by the positional change of extension. The importance of the application of these concepts to natural phenomena lies in the fact that it introduces the possibility of quantification and of description by means of mathematical formulae. We have confidence in science only when the data can be quantified and treated mathematically. Descartes created a new branch of mathematics—analytic geometry, and interpreted science as knowledge of quantity. Since the method he devised provided the means by which the data of science could be quantified, it became possible to define science in quantitative terms. But quantity is not an independent entity; it is only the key with which men open the store of scientific knowledge; it is an instrument to be employed in the pursuit of scientific knowledge.

It is all very well for us to say that all corporeal things are extension and that all change is motion, but if we continue on this level of abstruseness we may fail to grasp the full significance of what we are talking about. If we deduce four conclusions from Descartes' fundamental conceptions, and compare these with the conclusions of classical science, the matter will become clearer.

The first conclusion which we note is that Descartes' method was a sharp break with the classical distinction between the higher order of knowledge and the lower. The classical practice of assigning a static, hierarchical and unchanging status (such as we see in the family register) to every class of objects was now outmoded. The concept of extension included all corporeal objects, and that of motion included all change. All things were now looked upon in terms of their quantitative relationship; there was no longer place or need for a hierarchy; the stars in the firmament and objects on the earth received the same treatment; all were extension, and all their changes were motion.

Classical thinking had assigned different natures to different things—minerals had one nature, stars another, plants another. But Descartes discarded these distinctions and looked upon all things as being equal in nature. The mystical distinction among the natures of things thus disappeared. For example, respiration in the human body and the circulation of blood were no longer inexplicable, or virtually magic, phenomena; both could now be treated in terms of extension and motion. The circulation of blood in the human body was analagous to the working of a water pump; respiration could be likened to the blowing back and forth of the wind, and so treated as motion. The concept of quantity replaced that of the inherent natures of things, and it was now possible for men to observe everything in the same way, whether it was a living creature or a lump of ore.

Even though modern science has shown that Descartes' conception that all objects were to be explained the same way was an oversimplification, we must still credit him with having made an extremely valuable contribution to the development of human thought. Classic science prior to the time of Descartes had classified things into innumerable fixed, complex, and isolated kinds, with the result that man's efforts to understand his world were discouraged by the apparent unmanageability of the task. Descartes' contribution lay in the fact that he tumbled this feudal system of knowledge, and in effect made man's world susceptible to inquiry. Descartes' contribution to method consists in using the concepts of extension and motion to account for all natural phenomena. They are easy to grasp, and the introduction of these relatively simple concepts did much to dispel the ignorance which had so long prevailed when the world was regarded as consisting of so many mysterious entities that it was useless for man to try to understand it. A conception that did so much to throw light where there had been darkness, which encouraged men to concern themselves with practical application instead of looking on their world with mystified bemusement, is no small improvement in human thinking.

The second conclusion we note is that Descartes made a clean break with the Aristotelian concept of final cause—the purpose for which a thing exists, which governs all change, and which is the end toward which change is directed. Descartes discarded this concept, and asserted that there is no final cause in motion—that motion is no more than positional change of extension. The fact that now men did not need to concern themselves with the search for an unknowable final cause made more economical thought processes possible.

Aristotle's concept of final cause had always been responsible for difficulty, but the harm was compounded when the idea was adopted by theologians and made an instrument to serve the interests of religion. Descartes' discrediting of this concept of a fixed, mystical, and unknowable final cause, and his substitution for it of his concepts of extension and motion, was a most important contribution where practical human affairs are concerned. Let me give you an example. Philosophers such as Aristotle applied the concept of final cause to the human body, asserting that each part of the body has its own purpose. They said that human bodies are warm when they are alive; that when the heat goes, men become sick; and when the bodies become too cold, they die. Men can live only when the heat and the cold of the body are in balance. Since they believed that some part of the body supplies heat, some other part cold, they decided that the heart furnished the heat, the brain the cold. Of course this is an extreme example, and a ridiculous one. But it illustrates one of the dangers we run when we insist upon applying the concept of final cause. To justify the existence of a final cause people will resort to all manner of ridiculous arguments.

However, Descartes changed all this. He denied that change is governed by the final cause toward which it is directed, and instead explained change, or motion, in terms of antecedent cause. Every change, he said, is caused by something that happened before it. He found no need to think of the human body in terms of final cause, but rather in terms of motion—the motion of the blood, the motion of respiration, and so on. He applied the same methods to all other natural phenomena; one motion causes a subsequent one, and that one still another one, and so on indefinitely. Change is the relationship between a precedent cause and a subsequent effect.

The law of conservation of mass was formulated later—for example, the fact that when wood is burned, the weight of the remaining ash plus the heat generated in the burning together add up to the original weight of the wood. But before this law was discovered, it was foreshadowed in Descartes' argument that the motion of all corporeal things involves change in their volume, or extension. The total volume of things exists forever, and the sum of extension and motion never changes. This concept of quantitative relationship was so much more usable in dealing with natural phenomena than the concept of final cause had ever been that it soon superseded the older concept.

The third important conclusion to note is the importance of mathematics in Cartesian thought. Aristotle, when dealing with science, emphasized the classification of things according to their several natures, and disregarded quantitative distinctions, seeing them as accidents. For him, the nature of the chrysanthemum never changed, regardless of its size or color; the nature of the triangle did not change, even when the length of the sides or the size of the angles were altered. Descartes, on the other hand, devoted primary attention to quantity. If all objects are extension, and all change is motion, he asserted that both extension and motion could be counted or measured, and only when they are counted and measured can they be the data of science. Whatever cannot be counted or measured cannot be called science or included in it. The fact that Descartes dislodged the concept of species from the position of dominance it had held in Aristotelian thought is another of his important contributions to the development of thought.

It is undeniably true that students of the history of modern science frequently deplore Descartes' oversimplifications; but it is equally undeniable that modern science is greatly indebted to him. It was only after Descartes had demonstrated the importance of quantification, and after he had insisted that the subject matter of science must be susceptible to numeration and measurement, that scientists were able to give their central concern to the study of quantity and the use of formulae. It was not until Descartes had prepared the ground that the quantitative approach to science could grow and flourish. Prior to his time questions about truth, falsity, accuracy, and so on had to be dealt with in the absence of fixed standards according to which judgments might be rendered; but as a result of his work, standards were devised on quantitative bases, and truth was defined as quantitative accuracy.

We mentioned a few moments ago that Descartes demonstrated the fact that mathematics was the key with which man might unlock the store of scientific knowledge. His emphasis on mathematics stemmed from his concern with the concept of quantity, and he developed a mathematical methodology for the treatment of the data of science. In mathematics we start with the simplest theorems and symbols, with which we can deal with reason alone, apart from any involvement of our sense organs. The answer to a mathematical problem can be arrived at by the application of a few basic theorems; and such an answer can be checked by further use of theorems and symbols, and determined, without any uncertainty to be either correct or incorrect. The basic method of Descartes' thinking is to begin with the simplest theorems and to deduce the more complex from these.

Descartes employed mathematical reasoning, involving simple theorems in the initial stages, to determine answers to his questions; then he applied these simple theorems in combination with more complex ones, to the construction of far more complex new theorems. He viewed the process of constructing new knowledge as being completely the function of reason, and as wholly independent of observation. Thus he took the same attitude toward all the sciences—in any one of them one starts with definitions and then proceeds, step by step, to the deduction of new theorems, by which he meant the discovery of new truth. All this was done by reason, without any need for observation by the sense organs. The accuracy of the resulting theorem, or new item of knowledge, was always, he held, susceptible to confirmation or rejection by acts of reason. This is why we call this method the rationalistic type of thinking.

There is no need for us to labor the fact that, viewed from the vantage point of modern scientific progress, Descartes' attempt to deal with natural phenomena solely through the application of such a limited number of theorems was a mistake. Even in his own time there was controversy on this point. Descartes and his followers gave preeminence to the concept of quantity and to the function of reason; while in the next generation, the great scientist Newton placed equally great emphasis on observation, experimentation, and sense-experience. Newton was himself a great mathematician, but he did not exalt mathematics to anything like the all-important status which Descartes accorded to it. The empiricists eventually won the battle; still we cannot gainsay the invaluable contribution which Descartes made when he demonstrated the importance of quantitative methods and thus paved the way for the development of modern science.

The fourth conclusion to which I direct your attention is that Descartes disparaged sense perception, and regarded it as an unreliable method of gaining knowledge. Descartes was concerned with the quantitative aspects of things, and inasmuch as sense perceptions—sound, color, taste, smell, touch—are related primarily to qualitative distinctions, he feared that they would all but inevitably lead to mistaken conclusions, for the very reason that they are not subject to quantification.

In classic theories, man senses the property of weight through his muscles, color through his eyes, roughness and smoothness through his skin—that is to say that man can know the properties of things only through sense perception. But in Cartesian theory there are no such things as properties—weight, color, roughness or smoothness; these are merely the motion of external objects which induce psychological changes in man. Descartes totally rejected the idea that things have inherent properties. And since sense organs can provide only perception, which is not a basis for knowledge, man must seek out quantitative distinctions as a safeguard against his being deceived by his unreliable sense perceptions.

Descartes' deprecation of sense perception is significant, especially in light of the importance which classic science had attached to quantitative distinctions—distinctions of weight, color, smell, and taste—at the same time that it ignored the importance of quantitative distinctions. Descartes was determined that the emphasis which classic science had put upon sense perception should be superseded by a sounder and more usable approach to knowledge.

Descartes could not have foreseen the effect of his disparagement of sense perception on later philosophical developments. One effect was the dispute between rationalists and empiricists about the relative functions of reason and perception as sources of true knowledge. The other is the continuing contention between Idealists and Materialists. While Descartes gave his major attention to quantitative distinctions, he did not deny the existence of external objects. While Materialists have continued Descartes' emphasis on quantification, Idealists have gone to the other extreme and espoused the view that all the things which man regards as material are, in reality, constructs of the mind.

In our next lecture we will deal with the methods employed in Cartesian thinking. For the moment it is enough for us to mention once more Descartes' two major contributions to human thought: the first, his discrediting the ridiculous concepts of classical science; and second, his replacement of the classical concept of species with his more workable concepts of matter, and his substitution of his concept of motion for the classical method of classification and static distinctions among the properties of things.

Characteristics of Descartes' Thought

In the first two lectures of this series we elaborated upon the close relationship between the Greeks' conception of the universe and their method of thinking. The Greeks saw the universe as being hierarchical and systematic, and as being characterized by distinctions between the higher and the lower, the important and the unimportant. This concept of a hierarchical and systematic universe naturally influenced their method of thinking, causing them to emphasize definition, classification, systematization, and syllogism.

In the third lecture we showed how the Greek concept of the universe was discredited by Descartes, whom we have chosen as exemplar of the second type of thinking, the rationalistic. Descartes saw the universe not as hierarchical, but as equal; not as pluralistic, but as identical. All corporeal objects are extension, or volume; all changes are motion. Descartes employed these concepts of extension and motion to explain the universe; and his new concept of the universe naturally called for a new methodology, for a type of thinking that would be compatible with this concept of a universe characterized by equality in all its manifestations.

The concepts of intuition and deduction are basic to Descartes' methodology; but since he used these words in a particular sense quite different from that attached to them by other philosophers, it behooves us to clarify what he meant when he used them. Let us take intuition first. Many philosophers have treated intuition and reason as mutually exclusive concepts. They have accorded intuition a higher status than reason because of their belief that intuition can grasp things which reason can not know. Some philosophers even supposed that through intuition man may come into possession of mystical or supernatural knowledge. Descartes disagreed with all of them. In his usage intuition and reason not only were not mutually exclusive, but, on the contrary, intuition was a function of reason. It was the most direct, the easiest, and the simplest part of reason, that aspect of reason which can grasp an object most intimately and directly; in other words, when reason functions directly and without mediation, it is intuition. For Descartes, then, intuition was not higher than reason; it was merely reason functioning at its simplest and least complicated level.

Descartes posited two criteria for intuitive knowledge—it must be clear, and it must be distinct. The only knowledge that can be grasped through intuition, if it be true knowledge, must meet these criteria of clarity and distinctness. Let us illustrate with an everyday example. In a darkened room we cannot observe things clearly and distinctly because there is not enough light. We can, though, observe things clearly and distinctly in a room where the light is strong enough. But this is not what Descartes meant by clear and distinct; in his usage, a man can not achieve clear and distinct knowledge even when the lighting is perfect.

The clear and distinct knowledge of which Descartes was speaking is not knowledge derived from sense perception. Knowledge is clear and distinct only when it can be grasped easily and obviously, and when the object of intuitive knowledge can be grasped with such absolute accuracy that there can be no possibility of dispute about it. It is only when all men agree that the object is precisely what each one's intuition reveals it to be that it can be said to be clear and distinct. Ordinary sense perception can never provide knowledge with this degree of accuracy. It is beyond the bounds of the possible for everyone to have exactly the same concept about an object of sense perception; it is out of the question to expect that their concepts will not be subject to some degree of dispute.

Thus Descartes did not expect that clear and distinct knowledge could derive from sense perception; he was concerned with knowledge that is so clear and so distinct that one can readily see that it can be made the basis upon which subsequent knowledge can be built. For example, we can observe a table, and even use it properly; but our perception is not accurate enough to be taken as the basis of knowledge because it does not meet the criteria of clarity and distinctness. And why not? For the simple reason that sense perception can so easily be erroneous. A table in a painting, may, at a distance, look like an actual table, and we may have to come close to it to recognize that it is a mere representation on canvas. Or a man suffering from delusions may create a table in his imagination; or any one of us may see a table in our dreams. Such tables, of course, do not actually exist. These examples illustrate ways in which our sense perception may be mistaken, and the reason that it is not to be relied upon.

If the first reason that sense perception can not give rise to clear and distinct knowledge is that it is unreliable, the second is even more important. It is true that we know that this is a table when we see it, but this perception does not provide us with knowledge of the meanings attached to the table, or the elements of which it is composed. We can see only one side of the table at a time; there is always a part of it that is not subject to our perception; we can know the color of the table without knowing why it is this color instead of some other. Thus mere perception does not constitute knowledge which is clear and distinct. There are so many and such complex aspects to an object such as a table, that even a scientist cannot completely comprehend it.

These two reasons illustrate the fact that when we speak of clear and distinct, we mean two things: first, knowledge which is clear and distinct is recognized by everybody, and there is no possibility of disagreement about it; and second, knowledge, to be clear and distinct, must be so simple and so easy that it is obvious at a glance, and convincing beyond the possibility of a doubt.

We have been speaking of Descartes' deprecation of sense perception and his rejection of it as a source of knowledge. He would not say that we cannot recognize what is an object, or that we cannot know whether it is black or white; but he did argue that such recognition was not knowledge; that our senses could never tell us why one object is black and another white, and that therefore whatever we have, it is not accurate knowledge. In short, Descartes denied that it was possible for sense perception ever to result in reliable knowledge.

Then, we must ask, is there any possibility of intuitive knowledge which meets Descartes' criteria of clarity and distinctness, which is simple to grasp, and which can be immediately understood by everybody in exactly the same way? Descartes held that there was. Where, then, did he locate such knowledge? Descartes concluded that in mathematics man had access to clear and distinct knowledge; that *number* in arithmetic, and *form* in geometry met the conditions which he had laid down for intuitive knowledge.

For example, the number 99 is clear and distinct; it can be divided into 99 *ones*, and everybody understands it immediately and without the possibility of argument. In the same way we can understand the difference between the number *1* and other numbers: it is different from the number *2* or *3* or *10*; it is 99 less than the number *100*, two less than the number *3*, and one less than the number *2*. The meaning of the number *1* cannot possibly be confused with the meaning of another number. Number, thus, cannot be in error.

What is true of *number*, Descartes argued, is also true of *form*. Perhaps we do not get an immediately clear understanding of a very complex form, but complex forms can always be resolved into simpler component forms which anyone can understand clearly. In any form there are *points*, and this simplest of all concepts is readily comprehensible. We can also see how a *point* in movement generates a *line*, and a line in movement generates a *surface*. We can move in this way from the simpler to the more complex; we can also analyze the complex into its simpler elements. This is Descartes' clear and distinct knowledge.

Since Descartes was seeking knowledge which could be relied upon because it was clear and distinct, he felt that he must clear away the intellectual rubble which had passed for knowledge and which had stultified human intelligence. He cast doubt upon all knowledge out of the past which did not conform to his criteria of clarity and distinctness. When he inquired of traditional beliefs, habits, and presumed knowledge whether they were both clear and distinct, when the answer was "no" he insisted that these things should be the objects of doubt.

Descartes prescribed three methodological rules: first, one must not regard as truth anything that he does not know; second, one must abjure intellectual slovenliness and preoccupation when making judgments; and third, one must not pass judgment on anything that is not clear and distinct.

Descartes wrote a book in which he detailed the history of his doubting, and showed how he had gone about clearing the intellectual scene of the rubble which had earlier passed for knowledge. He described his own education in a famous school which had the highest standards of scholarship, and, applying his criteria of clarity and distinctness to what he had been taught there, concluded that the only subject which could stand up under this test was mathematics. All other subjects, including philosophy and science, fell short of meeting the criteria. He pointed to the disputes between philosophers and scientists over the centuries, and the sacrimonious debates between advocates of different schools of philosophy, as evidence that such knowledge was not clear and distinct, and could not, therefore, be relied upon. Descartes therefore adopted an attitude of complete doubt about everything he had learned in school except mathematics.

His travels throughout the countries of Europe intensified Descartes' attitude of doubt. He found that no two countries shared the same thought-patterns, the same laws, or the same customs. Something looked upon as sacred in one country might be decried as superstition in another, and vice versa. He came to the conclusion that there was nothing which was universally regarded as being true throughout the world; and this conclusion strengthened his conviction that there was no truth other than mathematics which could stand the test of his criteria.

Descartes applied his criteria to all instances of thought which came to his attention, and refused to accept anything as long as there was any possibility of doubt about it. Material objects he found to be unreliable as bases for knowledge; he could find only number in arithmetic and form in geometry to be clear and distinct. Even spiritual objects of knowledge he found unreliable, except the concept *I*. "I doubt; therefore I must exist." *I* am the subject of consciousness, and therefore a subject which is not susceptible to doubt. This *I* is the basis upon which the structure of spiritual knowledge is to be erected, just as *number* is the basis upon which material knowledge is to be built.

Let us move now from Descartes' concept of *intuition* which we have been discussing up to this point, to his ideas about *deduction*. Once again we must note that Descartes did not use the word in its ordinary sense, but employed it to describe a process quite different from that to which it customarily applied. When he used the term deduction, Descartes had reference to the process in which the simplest and easiest fundamental concepts are combined or brought to bear upon one another in such manner as to result in formation of other concepts which, while they are more complex, are nevertheless still clear and distinct. This process is exemplified in arithmetic and geometry, where steps in a given operation are sequential and unarguable. It is to this sort of sequential order which proceeds from the easy and simple to the more and more complex that Descartes applied the term deduction.

In ordinary logic when we speak of deduction we have reference to the syllogism—"All men are mortal; Socrates is a man; so Socrates is a man; so Socrates is mortal." But if we are not to be misled, we must keep ourselves reminded that this was not what Descartes meant; he was talking about "constructing" clear and distinct knowledge in a series of steps from the simplest to the complex. The building of a bridge offers a convenient analogy. Let us think of each stone in the bridge as representing a clear and distinct concept. When we put the stones in place to make the bridge, we must know the function of each stone; we must see each stone as a unit or atom, and build the bridge by placing the stones in proper relation to each other. If we can remember that intellectual procedures which move along these lines are what Descartes referred to as deduction, we will avoid unnecessary confusion as we discuss his methodology further.

Descartes had full confidence that his method would yield a great harvest of knowledge, and, indeed, that there were virtually no limits on the knowledge that could be derived from the sequential application of mathematical rules. Men are confused by and fail to understand ordinary natural phenomena, such as thunder, electricity, light, heat, the growth of plants and animals, and so on, he said, because these are so complex. But by his method of deduction, man could seek elemental knowledge, and by subjecting these simple elements of knowledge to mathematical operations, achieve understanding of the more complex phenomena. When, in proceeding from the simple to the complex, man finds each step clear, the entire process is thereby equally clear.

Nowadays when we look back on Descartes' insistence that all knowledge could be derived from the manipulation of initially simple mathematical concepts, we regard it as ambitious nonsense. The house he built did, indeed, collapse; but the foundation on which he built it endures. His insistence upon the necessity for quantification in dealing with natural phenomena, and his idea that "true knowledge is based in mathematics" constitute lasting contributions to human thinking. In contemporary physics, for example, scientists still use quantification when dealing with color, and we know that different colors are conveyed by light waves of varying length. If it were not for this quantitative relationship, it would be impossible to deal scientifically with the phenomenon of color. Science will always be indebted to Descartes on this count.

Now that we have finished discussing the basic concepts of Descartes' philosophy, I should like to direct your attention to some of the results of the application of his methodology. My remarks are not offered as criticism or attack, but to help you see the importance of Descartes' contribution to the history of thought.

The greatest single contribution lies in the fact that Descartes' insistence on applying the criteria of clarity and distinctness to all knowledge had the effect of simplifying the knowing process. Prior to his time innumerable traditional errors and superstitions cluttered human thought and hampered man's effort to know his world. In sweeping away this intellectual rubble and simplifying the knowing process, Descartes lifted a burden from mankind.

There was more to the matter, though, than the emancipation of human thought from the shackles of tradition and error, important as this contribution was; even more important was the fact that Descartes' methodology created confidence in man's power to think. The methodology of Aristotle, classification and systematization, left no room for creativeness; Descartes' notion that truth can be sought step by step, that knowledge can actually be created, was a dynamic one. It caused men to realize that human thought can exercise a creative function, and gave them a confidence in their power to think. This contribution marks an important milestone in the history of thought.

Another rather important point is the effect Descartes' emphasis on clarity and distinctness has had on the people of France. The clarity and distinctness of the French language, and of French literature and fine art, are a heritage from Descartes. To be sure, these characteristics are observable in the French even prior to the time of Descartes, but since his time they have been made explicit and are more consciously stressed, so that the French, probably more than any other people, emphasize clarity and distinctness, as opposed to ambiguity and obscurity, in their language, literature, fine arts, and religion. Descartes, as a person, was a retiring man; he even burned his books when they incurred the disapprobation of the Pope. We can be sure that he did not foresee the far reaching effects his methodology would ultimately have upon human thinking.

Still another point is that Descartes' rationalistic methodology, emphasizing as it did rational conception, and deprecating experience, gave a new importance to human reason, and made rational conception the most important source of knowledge. Cartesian deduction is the use of rational conception in the step by step construction of knowledge. Instead of starting with the experienced object in order to get to know it, one can immediately begin with reason, and build up knowledge step by step. The structure of reason is obviously identical with that of nature; otherwise nature would have to conform to the structure of reason. The fact that in Descartes' methodology reason was seen as being interior rather than exterior to man gave added importance to the conception of the structure of reason.

The empiricists rejected this concept. Descartes had pressed the matter too far. Some of his followers went even farther than he did—so far as to incur ridicule, as when their critics accused them of saying such things as that in telling jokes, one does not have to tell each individual joke, since when people understand the general conception of "joke," they will laugh anyway. This is, of course, an absurd example; but many rationalistic thinkers perpetrated absurdities almost as extreme.

A third point for us to consider is that Cartesian methodology calls for intellectual individualism; it emphasizes reason as the common possession of all men. The reason that people disagree is that their reason has been perverted by the wrong kind of education, or poisoned by superstition, or vitiated by preoccupation. Descartes held that all men had equal and natural ability to make sound judgments, and to distinguish the true from the false, until and unless these abilities were crippled or stunted by improper education or by acquiescence in traditional error and superstition.

Descartes used the analogy of a city at this point. If a city "just grows," by unplanned additions and accretions, it will inevitably become disordered and chaotic; but if the city, from its inception, is built according to a systematic and well-designed plan, it will develop in an orderly fashion. Descartes urged that each person should plan his own intellectual life, laying out the design for it as an architect might lay out a plan for a city; he urged that men recognize the unreliability of others' knowledge, whether they were living or dead, and see that reliance on such knowledge would result in an unplanned intellectual life that would be as chaotic as an unplanned city. He wanted every man to be able to plan, to doubt, to rectify error, and to cultivate his own reason. If each of us could do this, he thought, the society in which we live would naturally be a good one.

Descartes was a conservative man, and not a very brave one. He wanted to avoid trouble. He could not have foreseen that his method, his attitude of doubt, his insistence on sweeping away the intellectual rubble of the past, was really revolutionary; he would have been shocked if he could have known that he was actually a major pioneer of the French Revolution. But the men who did lead the Revolution had as one of their mottoes "We must reform existing social institutions on the basis of reason." Revolutionaries even reconsecrated some of the great Christian churches in France to "the Goddess of Reason." Even today we find a tendency in French literature to associate the ideas of "reason" and "humanity," and repeated reference to the thought that reason is a common human characteristic.

John Locke
Sensation and Reflection

In this and the next lecture we will discuss the third type of thinking, which, as we have already mentioned, is empiricism, of which we take John Locke to be the foremost exemplar.

But before we get to Locke, we must make a few remarks about Francis Bacon. Born some thirty-five years before Descartes, Bacon lived in the Elizabethan age, and was a countryman and contemporary of Shakespeare. This was a period of rapid development in England; mercantilism developed in the economic sphere, and literature flourished. Bacon was not a professional philosopher, but rather a famous lawyer, a successful politician (he was at one time Lord Chancellor), and a man of practical affairs.

Bacon lived in the late 16th and early 17th centuries, about a hundred years after America had been discovered, and when Europe was in the early stages of vigorous cultural development. The rapid development of the period—political development, social development, developments in intellectual life—demanded a new method of thinking, a method which would enable men to keep up with and to accelerate these developments, and to take advantage of expanding horizons.

Bacon, convinced that this was the threshhold of a new era, sought a new method of thinking which would advance and facilitate and enhance the developments he saw taking place around him. His time—the late 16th and early 17th centuries—was marked by the discrediting of many of the superstitions and traditions which had prevailed in Europe for centuries; his interests, therefore, were centered in secular rather than sacred concerns, in the problems of men rather than the refinements of theology, in nature rather than in transcendentalist speculation. He saw the need for a method which would enable men to deal with practical affairs in ways that would fulfil the promise of the new age, for means by which men might control nature and subject it to their service. His interpretation of the proverb that "Knowledge is power" was that it was possible for man to have the sort of knowledge that would enable him to control nature and make it serve his ends.

In an earlier lecture we referred to Descartes as an exemplar of rationalistic thinking, and mentioned the fact that his interests were centered almost wholly in theoretical study, and that he was not very much concerned with the practical affairs of society or with political problems. Nevertheless, Descartes was influenced somewhat by Bacon, and some of his remarks have a markedly Baconian flavor. At one point he called for the overthrow of traditional speculative philosophy, and for its replacement with a practical philosophy which would deal with flowers, the air, the stars, and the movement of the heavenly bodies. He averred that such a practical philosophy would enable men to understand the functioning of natural phenomena, and to subject the forces of nature to the promotion of human welfare. He declared that men are to be the masters of nature, its owners, and that they should not be owned by it. This argument sounds almost as though Bacon himself might have uttered it.

Throughout his career Bacon sought to devise a method of thinking that would be based in experience. He was bitterly opposed to, and vehement in his attacks upon, classical Aristotelian logic, especially the device of the syllogism. He attributed two major faults to Aristotelianism. The first of these was the fact that classical logic seemed to him to be a method of argument, not a way of thinking, a means of demonstrating the superiority of one's opinions or advocacies over those of another. He could see no warrant for a method which could be applied only in intellectual contest; what he wanted was a method which would give man control over nature. The second fault he noted was that the classical method exercised only the function of systematizing already existing knowledge, and that the practice of classification and systematization could never create new knowledge. Bacon was primarily interested in devising a method by which man could seek and find knowledge that was new, something that did not already exist.

Bacon held that these two faults stemmed from the fundamental fallacy of assuming that the order of nature was identical with the order of human reason, and from the fact that classical logic did not start with observable facts, and did not credit the experience of observation with being the basis of knowledge. In reaction to something he regarded as fatally fallacious, Bacon urged that all methods must first be based on facts, and that observation of facts must be clear, and that recording of observations must be exact and accurate. For him, reason, rules, and order all derived from facts. Man could determine the rules which govern nature, he said, only by observing the facts of nature.

Bacon's adaptation of traditional methods was to begin with observation of discrete facts, and then from observed similarities in many separate events, to arrive at generalizations—and thus he formulated his inductive method. This method of induction enabled him to derive rational generalizations from his observations of disparate facts. Bacon's method was influential in the development of modern science, which was already in the process of development during his life-time.

Bacon did not disparage reason; he did insist, however, that reason was a second step, to be utilized in organization and analysis only after the facts had been carefully observed. In one of his essays Bacon draws an interesting analogy between types of thinking and the activity of insects. He compares the rationalistic thinker who uses pure reason as a means of arriving at truth to the spider who spins her web from material extruded from her own body. The extreme sensationalist who randomly accumulates facts and who fails to apply reason to organize and analyze, and to derive meanings from the facts, he compares to the ant which busily scampers about, collecting and indiscriminately storing heaps of miscellaneous materials. His own method he saw as comparable to the operations of the bee, which collects pollen and nectar, and then digests and modifies the collected stuff in order to make it yield its hidden treasure.

We cannot support the claim that Bacon's inductive method was a direct and effective contribution to the growth of modern science, largely because he failed to work out its implementation. Modern science was in its infancy at this time, and Bacon did not actually formulate anything that we might call scientific method in the modern sense of the term. He did, by emphasizing the importance of experience, give impetus to the development of empiricism, which has been a dominating influence on British philosophy for the past three hundred years, just as rationalism has been the dominating influence in philosophy on the continent of Europe during the same period.

The date 1688 is a memorable one in British history. This was the year of the Glorious Revolution which overthrew the Stuart dynasty and repudiated its doctrine of the divine right of kings, and which, by augmenting the power of Parliament, transferred more power to the people themselves than had ever been the case before. John Locke's most important works were published at about this time, so it is reasonable to regard him as the philosopher of revolution.

Bacon had been concerned with the subjugation of nature, but Locke did not have any such ambition. He was more concerned with social and political questions than he was with investigation of natural phenomena, and soon became recognized as a philosopher of liberalism. Locke believed that every man had the ability to think, and that all should be accorded freedom of observation and of thought. He wanted to find ways in which men could have closer and more fruitful relationships, to determine the conditions under which men could love and appreciate each other, to discover means by which men could become able and disposed to cooperate and join themselves together in resistance to unjust power and in protection of their freedom, to identify what it meant for men to be citizens of a free nation.

Locke's thought had a profound influence on British liberalism, but it soon spread beyond the shores of England. It was a major source of inspiration to the men who guided the American War of Independence, as well as to the men who were responsible for the French Revolution. Locke is indeed the philosopher of revolution—of the Glorious Revolution in Britain, of the American Revolution, and of the French Revolution.

The Western world was torn by many wars in the 17th century. At mid-century civil conflict raged in Britain, and there were protracted wars in many places on the continent of Europe as well. Some of these were primarily political in nature; others were religious wars. War, of course, is evidence and consequence of sharp divergence of opinion and belief. The bloody wars which raged for so much of the 17th century were, in many cases, fundamentally religious wars, but religious differences have political overtones, and it is thus possible to view these wars as having been political in nature.

Since it was obvious to Locke that human disagreements were a fundamental source of armed conflict, he set himself the task of exploring the nature of opinions and beliefs and finding out how they were formed. He wondered whether beliefs and opinions were the result of thought processes, and thus susceptible to control by changed methods of thinking, or whether they were beyond the province of thought. He wanted to see whether, and how, he could account for the fact that so often discussion of beliefs and opinions was impossible because men misunderstood each other.

If he was to find out whether opinions and beliefs were or were not subject to man's thought processes, Locke had to explore the nature of thinking, establish limits, and determine what kinds of things man can know and what he cannot know. Locke's position on knowledge was the same as Bacon's, namely, that knowledge is derived from accurate experience; but the difference between the two men was that Bacon did not undertake to formulate a theory of experience. Locke's approach to the problem of the nature of experience was through psychology, and the fact that he explained experience from a psychological point of view was undoubtedly one of the reasons that his explanation carried such tremendous weight.

Locke's logic was based in psychology. In everyday life it is easy enough to see that some beliefs exist among people, and that others do not; but it is not nearly so easy to know *why* people hold the beliefs that they do hold. We have to inquire into the nature of belief, into the function of mind. We need to find out how beliefs originate. It is only after we get answers to such problems as these that we can hope to do anything about beliefs. But understanding of these problems calls for thorough investigation of mind and its operation. We must know the capabilities of intellect and its limitations before we can pass judgment on particular beliefs. Without such understanding we might easily behave like dictators and resort to methods which free men would repudiate.

In his exploration into the nature of belief, seen from the psychological point of view, Locke divided experience into two categories—first, sensation, or perception of external objects, and second, reflection, the activity in which the self observes its own state of mind, its own feelings and thoughts. According to Locke all human experience is embraced in these two categories; but the second, reflection, is based in and arises from the first, sensation. Sense impression of the external world must lead to introspective observation of the workings of one's own mind. Because these two processes are the only methods by which we can understand experience, they constitute the criteria against which we test and judge all beliefs and opinions. If, out of inspiration I propound a new school of thought, Locke would insist that I be able to say where I got my ideas. He would ask whether my ideas could be analyzed into obvious, simple, and precise experiences; and if they could not be, he would say that my position was untenable, without foundation, and therefore that it was not reliable knowledge.

Locke developed his thought in a number of brilliant essays in which he set forth his position that all sound ideas, no matter how fantastic they might seem, or how noble they might be, must have their bases in facts, in our experience with the perceptible world around us. Any idea without such a foundation is not reliable and must not be constituted a basis for belief. Because this skeptical attitude toward speculation is characteristic of the thinking of the British people, we can look upon Locke as representative of his background. We can also note that on the one hand Locke is a successor of traditional philosophers, while on the other he is a pioneer of modern thinking. He is a successor in the sense that he developed traditional philosophy in a definite direction; and he is a pioneer in the sense that he paved the way and provided some of the basic tools for the development of modern thinking.

Locke himself regarded his book, *An Essay Concerning the Human Understanding*, in which he discussed the problem of knowledge, as his most important work. The motivation for this book lay in the many and peculiar difficulties he encountered in trying to carry on discussions with his friends—difficulties which finally rendered further discussion impossible. Locke was curious about the source of these difficulties, and speculated upon the possibility that they stemmed from some characteristic of the human understanding. Until and unless we can discover the limits of human understanding, Locke held, it is not possible to say what the human understanding is capable of, and what it is not; and until we know this, it is unlikely that we can carry on fruitful discussion very far.

Thus Locke's purpose in writing this book was to explore the limits of human understanding. Matters which lie beyond these limits cannot, he held, be known, and speculation about them leads to illusion. Locke was implacable in his rejection of decisions which are arbitrary or illusory—of anything, in fact, which was not ultimately based in our observation of the world around us. In his view, any theory worth holding must be based in experience. His philosophy eschews as illusion all that lies beyond the limits of human understanding. As far as Locke was concerned, it was not necessary for the mind to know everything; our knowledge is sufficient if it serves the purposes at hand. It is not necessary to know all about behavior in order to regulate our behavior effectively. Even incomplete knowledge, enlightened by the mind can serve as a candle, which, while it may not shine brightly, can provide enough illumination to enable us to get a clear view of the problem at hand. When we have enough light to enable us to do what we need to do, there is no point in being ambitious about achieving complete knowledge.

Today we have talked about the background and general outlines of Locke's philosophy; we will have to leave discussion of details of his method until our next lecture. But before we conclude, we must look at those things against which Locke directed his most vigorous opposition. The first target against which he directed his criticism was the doctrine of innate ideas. Since Locke's position was that all knowledge is derived ultimately from experience, it was altogether natural that he should repudiate this Platonic doctrine; but there was another reason for his determination to discredit it. The doctrine of innate ideas had become a weapon for the defense of arbitrary authority, of superstition, and of ridiculous theories. Men in authority argued that their actions were justified by ideas that were pre-existent and innate, which did not call for thinking, and which could not be investigated. In other words, the doctrine was invoked as a means of preventing people from studying, from observing, and from thinking; it served as justification for regarding certain general principles as being equally applicable at all times and in all places; it was the means by which authority sought to restrict freedom of thought.

A few minutes ago we noted that the wars which raged during this period, both in England and on the continent, were the results of disagreement in religious beliefs and in political opinions. But both in politics and in religion, men resort to the doctrine of innate ideas to justify their claim that a given dogma is sacred, not subject to doubt, and immune to criticism and investigation. Since this doctrine is the very antithesis of the freedom of observation and investigation which was so basic to Locke's position, it is easy to understand his implacable opposition to it.

Locke's philosophy is reflected in his social and political theory. As an advocate of a philosophy of liberalism, he had to reject the doctrine of innate ideas, if, for no other reason, because those in positions of authority appealed to it as warrant for their prerogatives and privileges. Locke rejected arbitrary authority and worked to restore freedom; and in his eyes, freedom of thought was the fundamental freedom, without which all other supposed freedoms are without basis, and therefore illusory.

The second target for Locke's attack was the abuse of language, which he viewed as another weapon in the arsenal for the defense of arbitrariness, superstitions, stupidity, and ridiculous theories. All sorts of meaningless theories have established themselves by the misuse of language; their proponents resort to verbiage which may superficially seem scholarly, but which, when subjected to analysis, turn out to be empty of meaning and unworthy of attention. Words properly used, Locke said, are like servants who carry out the desires of their masters; but when misused words can constitute laws which are ambiguous and confusing and beyond understanding.

The most critical area, the one in which language is the most subject to abuse, Locke pointed out, is in connection with terms employed when men talk of morality or religion. Much of what is written in these fields is just so much paper, and many scholars, misusing language, have written volumes filled with empty dispute; they have spent time and energy with results that are largely useless to intelligent men. Locke insisted that language must be used more carefully, and that obstacles created by the abuse of language must be cleared from the way, before men can establish criteria against which they can intelligently judge their society. He was especially insistent about the need for rigor in the use of terms which apply to morals and religion, to the end that these could become clear and be used in worthwhile discussion.

In our next lecture we will discuss more in detail the methods which Locke employed in his philosophy.

Characteristics of Locke's Thought

In the first two lectures of this series we discussed Aristotelian logic, or the logic of systematization; in the next two, we dealt with Descartes as the exemplar of rationalistic logic; and in the fifth, we took up empirical logic, particularly as this is represented by Locke, a philosopher whose major work came at the end of the 17th century. Locke's position was that experience is the only source of knowledge, and that various abstruse concepts such as that of the innate ideas and so on, have more often than not led to misconceptions, and have resulted in men using undefinable terms to explicate complex but essentially meaningless ideas in totally confusing fashion. This was as far as we could go in our last lecture; this time we will discuss the methods employed in this type of thinking, or the epistemology of empiricism.

The type of thinking which Locke represents proposes a method based in the conviction that man has "inborn ability." This concept is not to be confused with the doctrine of innate ideas, which Locke rejected out of hand. Holding that all knowledge derives ultimately from observation, Locke likened the human mind at birth to a blank sheet of paper upon which observations of the world would henceforth be recorded. Observations were of two sorts—on the one hand, of external objects, on the other, of the operations of one's own mind—and these were the only sources from which man could gain knowledge.

But even though Locke denied the possibility of innate ideas, he did assert that every child is born with the ability to seek knowledge and to acquire mastery of the methods by which knowledge is to be gained. In dealing with this inborn ability to build knowledge on the basis of experience, the first step is to know its functions. According to Locke, this ability, or *mind*, exercises three functions.

The first of these functions is that of complexion, by which Locke meant the function of association, or of combining—of bringing simple ides together and composing a complex idea out of them. As an illustration: in our search for knowledge, we cannot depend solely on our sense organs, since they yield only perceptions which may be unsystematic and chaotic. Eyes can see only color, such as red or white; ears can hear only sounds, such as high and low tones; and hands can only touch and tell us whether a surface is smooth or rough. These perceptions in and of themselves are useless; it is only when mind functions to bring them together that we can know, for example, that this object which we saw and felt is actually a desk. This is Locke's function of complexion—the combination of elements of perception into a meaningful whole.

The second function is that of comparison; the mind functions to compare two ideas or two sense perceptions which exist at the same time in space. For example, the mind functions to make the tea-pot, the glass, and the ink bottle which are on the desk all have simultaneous existence. Along with this, there is the sequence of time, which means that we see this object first, and then that one. This is another case of the function of mind which we call comparison. It is this function which contributes to our understanding of the cause-effect relationship. When we slap the table, we can infer that the impact of the hand, as cause, will produce sound, as effect. This is a simple matter, quite different from what we ordinarily mean by the cause-effect relationship. Because mind exercises the function of comparison, it can detect the time order of cause and effect. There is nothing remarkable about this; it is merely one of the functions of mind.

The third function is that of abstraction, or the selection of and concentration of attention upon one of many characteristic qualities of an object. If, for example, we say "This table is high," we are selecting the characteristic of height, or the idea *high*, and ignoring others. In the same way we select or abstract the idea *man* from our experience with many men, and the idea *tree* from our observation of many trees. Sense perception as such does not convey any such ideas as *high, man* or *tree*; these ideas result from the mind's function of abstraction, from the process of selecting one characteristic among many, focussing attention on that one, and ignoring others. This is more important than it may sound, because Locke did not recognize classifications as having objective existence, but held instead that generality and universality existed only as the results of mind's function of abstraction.

Locke's refusal to grant the status of real existence to universality is a milestone in the history of philosophy. Many earlier philosophers had emphasized the concept of universality and had assigned it a position of preeminence in their schemata. We recall, for example, that both Plato and Aristotle attached no value to individual objects, holding that the meaning of an object derived from the universality under which it was subsumed. Even the French philosopher, Descartes, held the same view. But Locke took a diametrically opposed view on this question, and insisted that it was only individual objects which had the status of real existence, and that universality was nothing more than a convenient product of mind's abstraction.

This conception of knowledge not only paved the way for a whole new era in human thought, but also exerted incalculable influence on social and political theory. In Locke's philosophy only the individual person has the status of real existence; society and the state are merely convenient abstractions created by the operations of human intellect; law, morality, and other such concepts are likewise artificial generalities or universals brought into being by mind through its function of abstraction. Only the individual person has any real, practical existence.

Upon the general and beginning aspects which we have been discussing, Locke proceeded to construct his method of analysis. Believing that every complex idea comprises simpler and more elementary ideas, Locke argued that the only way of determining the validity of a complex idea was to analyze it into its simplest component ideas. When these simple ideas are identified and judged, it is possible to judge the truth or falsity of the complex idea which, in combination, they compose.

Philosophy, for example, deals with a multitude of complex ideas such as time, space, matter, soul. Ethics treats complex ideas such as justice, humanity, and the idea of essential right in politics. Locke thought that scholars had been irresponsible in the ways in which they had employed such complex and abstract ideas, producing confusion rather than clarification, mystification rather than understanding. His method of analysis, he contended, would make it possible for people to understand such complex ideas. A complex idea could be analyzed into its simplest components, and when the meaning of each simple idea was clarified and made explicit, then people could, without difficulty or confusion, understand the complex idea.

Locke insisted that no matter how complex an idea might be, it could be analyzed into simple component ideas. An example might be a house. What is it? It can be seen to be composed of bricks, stones, timbers, tiles, and so on. When we have learned about all the materials that went into the building of the house, and know how it was built, we can understand the structure and its contents. It is the same with ideas—the most complex can be analyzed, and when the simple components are understood and judged, the validity of the complex idea can be assessed. In earlier times people were often confused and deceived when they had high-sounding terms which they did not know how to analyze thrown at them. If they had known, they could have recognized their truth of falsity as readily as they understand the house.

We must note two aspects of Locke's method of analysis. One is that it was primarily a method of criticism, a method which, by means of analysis, subjected to critical scrutiny the many complex ideas which prevail in a society, and which, because of their abstruse nature, cause confusion and misunderstanding. Locke proposed that all such ideas be analyzed into their simple components and examined critically so that the degree of their validity might be determined. The other aspect for us to note is that Locke's method of analysis is an historical one. Analysis includes exploration into the historical relationships of the idea, and of the roles that it has played. It atomizes the structure of the complex idea, and analyzes the origins of each element in it.

The very simplicity of Locke's method creates the danger that we may fail to appreciate its historical significance. We must remember that Locke lived at the end of the 17th and the beginning of the 18th centuries, during a time when Western culture was in a period of transition. The culture of liberalism had been developing for two hundred years before this period, and already, in Locke's day, was a strong influence; but at the same time, traditional European thought and superstitions, a heritage from the Medieval Age, continued to dominate many areas of human thought. Locke lived at a time when medieval traditions and modern liberalism contended for supremacy. The new culture existed, it is true; but traditionalism was also very much in the scene. Locke, as the philosopher of liberalism, forged an important weapon for the advancement of the new and the eventual rout of the old—and this weapon was his method of analysis. This method enabled men to subject to critical analysis the traditional institutions, ideas, and superstitions which they had inherited from the past, and to determine their origins and to discern their shortcomings. This is the reason we call Locke's method an important weapon in the war against superstition.

Although Locke died at the beginning of the 18th century, his influence throughout that century was a dominant one. It affected England, but was even more influential in France. For much of the Western world, the 18th century was an age of destruction—that is to say, an age of reason during which traditional institutions, traditional thought, and traditional religion came under every form of attack. The intellectuals of the 18th century applied the term "The Dark Ages" to medieval times, and called their own century "The Enlightenment." They made great use of Locke's method to throw light into the darkness. This method was applied not only to revolutionize intellectual life, but was equally applicable in social and political affairs. No institution escaped analysis, critical examination of its origins and its contents, and rigid assessment of its worth. When such examination disclosed faults and contradictions in inherited institutions, it was relatively easy to discard the institution and replace it with another. Locke's influence during this period was incalculable.

Thus far we have been talking about the application of Locke's method of analysis in understanding a complex idea and determining its worth; we turn now to his method of seeking knowledge. Locke's definition of knowledge was that it was the determination of the degree of agreement or disagreement between two ideas—surely a simple definition, and one easy to understand. For example, when we assert "the glass is white," we must determine whether there is agreement between *glass* and *white*; or, if we say "the glass is not black," we must be able to show that this *glass* does not agree with or correspond to *black*. This illustrates what Locke meant when he said that knowledge consists in determination of agreement or disagreement between two ideas.

Let us look at an example. If we ask what the relationship is between the authority of government and individual freedom, the meaning of the question is by no means clear. Let us try a simpler question, "How much longer is this house than this desk?" This question is not clear either, and we can not answer it right away. But there is a way out; we can take a meter stick and find out how long the house is; then we can measure the desk with the same meter stick, and by comparing our measurements we can know exactly how much longer the house is than the desk. This method of getting knowledge is to analyze each complex idea into simple ideas which are easy for everybody to understand. The application of this method of analyzing matters into their simplest components makes knowledge accessible to all; even the man in the street can observe and understand.

So much for knowledge; now let us look at Locke's ideas about reason. Reasoning, for Locke, was quite a different process from what it was for Descartes and Aristotle. Just as by knowledge Locke meant the determination of agreement or disagreement between two ideas, by reason he meant investigation into the agreement or disagreement among more than two ideas, or even among an indefinite number of ideas. Fundamental to Locke's interpretation of reason is his insistence that reason cannot skip around over a domain, but must proceed methodically step by step. If, for example, we are dealing with a sequence of twenty ideas, we cannot start with the first and second, and then skip over the others to the twentieth, because to do so would be to give rise to misunderstanding. The proper method is to start by comparing the first and second ideas, and then inquire into the agreement or disagreement determined in this comparison with the third idea, then compare the result of this operation with the fourth, and so on, until we reach the nineteenth, and then the twentieth idea. Such procedure brings assurance, and prevents disagreement; it is like a chain in which each unit is linked to the one before it and the one after it. It is an historical method in which, as each step is performed, everyone understands. In short, it is a way of making something which is initially difficult and complex into something that is easy and simple, so that anybody can understand it.

Let us use one of Locke's own examples to help us understand his method of reasoning. He told of an old woman living in a small village who was just recovering from a fever. As she was getting ready to go outdoors wearing only a light dress, a friend told her that the weather was changing and that there was quite a bit of wind; that when there was wind, it might well rain; and if she was out in the rain, she'd get wet. Since she was wearing such light clothing, if she were to get wet, she might catch cold. And a cold, coming so soon after her fever, could develop into pneumonia. When her friend spoke to her this way, the old woman decided not to go out. But suppose that her friend had skipped from "rain" to "pneumonia," omitting the intervening remarks. It is quite possible that the old woman wouldn't have understood, and she might not have heeded the advice. Locke used this as an example of the method of reasoning employed in everyday life by ordinary people, and called attention to the difference between this and syllogistic reasoning with its prescribed major premise, minor premise, and conclusion.

Locke went on to point out that the reasoning used by ordinary people was just a matter of understanding the relationship between one idea and the next one, and making commonsense connections between these relationships. There is not only no need to resort to the syllogism; if the old woman's friend had cast his advice to her in the form of the syllogism, the old woman probably wouldn't have understood him. The syllogistic method is not normally employed by ordinary people. Even Aristotle's own thought, Locke pointed out, was not totally syllogistic, adding caustically that God had not created man to be a mere body without thought until after Aristotle had so arranged it.

Locke deprecated syllogistic reasoning, and endorsed a method of reasoning which differs markedly from traditional and classical patterns. Traditional reasoning required as a major premise a proposition which stated a universal or general truth, such as "all men are..." or "all animals are..." and so on. Traditional reasoning begins with the indispensable statement of a general truth as a major premise. Even Descartes used this formula. But Locke denied the need for a universal major premise, and insisted that reasoning is the establishment of relationships among more than two particular ideas. When all the separate relationships are clearly understood, the act of reasoning is complete. The remarks of the friend who warned the old woman in the village, "change of weather...wind...rains...wet... sick..." are connected relationships. This empirical method differs from the traditional in that it denies the real existence of universals, regarding them as constructs of man's mind which serve only as conveniences in the processes of thinking and reasoning, and looks upon individual objects as the only actually existent entities.

Locke's position was that all human behaviors and actions have their origins in knowledge and thought; thus, if a man takes action on the basis of a mistaken idea, his action will also be wrong. Hence the importance in this type of thinking of concise ideas. Hence, also, the emphasis on the individual object, and the importance attached to accurate observation of discrete objects. It is only the individual object that can be observed by the senses. Empiricism rejects universals because they cannot be the objects of observation. *John*, as an individual person, is observable; *mankind*, on the other hand, cannot be observed; as a universal it is only a construct of the human mind, and does not have objective existence. Locke's insistence that all experience must be observable accounts for the importance he attached to the individual, and his deprecation of abstruse generalities.

This is the essential characteristic of the empirical method; it was designed to free men from the tyranny of non-existent universality, and to eliminate the ambiguity which results from the use of undefined or ill-defined abstractions, and to encourage men to concern themselves with individual objects. In other words, it calls upon men to make accurate observations of existent entities, and thus to achieve clarity in their ideas. This is the central element of empiricism; other questions derive from this thesis, are subordinate to it, and are relatively minor.

My few remaining comments on this type of thinking are also relevant to the experimental type of thinking which I will discuss with you in the next lectures in this series. I think that it is important for me to make these comments now, because there are so many similarities between the sensationalistic thinking which we have been discussing and experimental thinking, about which we will be speaking in the next two lectures. Both of these types of thinking claim that all knowledge derives from experience, and it is not always easy to distinguish clearly between the two. For this reason I want to call attention to some of the shortcomings in sensationalistic thinking, so that it will be easier for you to discern some of the fundamental distinctions between it and the experimental type of thinking.

The first and basic fault of the empirical method is that it is merely a method of criticism, not a method of construction. It is easy enough to analyze traditional institutions, traditional thinking, and traditional religion; but mere analysis does not contribute to the creation of new ideas, or to the prediction of the future. When the need is for planning the future and constructing systematic plans of action, mere analysis is not enough. Locke's method of analysis was useful in destroying the old; it was inadequate for building the new.

Why is it that the method of analysis is a good one for clearing the decks of the accumulation of tradition, but not useful for the reconstruction that must follow destruction? The basic reason lies in the empiricist's interpretation of experience. Locke looked upon experience as an unending succession of separate and discrete observations; he saw it as though it were uncounted gobbets without organic relationships. For him, organization of any sort was artificial, and in no sense characteristic of experience itself. Ideas such as time and space, and all the others, were constructs of man's mind.

This interpretation of experience was carried to extremes by some of Locke's disciples, especially by David Hume. Hume regarded experience as consisting of innumerable small, isolated, unrelated elements; and this view resulted in utter skepticism in which there is only probability, never necessity. Consistent application of this view would preclude the possibility of the development of science or the discovery of truth, since one of the characteristics of science is the establishment of demonstrable relationships among the facts of experience, and the derivation of laws which account for these relationships. If all relationships among facts were products of individual minds, there could be no science. And in his ethics, Hume, recognizing only the existence of the individual person, saw each man inevitably seeking his own advantage and interest. Rugged individualism was the only possible consequence of such a view. Thus we can see that when experience is regarded as being composed of separate and unrelated particles, hurtful consequences can ensue.

There is still another grave fault in empiricism, which is its view of experience as being passive rather than active. We see this when we look at Locke's *tabula rasa* theory, the view of the human mind as a blank surface which received impressions from without, which was acted upon, without itself acting. We know now that this is an inadequate explanation; that experience is, in fact, active and creative. We will talk more about this aspect of knowledge in our next lecture.

Experimentalism, Answer to the Conflict Between Empiricism and Rationalism

In this seventh lecture of this series, we come to the fourth and final of the types of thinking we said that we would cover. You will recall that we dealt first with the systematizing type of thinking which flourished among the Greeks; then we took up the rationalistic type, which has been so influential, especially on the continent of Europe; third, we came to the empirical type of thinking; and now we are ready to deal with the experimental type of thinking. In the earlier lectures we have always dealt first with the background and origin of a type of thinking, and then in a subsequent lecture with its methodology. Staying within this pattern, we will talk today about the background and origins of the experimental type of thinking, and will leave until our next lecture discussion of its methodology.

Although we selected Descartes as the representative of the rationalistic type of thinking, and Locke as the representative of the empirical type, we must remember that they are *representatives* in the literal sense of the term; they were not by any means the only philosophers to use, or to contribute to the development of these types of thinking. For two hundred and fifty or sixty years, from about 1600 until 1850 or 1860, there was sharp philosophical contention about the roles played by *reason* and *perception* in the process of gaining knowledge. The Rationalists claimed that many principles are universal and general, that they are innate, and can only be disclosed by reason, and that they had nothing to do with sense perception. The empiricists, of whom Locke was representative, held the opposite view, namely that all ideas, no matter how complex and difficult they might be, have their ultimate basis in experience, and that knowledge which is not derived from experience is not worthy to be called knowledge. This dispute raged until the mid-nineteenth century.

As we review these types of thinking today, I wlll try to help you understand the dynamics which have driven the proponents of these two types of thinking—the Rationalists and the Empiricists—into such sharp and persistent dispute. Let us look first at the dynamics of empiricism.

The first driving force which we note in empiricism is its insistence that knowledge is not the prerogative of a minority, but that every man has the ability to derive knowledge out of his own experience; that, as long as observation is accurate, knowledge is equally accessible to all people. There is thus no basis for discrimination between specialists and scholars on the one hand, and the commonalty of people on the other, insofar as acquisition of knowledge is concerned.

In the second place, the Empiricists argued that total dependence on reason could result only in illusion and hallucination. Experience is real, concrete, subject to verification. It is true, they admit, that the scope of experience is relatively narrow; and there are, indeed, matters which are not embraced in experience; but on the other hand they point to the fact that man is safe, and protected from the dangers of illusion and error, as long as he confines his efforts to the realm of experience.

In the third place, the Empiricists put great store by the fact that experience and sense perception are aspects of life as man lives it in his day by day existence; they deal with human concerns. From the time of Bacon, the British Empiricists have had as a major concern the control of the forces of nature and their application to the improvement of human life. Thus we see that Locke's empiricism emphasized experience as a source of knowledge that could be applied to the practical affairs with which men are concerned.

The Rationalists adopted a diametrically opposed point of view. As was the case with empiricism, there are three arguments advanced by the Rationalists at which we must look. In the first place, the

Rationalists argued that experience is unstable, always changing, and hence not a reliable source of knowledge. For example, they pointed out, when a man finds himself in unusual circumstances, or when he is ill, his experience is of a different nature and quality than it is under ordinary conditions. Inasmuch as experience is subject to such wide variation, it cannot afford us appropriate guides for our behavior. They thus concluded that the only dependence man could justify was dependence upon reason.

In the second place, the Rationalists denied the claim of the Empiricists that their emphasis on the practical application of knowledge was the chief strength of their position, and charged that in actuality this was a weakness rather than a strength. Since the scope of experience is admittedly very limited, they argued, its practical application is likewise limited to the mechanical and material aspects of life. Man's concern with higher spiritual and ideal matters, they insisted, is beyond the scope of experience and sense perception, and that therefore to attribute preeminence to experience and to deprecate reason is to neglect the higher and spiritual aspects of life.

In the third place the Rationalists argued that when men rely wholly on experience, they put themselves in a position to be hampered by tradition. All experience, they said, is limited to the past, and cannot, therefore, provide perspective for planning the future or for deriving guidelines for living. They accused the Empiricists of being slaves of the past, and of ignoring the possibility of arranging, planning, and building for the future. Since the future is unpredictable, effective guidance for it cannot come out of observation of present experience. It is only by resort to reason, they insisted, that men can plan for, arrange, and build for the future. Experience is of no avail for the future; reason, on the other hand, affords guiding principles for both the present and the future.

Why do we find it necessary to explore the dynamics of the contention between the Rationalists and the Empiricists? It is because understanding of the strengths and weaknesses of rationalism and empiricism will make it easier for us to deal with the new concept of experience which has been developed in recent decades. This new concept of experience preserves the strengths of empiricism, while avoiding the weaknesses which were the targets of the Rationalists' criticism. It can resolve, at least for the time being, the dispute which has raged for the past three hundred years, and enable us to get down to the business of systematically constructing new knowledge—an important undertaking, and a difficult one, too. The intellectual warfare between the Rationalists and the Empiricists was not in vain; it demonstrated an overriding need for a new concept of experience. Let us see whether the new concept that has been developing in recent decades can resolve the dispute, and meet the objections advanced against each other by the Rationalists and the Empiricists.

We will deal now with three developments that have taken place in the recent past and relate these developments to the emergence of this new concept of experience. These events have resulted in a radically changed view of experience, and have enabled us to revise and expand the Empiricists' concept of sense perception, and to reconcile it with an updated view of the function of reason.

The first of these events was the appearance on the scene of the theory of biological evolution. This is a fairly new theory; it was only sixty years ago, in 1859, that Charles Darwin formulated the theory in his *Origin of the Species*. But what does evolution have to do with experience? The answer is simple: until Darwin advanced his theory, people were prone to regard the sense organs as being passive, as having been created for the purpose of seeking knowledge. Even the brain and the nervous system were regarded as being inactive, and as having only the function of thinking. But Darwin's theory required that the nervous system be regarded as an instrument of biological evolution. As was the case with the body, the evolution of the nervous system was now seen to have been on a step by step basis, and to have taken place in responses to changes in environment.

The concept of biological evolution provides a history of the creatures of the earth that is a long and interesting and exciting story. In the beginning simple animal forms exercised only the most elementary functions required for their adjustment to their environment. As environments were altered, more complex adjustments were called for; creatures which could make these adjustments survived, those which could not disappeared. Over the eons increasingly complex activities were necessary for adjustment to varying environment, and this process eventually produced animals which possessed the structure and exhibited the behaviors that made them "higher" animals. We can thus conclude that the respiratory system, the digestive system, and the characteristic musculature of animals developed as a result of adjustment to changing environments over the period of millions of years. The same thing applies to the sense organs—eyes and ears are as much the products of evolution as are fins and claws. Living creatures have sense organs not for ornament, but rather for increasing their power to survive. These organs are instruments for living.

Let us look at the eye as an example. We were not provided with eyes just so that we could seek knowledge. Long before man appeared on the earth, his non-human ancestors developed eyes so that they could see and avoid dangers, protect themselves and their young, escape from their enemies, and locate food. And just as the eye was an instrument for living, so was the ear, the nose, and the other sense organs. Even the brain had functions as an instrument of living, long before our ancestors began to use it for seeking knowledge and for forecasting and planning the future.

This interpretation of the function of sense organs, recognizing the eye, the ear, and the nervous system as instruments for living, and not just as the source of knowledge, has resulted in drastic transformation in our concept of knowledge. Knowledge is not something apart from, or added to, life; it is a means of living. The long contention between Rationalists and Empiricists about the roles played by sense perception and by reason stemmed from the fact that both camps attributed intrinsic value to knowledge, and ignored the fact that actually its only value lay in its application to life's problems. A traditionalist defining *hand* would concentrate on description of the structure of a hand; but the thing that is really important is to inquire into what the hand can *do*.

In older traditions knowledge was regarded as though it were a sort of mirror which reflected reality. This view gave rise to inevitable dispute. The Empiricist claimed that his mirror was clear, and that it reflected true reality; but the Rationalist retorted that the Empiricist's mirror provided only a surface reflection, and could say nothing about the deeper and more precious part of reality.

Within the context of biological evolution, however, knowledge is nothing like a mirror reflecting reality; instead it is something to be used in every aspect of life. Both perception and reason contribute to living. Knowledge enables a creature to be alert to danger, to escape from it, to locate and grasp objects that can be useful to him; it is not a mechanical thing such as a mirror which reflects reality. Thought and knowledge can help us foresee and get ready for the future by utilizing the meanings of what we have already learned. Thought and knowledge are not things of no use, nor are they the mirror which reflects true reality. This takes care of one element in the dispute between Rationalists and Empiricists.

The second development was the appearance on the scene of a new psychology. This development was closely related to and influenced by the theory of biological evolution; we could, as a matter of fact, discuss them together as two aspects of a single development, but in the present context there are reasons for dealing with them separately. The weakness of empiricism is that it regards perception as the only material of experience, so that experience can never rise above mere perception. The new psychology rejects this interpretation of experience, and defines sense perception as a stimulus which invites the creature to act. For this reason we speak of this new psychology as Motor Psychology.

What is this motor psychology, and how is its interpretation of sense perception different from that of traditional psychology? In traditional psychology sense perception is the only condition of knowledge; but motor psychology regards sense perception as merely the stimulus which evokes reaction by the creature. The movement of the limbs, the focussing of the eyes, are both the result of sense perception serving as a stimulus. Each perception has the function of directing or inhibiting behavior. For example, when a man crosses the street, he must use his eyes to observe the traffic and use his feet to walk, and do both at the same time. We know now that our sense organs are not merely passive receptors; they function all the time to direct the creature's behavior—in our example to enable the man to cross the street safely. When one carves wood with a knife, he must use his hands and his eyes at the same time, each perception having the function of directing his movements so that the undertaking may go forward step by step to completion.

The Rationalist's criticism of the Empiricist's position on perception is that it provides no basis for systematization; that it is like a person whirling around madly until he falls to the ground in a faint. This criticism is too harsh; but it is true that when perception is taken out of connection with its application, it is not systematized. In motor psychology the function of perception is to direct the action of the creature; each perception is potentially an aid and impetus to action; thus what might otherwise be blind perception can be systematized. When a man stands in his doorway, looking around and waiting for a break in the stream of traffic so that he can cross the street, he has a host of perceptions, but he consciously organizes and systematizes them.

The third development was man's discovery of new means by which he could systematize and organize his thought and his knowledge. When man understands the functions which thought and knowledge perform, he can then grasp the real meaning of both thought and knowledge. The basic fallacy underlying the old dispute between the Rationalists and the Empiricists did not become obvious until scientific thinking appeared on the scene. People in the past had no opportunity to achieve understanding through the use of systematized and organized knowledge; and there was no possibility of formulating the scientific method of thinking until modern science developed. Thus, the new concept of experience about which we have been talking is a fairly recent development.

We can say, then, that the third important development was the formulation of the scientific method. We will discuss this at greater length in the next lecture, but at this time we should mention a few important considerations. When we look at the matter from the viewpoint of the scientific method, the Empiricist was mistaken when he repudiated the idea of the universal or general principle. Without general principles there could be no science; we must have them. But when the Rationalist exalted the concept of the general principle and made it all-important, when he saw it as having value in and of itself, he went too far. The value of a general principle lies in its function of organizing and systematizing otherwise chaotic masses of perceptions, so that meanings can be derived which can effectively guide further action. This is certainly an important function; but it does not change the fact that a general principle has value as an instrumentality, and that in and of itself it is valueless.

The use of a principle or a law is to organize chaotic masses of facts, to systematize them, to connect them, and to make it possible for meanings to be derived from them. Perceptions are useless until they are organized according to one principle or another. Can a man become a scholar simply by memorizing the card catalog in the library? When we admit as we must, that general principles are essential to the systematizing and organizing of sense perceptions, we are acknowledging that in this regard, at least, the Rationalists were right.

But the Rationalist was wrong when he exalted the concept of the general principle and saw it as being independent of the restrictions and tests of experience. Although we can not get along without resort to general principles, any principle must be subject to the test of science, and only when it has been so tested can it be regarded as valid. A principle that is not borne out in scientific testing must be revised or replaced. The Rationalist could not possibly have been right when he claimed that general principles are transcendent of experience.

Let us look at a recent example which illustrates what I have just said. For two hundred years Newton's law of gravitation was regarded as perfect, as having universal application; but even this law of gravitation has had to be modified. The German scientist, Albert Einstein, published his theory of relativity, remarking at the time that he thought that it was probably correct, but that he couldn't be sure until the next solar eclipse. If his theory were correct, certain phenomena would be observed at the eclipse; and if these were observed, this fact would establish the validity of his theory. When the eclipse occurred, the phenomena which Einstein had predicted were observed, and his theory was established. The general law of gravitation which had been accepted as perfect for more than two hundred years was modified within a few minutes. I believe that we can say without further argument that any general or "universal" law or principle must be subject to modification when experience demonstrates its inadequacy.

Now I will try to pull together some of the things we have been saying. At the beginning of this lecture, I commented on the view of experience which notes that it is limited to the past; and that when we just accumulate experience of the past, and cannot use it to direct the course of future events, all that it can do is to reflect the past; it cannot create the future. But I have tried to show you a new concept of experience, and have discussed the three major developments which made it possible for us to see experience as living, as a phase of the forward movement of life and as having application in the future. When we see that in one activity we both recall the past and move forward into the future, we have disposed of the Rationalist's allegation about the weakness of empiricism.

Past experience is memory; we can do nothing about it. The only thing which is subject to our control is the future. There are two ways in which man moves toward the future: by blind trial-and-error, or by consciously planning his future on the basis of his past experience and his projected desires. When experience is seen as living, and knowledge is recognized as an instrumentality for living, we can make plans for the future, and not just drift into it. This is the reason that the experimental type of thinking places so much emphasis on logic, since we know that effective organization of past experience is impossible without logic. This is a central feature of experimentalism. The Experimentalist hopes to construct methods which mankind can use as instruments with which to control the controllable part of the present, and to make intelligent plans for conscious movement forward, step by step, into a partially foreseeable future.

Characteristics of Experimentalist Thought

In the last lecture we made three important points about experience. First, experience is life, and life is a continuing process, embracing past, present, and future. Basing preparation for the future on past experience means a continual transformation of the old into the new. Second, since we are engaged in this transformation, man's success in coping with the future depends upon the accuracy with which he can foresee it, and the degree to which he can control it in the light of his past experience; and his chances of success are enhanced when he utilizes systematized knowledge and organized behaviors. Third, the problem of method is not solely one of theoretical reasoning. Reasoning is essential as an instrument for ordering the present in such ways as to provide the maximum foresight into the future. The problem of method is, therefore, more a practical one than a theoretical one. These are the three most important conclusions which we reached in our first lecture on the experimental type of thinking.

Today I am going to introduce our discussion of the methodology of this type of thinking with an example so familiar and so simple that even those people who have never studied logic or philosophy can understand it and see its application. This particular example is not necessarily characteristic of this or that type of thinking; the point is that it is a method—one which ordinary people apply unconsciously, without even recognizing it as method. We spoke earlier of the man who had to cross the street when traffic was heavy. The activities in which he engages can be looked upon as representative of the activities of living—there are many situations in a man's life which are quite similar to crossing a busy street. Life is a wide street, involving great distance, and many complications and dangers, and it is by no means easy for a man to traverse it. We will examine this illustration first, then proceed into a discussion of the method employed in this everyday situation.

The first thing the man does when he wants to cross the street is to observe; he looks the situation over to see how many cars are coming in either direction, to estimate when the street will not be so crowded, and to decide how long he should wait before trying to cross the street. The first step, then, is observation; but let us note how different this is from the view of observation taken by empiricism, the third of the four types of thinking covered in this series of lectures. In the first place, observation in this instance is spontaneous, not passive; it is not, as empiricism would have it, simply something the mind receives from the external object and imprints, as it were, on a blank sheet of paper. On the contrary, this instance of observation is purposeful; the man uses his eyes to look up and down the street, his ears to hear the traffic noises, for the purpose of planning his intended action of crossing the street. In the second place, the observation which we are talking about does not cease with mere perception; it is applied, and becomes the material of inference. It does not take place for its own sake, as might be the case with a photographer who snaps the shutter of his camera and is content with the impressions made on his film. Observation in this case is thus quite different from what the Empiricist meant when he talked about observation.

The next step after observation is inference. We are so used to making inferences that we may fail to recognize this as a problem. But inference is, in fact, a problem when we are dealing with logic; it is the activity by which we move from the present to the future, or, in our example, by which the man decides whether he can safely cross the street. Inference is the process by which we move from the known to the unknown, to the future from the present. Inference is possible only when we have had past experience comparable to the present situation, since it is a comparison to similar past experience and the present situation—again, in this example, in order to decide when one can cross the street. If the man hasn't crossed streets in the past, he cannot safely make inferences in this case, because he has nothing to compare with the present situation; and it is only by making such comparison that he can infer the future from the present.

The third step of the method is action following inference. Observation provides the material on which one can base an inference, or judge the situation. The third step is to act on the basis of inference, that is to put one's judgment to the test. After the man in our example renders a judgment, he may wait where he is for half a day, he may rush across the street forthwith, or he may decide to stay where he is until the traffic thins out—but whatever he decides he is acting on his judgment, and this is the third step in this method of thinking. It is this step which constitutes the essential difference between experimentalism and other types of thinking, because none of the others have ever included the taking of action as a part of their method of thinking.

Why do we insist upon including action as a step in our method of thinking? For the simple reason that taking action is the concluding step in the series. A man who observes and infers, and then fails to put his inference into action, has no way of knowing whether his inference is valid—in this case, of knowing when and whether he can safely cross the street. After he has acted on his inference, he is in a position to know whether it was a valid one or not. Maybe he is near-sighted, and has made an inaccurate observation and an erroneous inference, and he may be hit by a car. Or he may have miscalculated, gauging the speed of a car as though it were a cart, and then he rushes across the street into unforeseen danger. If he crosses the street safely, he can conclude that his inference was correct; if he doesn't get across, or barely escapes being hit, he knows that his inference was in error, but he can review it, find out where he was wrong, and guard against making the same mistake the next time. This case illustrates the fact that action is the proof of theory; action is a practical proof; action is the basis on which we determine the correctness or incorrectness in the first and second steps. Without this third step, action, we have no way to determine whether our observation and our inferences were or were not correct. This is the reason that we include action as a requisite step in the experimental method of thinking.

The reason I have used such a simple example is to demonstrate the fact that the scientific method is the method used by ordinary people in their everyday living. The difference between the example I used and the more sophisticated procedures followed by scientists is one of degree, not of kind; qualitatively they are the same. When it is employed in scientific investigation, the method is more rigorous and consciously systematic, but essentially it is simply a refinement of the commonsense method of thinking which people generally use in their everyday affairs.

Let us look for a moment at the respects in which the scientific method used consciously and carefully differs from commonsense. There are two weaknesses in everyday observation: first, people in general are prone to devote too much attention to the gross and external aspects of an object—its volume and its surface characteristics; and second, they tend to neglect aspects of the object which are not immediately obvious. The scientific method avoids these weaknesses because it requires more thoughtful and thorough observation. Aspects which can not be observed by the unaided sense organs are observed with the aid of artificial instruments such as telescopes and microscopes, so that every significant feature of the object is brought into the picture.

In making their observations scientists employ many sorts of instruments—the telescope, to observe things out of range of unaided eyesight; the microscope, to observe objects too small to be seen with the naked eye; the spectrograph and spectroscope to study and analyze light; the thermometer to measure temperature; the barometer for measuring pressure and forecasting the weather, and hundreds of others. But even the detailed observations which the scientist can make with the aid of these instruments are not enough; he refines his observations even further by mathematical calculations, so that even the smallest particles are subjected to observation. Thus the essential difference between commonsense and the scientific method is that the latter makes observations in much greater detail than the former.

The important point here is that a scientist observes with a purpose. Some other types of thinking also stress observations; but only in the scientific method is observation always undertaken for a purpose. It is a tool which we employ to help analyze facts or identify difficulties. A scientist never observes aimlessly; he always has a problem in mind. In commonsense observation people are often content with crude judgment, fail to analyze the situation, and do not consciously seek to identify difficulties. But in observation conducted according to the scientific method, the scientist checks his observations carefully with reference to the purpose for which they are undertaken. This is why we say that observation is an instrument which guides us to the second step of thinking.

A good illustration of the scientific method, in which observations are made for the purpose of identifying difficulties and analyzing situations, is the procedure followed by a physician when he makes a diagnosis. A doctor does not write a prescription solely on the basis of what his patient tells him; he uses instruments to take the patient's temperature, to examine his feces, and to analyze his urine. It is only after he has made these examinations that he writes his prescription; without them he could not be sure about the nature of the patient's illness.

Modern science is like traditional science in attaching great importance to observation, but differs from it sharply in recognizing that observation alone cannot solve a problem. It is a mistake to seek a solution to a problem merely by observation; observation is merely the means of supplying needed information, of locating and identifying the problem. In other words, observation can bring the problem into focus, but cannot solve it.

Traditional science explained a falling body by saying that it was heavy, a floating one by saying that it was light. The traditional scientist arrived at his interpretation of events on the basis of his sense perception. But when a modern scientist investigates falling or floating bodies, he recognizes that heaviness and lightness are results, not causes, and that the cause is the law of gravitation. He understands enough about gravitation to know that the weight of an object will change if it is projected beyond the gravitational field of the earth, and that on Mars or Venus it would have a different weight because the force of gravity on those planets is different. The same thing is true when he deals with light. The ancients treated light as a problem, but we have discovered that it is a form of energy, and that the speed with which it moves can be measured. Observation points the way to problems and helps us to know what they are; it does not provide answers.

Since mere observation cannot provide the solution to a problem, no matter how accurately it is conducted, the necessary next step is inference, the process which leads from the present to the future, from the known to the unknown. Every inference is a sort of adventure. Another difference between the scientific method and ordinary commonsense is that the former controls the adventure more carefully, and thus reduces the danger involved. The more rigorous the method the less the danger. Safeguards against danger constitute one of the important problems of the scientific method. There are two ways in which science minimizes danger, each of which we will now discuss briefly.

The first means by which the danger of error is reduced is rigorous reexamination of concepts, or the breaking, we might say, of intellectual habits. In our example, the man crossed the street on the basis of his past experience; but if his past experience had been in a village and he has formed habits on that basis, he could get into real trouble crossing a busy boulevard in a large city. He needs to break his old habits and approach the problem of getting to the other side of the street on other bases. Old familiar ways of looking at things, fixed intellectual habits, if we want to call them that, restrict the range of possible action when one is confronted with a new situation. The ancients believed that the earth was flat, and static, and that the sun moved around the earth every day. But now we know that the earth is a sphere, and that it takes three hundred and sixty-five days for it to move once through its orbit around the sun. The erroneous interpretation of the ancients persisted through the centuries because they were content with the explanation they had, and had "got into the habit" of believing that the earth was flat and that the sun moved around it. Thus the most important thing that the scientific method can do to reduce the danger of error is to reexamine concepts, to break old intellectual habits, to make comparisons, and to arrive at explanations which take account of all the facts ascertained through observation.

We can get rid of outdated ways of looking at things, of fixed experience, of ingrained intellectual habits, only by constantly expanding our experience and continually comparing one idea with another in order to select the better one. Because systematic science is the result of constant comparison of innumerable materials and experiences, it cannot be produced by individual effort; it is a social product. Science has no nationality; it admits no prejudices. Scientific discoveries made in one country are soon applied in another. An untutored person in a tropic land could not be expected to know that water can freeze, and that at low temperatures other liquids can become solid; but as he becomes familiar with science, he can comprehend these phenomena. Because science deals with so many materials and phenomena, and because the results of scientific investigation can be communicated and disseminated, people can break old intellectual habits and discard outmoded concepts even when they are not in position to make their own direct observations.

Just as the first means by which science reduces the danger of error is the continual comparison of ideas and concepts, the second is the formulation of general principles by means of which we can understand cause-and-effect or sequential relationships among events. The function of a general principle or scientific law is twofold: to organize discrete objects and events in systematic order so that we can deal with them more effectively and exercise greater control over them; and to provide a basis upon which we can, with assurance, infer future developments. With the guidance of such general principles and scientific laws we can move into the future with greater confidence.

We must remember that the value of the great number of general principles and laws which science has established lies in their application in experience. We organize complex experiences and from them derive general principles which we can then employ as a check on our later inferences. Again, an illustration of this checking of inferences against principles is the physician treating a patient. If the doctor concludes that the patient who complains of a stomach ache is suffering from a duodenal ulcer, he is not acting solely on the basis of his observations. He is aware of the conditions under which ulcers occur; and he is also able to fit the patient's symptoms into the general pattern which medical science has established. His diagnosis is based both on his own observation of facts and on a general principle against which he judges the facts. By utilizing this principle he reduces the element of danger, and is in a better position to make a prognosis.

Now that we have looked at the differences between the experimental type of thinking and the other types we have discussed, we can see that it is superior to any of the others. Experimental thinking does, to be sure, emphasize systematization and classification, but as means, not as ends in themselves. And, along with rationalism, it emphasizes general principles and laws, but again, not as ends in themselves, but as convenient guides for making our inferences.

Now for the third step in this type of thinking, action. Neither observation nor inference, or even the two taken together, are true knowledge, no matter how rigorously controlled and how accurate and detailed they may be. True knowledge does not occur until observations and inferences have been tested in action. Action is the test of the truth or validity of observation and inference; and until they are subject to this test, inferences are at best hypotheses.

Scientific experiment is action carried on with precision. The validity of a principle is established when events conform to predictions implicit in the principle, and only then. Truth can be determined only in experiment. Experimentation is disciplined practice, and is not anything like the performance of "exercises" by school children. The purpose of experimentation is to verify or demonstrate the need for changing a formulated principle, and of thus determining whether it affords an adequate basis for confident prediction of future events. The success of an experiment depends upon both the accuracy of observation and the soundness of inference.

I can summarize what I have been saying about the experimental type of thinking in two short sentences. First, its purpose is to make knowledge and principles more practical, and not to produce useless or "ornamental" knowledge. And second, it is a way of rendering human behavior more intelligent, more effectively controlled by reliable knowledge, and of reducing the incidence of blind trial-and-error type behavior.

As we look back in history, we find many theories not worth the paper they are printed on, and innumerable instances of human behavior based on blind acceptance. When we consider these things, we are forced to the conclusion that the experimental method holds out the only hope of human welfare and progress.

THREE CONTEMPORARY PHILOSOPHERS

THREE CONTEMPORARY PHILOSOPHERS*

William James

I

The first of the three contemporary philosophers of whom I will speak is William James, a compatriot of mine, who was, as you all know, the pioneer of Pragmatism. The term "contemporary" means "living at the same time," and since James died in 1910, it may not be, in a strictly literal sense, correct to call him "a contemporary philosopher." However, since the effects of his thought and the development of his ideas are only now having their full impact, we can view him as a contemporary, in spite of the fact that his works were published in the twenty-year period between 1890 and 1910.

The most important among James' works is his first book, *Principles of Psychology*, which was published in 1891, and which runs to more than a thousand pages. There are two reasons why this book is so very important: first, this volume includes the bases of the philosophy which James was to develop later, since his philosophy was founded in psychology; and second, James' philosophy is scientific, not speculative, and the scientific element of this philosophy is not

* A series of six lectures delivered in Peking, March 1920.

physics or biology, but rather psychology, the science which takes human nature as its subject matter. This fact is of the utmost importance. James' major interest was in learning about man and human nature. The psychology which he formulated is scientific; it begins with human nature and human experience. In this formulation, James eliminates with one stroke all the traditional "problems" which have interfered with man's effort to understand himself, and demonstrates that they are not, in fact, problems at all. This is the distinctive aspect of a kind of philosophy which is built upon a foundation of psychological theory which is thoroughly scientific in its nature.

James' career was primarily that of a scientist, but he was also a highly gifted student of painting, and had considerable training in painting in oils. His brother, Henry James, has, during the past thirty years, enjoyed the reputation of a major novelist, a reputation which has persisted since his death only a few yeas ago. James was born into a family which had a tradition of artistic achievement on a high level; he, himself, possessed both talent and training in the arts; hence his psychology is much more than a mere "anatomy of human nature." One of his unique characteristics is that, possessed of the spirit of the artist, he sees the function of the mind in terms of drama, and records his insights as though he were writing for the theatre. He rebukes traditional philosophers for having adopted the view that philosophy was argument, and succeeds in his own case in presenting philosophy as vision. When philosophy is looked upon as argument, numerous philosophical "problems" occur simply to keep the argument under way; but when we recognize philosophy as vision, it can possess both the values of art and the excitement of literature.

Since James deals with psychology as an artist-author, his psychology and his philosophy are vital; instead of being dead and dreary, they pulse with life. They are organic. James' primary dissatisfaction with traditional psychology lies in what he sees as a tendency to replace the state of mind of the participant with that of the observer, the psychologist. In his view, traditional psychologists substituted their own outlook as spectators, who, detached and uninvolved, could have no real knowledge of the process which they observed, for that of the participant, the person within whose organism these processes were taking place.

In a short article, "On A Certain Blindness in Human Beings," which he wrote late in his life, James maintains that it is impossible actually to penetrate another's mind, and that the observer can approximate the truth only by imaginatively putting himself in the place of the other; that otherwise one will understand no part of the truth. In this article James emphasizes the necessity of one undergoing the experience himself as a condition to understanding it. This was the reason that James had such great admiration and respect for the poet, Walt Whitman, who had been able to discard the conventions of literature and build his poems around the common and elementary actions of everyday human beings. Our education, especially with regard to literature, has led us far afield from life as it is lived. Our literature is replete with abstract words and with figures of speech which are empty of meaning because they are so far removed from our experience and our actual responses to life. James contends that this had led us to overlook the common and elementary aspects of experience, and that it has thus resulted in "A Certain Blindness in Human Beings."

James emphasizes the common, elementary, and fundamental aspects of human behavior, while at the same time he focusses attention on distinctive characteristics of individuals. Individuality is emphasized throughout his philosophy. He rejects philosophical monism which holds that all truth is ultimately one. In his article, "On a Certain Blindness in Human Beings," one paragraph reads:

> "Hands off: Neither the whole of the truth nor the whole of the good is revealed to any single observer, although each observer gains a partial superiority of insight from the peculiar position in which he stands. Even prisons and sick-rooms have their special revelations. It is enough to ask of each of us that he should be faithful to his own opportunities and make the most of his own blessings, without presuming to regulate the rest of the vast field."*

It is of the utmost importance that we keep in mind the fact that James does put so much emphasis on the common elements of human

---

* William James, *Talks to Teachers on Psychology: and to Students on Some of Life's Ideals*. New York: Henry Holt and Company, 1919. Page 264.

nature on the one hand, while, at the same time, he stresses the importance of individuality and rejects absolutism, because in his later period, his philosophy is based almost entirely on these two points. He coined two terms which have since come into common usage: *Radical Empiricism*, which denotes his emphasis on the fact that experiences of human beings are elementary and they cannot be subsumed under general and abstract terminologies; and *Pluralism*, which is the term he employs to denote the fact that human experiences are individualistic in character, and that they are not to be regarded as instances or evidences of absolute and eternal principles. Late in his life James advocated a "pluralistic universe," as an alternative to monism, of which he writes with distaste as a philosophic justification for "a block universe."

After this very general introduction I shall now outline the fundamental concepts of James' psychology, and these can then serve as the basis of our next lecture in which we will discuss his philosophy. In his psychology James applies the evolutionary hypothesis to human emotions, feelings, perceptions, and so on. Darwin had published his *Origin of the Species* in 1859, just sixty years ago, the book in which he propounded the theory of evolution which precipitated a major revolution in Western thought. James, who was Darwin's contemporary, was the first man to apply the evolutionary hypothesis to psychology.

In his earlier books, James notes that very few people recognize the fact that man's intelligence derives from his practical experience of undergoing and suffering. The application of the evolutionary hypothesis to psychology seems initially to reduce all functions of the mind to the category of response. An example of simple response is closing the eyes when they are stimulated by a bright light. There must be a response within the organism whenever a stimulus occurs from without, no matter whether such stimulus is simple or complex. Another example: when someone stands in our way while we are walking, we automatically step aside and yield to him. The nature of all such responses is action, not knowledge; we respond to the external stimulus by acting.

James contends that knowledge plays only a minor role in the huge range or response to stimuli. Responses in lower animals can be easily observed, since their reactions to stimuli are of immediate practical use. The same thing is true to a lesser extent in the behavior of higher animals. When we come to the human level, the problem of knowledge is, then, not one of theory, but one of practice, which means "how to do."

James sees knowledge as a phase of mental functioning. On the one hand, there is the stimulus from the environment, while on the other there is the response by the organism. Knowledge is nothing more nor less than the mediating process which occurs between the stimulus and the organism's response to it; its function is to determine the response appropriate to the stimulus. Knowledge is the selection of a response that can adequately cope with the stimulus. It is not independent of, but is intimately involved with both stimulus and response. Man has garnered so much knowledge from the innumerable stimulus-response activities in his experience that he has fallen into the trap of assuming that knowledge has value in and of itself. But as a matter of actual fact, we can gain knowledge only by controlling the stimulus on the one hand, and by selecting our response on the other. The importance of knowledge conceived thus as a mediating process lies in the fact that it "slows down" both the stimulus and the response, so that the organism can take time to plan. In the absence of the mediating process of knowledge, we would frequently make mistaken responses to stimuli; with the benefit of knowledge we can act more confidently. For example, a moth is attracted toward a flame, flies into it, and is burned to death; but a child knows that the flame is fire, and that if he touches it, his hand will be burned; and an adult knows that when he gets too close to the fire, his life will be endangered, so he stays away from it. A man with common sense knows that fire can be extinguished with water; and when this knowledge is refined, he knows how to take precautions by having water available where fire may occur. That's what we have fire hydrants for. The scientist studies the phenomenon of burning, and describes the chemical changes which take place when matter burns. Thus our knowledge becomes extended and enlarged, but in fact it remains the process which mediates between the stimulus and the response.

The manner in which James deals with the function of mind is evidence that his psychology is based in the evolutionary hypothesis. He notes that the functioning mind is characterized by two phenomena: first, the organism acts with reference to a future purpose; and second, it selects the methods and instruments by means of which he can hope to achieve this purpose. In the absence of these, James tells us, there is no mental function. Now these two aspects of mental function have traditionally been called "willy"; and so most people call James a "psychologist of will" as opposed to a "psychologist of knowledge." But James differs from the traditional psychologists of will in that he makes use of the theory of evolution to integrate knowledge with will. When knowledge, emotion, and will are integrated, and when the organism is directed toward a future purpose, it must have been able to formulate such purpose in advance, or else it could not experience satisfaction. All surprise, happiness, pleasure, and anger arise out of the organism's success or failure in achieving this purpose through its overt activities.

We have been discussing the introductory aspects of James' psychology in rather general terms; now let us look at a concept that is uniquely Jamesian, that is, his "stream of consciousness." Before James, people looked upon consciousness as though it were some sort of mixture of individual and discrete experiences; or, at most, they regarded it as something which is "constructed" in much the same way that a house is constructed. James, however, instead of comparing consciousness to a structure of component experiences, or as an amalgam containing many individual and discrete experiences, sees consciousness as a stream which flows constantly forward. This concept is the most important single one in James' philosophy. Many of the other concepts which characterize his philosophy, his emphasis on individuality, on change, on evolution, on adventure, and on freedom of action stem from his likening consciousness to a stream of water. James notes that when people before him had treated consciousness as an accumulation of isolated and inanimate building blocks, they obviated the possibility of viewing it as a stream of water, ceaselessly flowing. These people might possibly have visualized a glass of water, or a bucketful of water, or even a large jar of water, but never a stream of unending motion. But in James' view, all impressions of the mind are incorporated into this stream of consciousness;

each impression is connected with all the others, and none exists in isolation from the others. Rather they all exist as part and parcel of one inclusive stream of consciousness.

James insists that one of the greatest mistakes of the past was psychologists' practice of conceiving of mental functions in terms of physical objects; and, being misled by the fact that these physical objects were comparatively permanent and changeless, inferring that human consciousness was also permanent and changeless. They did not appreciate the fact that the stream of consciousness moves ever forward, is always in the process of changing. This desk may be the same today as it was when we saw it yesterday; but *we* have changed, so the desk cannot exist in our consciousness in exactly the same way in which it formerly did. The consciousness of one person is never exactly identical with that of another; and we cannot interpret either of them in terms appropriate to physical objects. More than this, the physical object can be separated into its parts; this cup, for example, has a mouth, a handle, and a bottom; but our consciousness is of a cup as a whole, and not as the sum of its parts. James employs the example of lemonade. We know that lemonade is composed of lemon juice, water, and sugar; but when we drink it, our consciousness is of lemonade, and not of its ingredients. A physical object may remain the same, but our consciousness cannot. The former can be separated into its parts; the latter cannot.

You may think that we have been speaking in trivialities, but if you grasp the full import of this concept of "stream of consciousness," and look at the effects it is having in philosophy, you will realize that it isn't trivial at all. There are at least two important respects in which this concept is changing philosophy. The first is that it affords a novel way of dealing with the ancient problem of the one and the many, of unity and individuality, or of monism and pluralism. James shows us that people were laboring under a misapprehension when they feared that the concept of pluralism would lead to chaos, and when they therefore insisted upon forcing all experience into one mold of system and unity. But as a matter of fact, if we change our viewpoint and see human experience as a stream of consciousness which runs ceaselessly, there is need for both monism and pluralism in interpreting the phenomenon. In any case, human experience has ceased to be a "thing," a dead concept; it is a living entity, and may be examined in a monistic frame of reference, or in a pluralistic one, as the nature of the occasion demands.

The figure of running water is both simple and complex. To take a single example, we may say that the water of a huge river rushing toward the ocean also contains mud; but as it flows forward, the mud settles and the water becomes clear. When we look at consciousness as a stream, we can see that it can be unified, but that it can also be pluralistic, according to the demands of the occasion. For example, when we are laying out a complex plan of action, we must take everything into consideration—and this is a case of our consciousness being unified. But when we are confronted with a difficulty, we must perforce analyze the difficulty point by point, and it behooves us to find out as many methods and opinions as we can, and this instance of employing consciousness as an instrument by means of which we deal with our environment is pluralistic. Therefore, the question of whether the universe is monistic or pluralistic is no longer really a problem. The only real problem is the determination of the circumstances which call for application of the principle of unity, and of other circumstances which require application of the principle of pluralism.

We have been dealing with the first effect of James' new concept, what it has done to the problem of knowledge. Formerly when people regarded knowledge as a copy or a picture, their questions had to do with the correspondence of our impression with the real object—the most persistent problem in the history of epistemology. How, for example, does our impression of a cup correspond to the real cup? James notes, however, that when we look upon knowledge as a stream of consciousness, we need no longer consider whether our impression of the object actually corresponds with the real object; we ask only whether the impression we have can lead us to other experience. If it can, it is real.

Let us take one more example, this College of Law in which we are meeting. Some people have a clear and detailed perception of the building; some have only vague impressions; others may not have even such vague perceptions, and may have noticed no more than the entrance hall; blind persons may perceive only the bell which signals the beginning of classes; and still other people may not have any impressions even of the entrance to the building or the sound of the bell—their only perception may be of the term, "College of Law." According to James, all such perceptions are correct, because each offers us some experience with the College of Law. Were we to insist that our perception of the College of Law had to correspond in every respect with the real building, we should have an extremely difficult problem on our hands. But the only purpose of perception is to produce anticipated consequences. This concept is of central importance in the epistemology of Pragmatism, as well as in its theory of truth, since Pragmatism regards both knowledge and truth as bridges which enable us to approach our purposes.

In our next lecture we will discuss the application of James' psychology to philosophy.

II

The problem which has been the source of the most disputation in the history of philosophy is the origin of knowledge. Some people hold that knowledge derives from experience; but many others contend that even though experience is important, the universal principles upon which truth is based cannot be derived from it, but must, of necessity, come from some other source.

Everybody agrees that certain knowledge comes from experience—such facts that sugar is sweet, that snow is white, or that fire can burn. But they will not agree that abstract knowledge, such as the axioms and laws of arithmetic, algebra, and geometry, or such things as the law of conservation of matter in physics and chemistry, or the concept of cause-and-effect in philosophy, or the moral laws of ethics, can be derived from experience. Their point is that such laws and principles are necessarily true, totally apart from experience. They point out that while the truth of such propositions as "2+2=4" and "the sum of the three angles in a triangle is equal to two right angles" can be verified through experience, they are not derived from it.

People who argue in this vein arrive at the conclusion that our knowledge of such universal laws and principles is innate. The empiricists were hard put to refute this conclusion until Herbert Spencer made use of the theory of evolution to show that universal truth can also be derived from experience. Spencer admitted that no one individual could arrive at absolute truth through the experience of one lifetime. But he held that as man evolved from lower animals, and made the transition through savagery to civilization, the totality of human experience through the ages has resulted in certain truths being so universal and so commonplace that man has come to regard them as absolute, and his knowledge of them as innate. Even with the change of environment certain laws and principles continue to have validity, and they are appropriately labelled "universal." Their truth, after repeated revision and restatement, becomes all but absolute, and we can utilize them to explain the regular natural phenomena within the framework of time and space. They are still, however, the products of man's total experience through the ages.

I mention Spencer at this juncture because somewhere in his *Principles of Psychology* James refers to this contribution. While James takes Spencer's argument as his point of departure, he develops the idea further. Spencer's concept is important in itself; but, far more important is the application which James makes in his philosophy. James differs from his predecessors in that on the one hand he goes far beyond the concept of empiricism which takes knowledge to be completely passive and external, while on the other hand, although he recognizes that truth comes from within, he repudiates the concept of idealism which asserts the existence of a higher, particular, and transcendental sphere from which man derives his laws and principles.

James holds that general principles originate neither in the particular nor from without, but incidentally. Initially man may have engaged in discussion and told jokes; ultimately the material of these discussions and jokes may have evolved into general principles. It is true that the mind is relatively passive in its reception of certain kinds of knowledge, such as the fact that a fish taken out of the water will die. No one, however, has ever directly experienced the principles of arithmetic, physics, or chemistry. No one would contend that our knowledge of the atom is derived from external experience; it is, rather, the result of incidental reasoning which occurs internally.

As an example, the earlier empiricists asserted that our knowledge of number is derived from experience, just because we have become accustomed to counting "one person, two persons," or "two cups, three cups." James observes that on the other hand, number is arbitrary. Let us take this teapot as an example: we can say that this is one teapot. But when we remove the cover from the teapot, we have to use the number two—one for the pot, two for the cover. And if we detach the handle from the teapot, we have three things—one the pot itself, the other two, the cover and the handle. We can count one, two, or three, even with the same teapot, depending on the way we wish to count. In the same way, if we take a tree as an entity, we say that there is one tree; but if we are concerned with the trunk and the branches, the number may become fifty; and if we are thinking about the leaves, the number may become five thousand. Thus it becomes obvious that our knowledge of number is not passive; it is, rather, the result of the connections we make between the external object on the one hand, and our internal reasoning on the other.

The practice of classification is an obvious example of an activity which goes beyond mere perception; classification is clearly an invention of man. If we had to depend on perception alone, our classifications would be very crude and elementary, and detailed taxonomy would be an impossibility. As it is, we often classify two organisms which exist thousands of miles apart in the same genus, while we place other organisms which grow side by side in entirely separate genera. The very procedure of classifying is thus not a matter primarily of perception of the external world, but a human invention, based on experience. James points out that many of the jokes of a comedian, many of the laws of a politician, or the creeds of a moralist, may turn out to be inadequate or inappropriate when their practical application is attempted. Their applicability is subject to empirical verification. Any ideal in itself is arbitrary; man cannot be confident of its utility until he has subjected it to empirical verification.

Three important points are suggested in James' treatment of the philosophical problem of whether knowledge originates in experience, or whether it is innate. The first point concerns the origins of all ideals. James rejects the position of the earlier empiricists who held that all meanings are derived from sense perception of the external world, although he does admit that some ideals do so originate. James compares the experience from without to the guest who enters the house through the front door. But, he points out, that the mind has, as a house does, a back door, which also affords access. He shows that ideals and general principles have two sources: the first is the experience which enters through the front door, the second is internal reasoning, which is arbitrary, and which enters through the back door. When we hear a bell ring, our experience of the sound comes through the front door; but when we take quinine, the ringing in our ears comes in through the back door. The external object can be given the opportunity to enter our mind, but thought itself comes from within. The origin of ideals can be likened to the production of a completely new substance by mixing medicinal powders and certain liquids. All general principles in ethics, aesthetics, and science can thus be compared to the compounding of a prescription. The idealist is correct when he refuses to acknowledge that ideals and general principles arise from external perceptions; but he is wrong when he insists that there exists a higher and transcendental power from which they must derive.

James tells us that knowledge from both these sources can have significant effects. Man can invent ideals and general principles. Such ideals and general principles, coming in through the back door, as it were, and thus being arbitrarily contrived by the mind, may possibly be mere illusions; and yet there are cases in which such illusions could be more important than the guest who comes through the front door.

From this concept a second point can be derived, and this is that occurrence of incidental thought may arouse an interest or a desire which can excite the mind. Those who happen to like music may become musicians; those who react strongly to rhythm may become poets; those who enjoy observing and classifying may become scientists. Because interest is what incites someone to do something, desire and enthusiasm in mind and will are of tremendous importance.

The third point has to do with the problem of the truth or falsity of knowledge. James tells us that we need not worry about the origin of ideals and general principles; that the guest who enters through the back door may be a welcome one, and that the one who comes in through the front gate may turn out to be an enemy. The values of ethics, theology, and science cannot be determined by designating the door through which they enter; these values can be appraised only by their application in experience, by finding out whether they work as they are intended to do, by seeing whether they can help us toward satisfactory solution of our problems, by determining whether they can lead us to further experience. The theory that can do these things for us is true; the one which cannot is false. James suggests that the major difference between his predecessors and himself is that the former looked toward the origin of ideals and general principles, while he himself looks toward last things, toward fruits and consequences. It is these last things which determine the truth of ideals and principles—not their origins.

Such a concept is in harmony with James' basic concepts which we discussed in our first lecture. James is not concerned with knowledge as a copy of the original thing, but with its usefulness as an instrument. In fact, it does not matter whether our knowledge of a given object is identical with the real object. What is important is that this general idea or thought is more useful to us than another in our struggle to achieve a purpose. It makes no difference whether one idea is more nearly like the real object than another, because ideas and thoughts are meant to be applied, and are judged on the basis of such application. We can ask whether this knife can kill, or whether it can be used in preparing food, but there is no point in asking whether it is like a "real" knife or not. Its value lies in what we can do with it, and not in its resemblance to a "true" knife.

The three points we have just discussed are of fundamental significance in James' philosophy. The first point, dealing with the origin of ideals, is basic to his Radical Empiricism. The second point, concerning desire and will infused with knowledge, is developed in his *Will to Believe*. The third point, the instrumental judgment of meaning, has particularly influenced the basic concept of his Pragmatism.

As we pointed out in our first lecture, Radical Empiricism is the term James coined to indicate his recognition that all experience is real. It is a radical departure from the position of traditional empiricism which regarded experience as the passive impression of external objects upon human consciousness. In James' Radical Empiricism, experience is active, adventurous, changing, forward-moving—a conception immeasurably broader than the one it supplanted. For James, the rudeness of experience is an aspect inherent in the nature of experience itself. There can be no single concept which can embrace the entire universe. Truth and its consequences, good and evil, suffering and enjoyment, peril and safety, success and failure—all these are facts which occur in experience. James sees experience as something rude, uncertain, and transforming.

The second part, the theory embodied in James' *Will to Believe*, has been unacceptable to many people because traditionally people have believed that truth is discovered through the exercise of pure reason, not by dealing with objective facts. James defines belief as the will to act, and asserts that the more complete the belief, the stronger the will to act, and hence, the less hesitation. Behind all true theories of mathematics, physics, chemistry, and so on, there must exist the will to make the world more intelligible. Underneath human reason exists irrational will. All truth about the universe has come into being because of man's emotional satisfaction at having his world made more intelligible when aspects of it are elucidated by new theories. Therefore, we can say that underneath all philosophy and science, there is this reservoir of irrational will.

Many of James' critics ask what right we have to believe if we have only the will to believe, but no objective evidence to support our beliefs. James retorts that this begs the question, that man could never do anything at all if he waited until he had collected all the necessary evidence. We must believe in something first, he says, and then proceed to look for evidence. We do not have enough evidence, for example, to know whether the word is essentially good or intrinsically evil. The only thing to do is to take one of the alternatives as an assumption, and seek the evidence to verify it. When we meet a new friend, we have no way to tell whether he is a good person or otherwise; but could we argue that we should never make new friends just because we cannot know whether they are good or bad men? After we have had enough association with him, we can tell whether the new friend is one we choose to keep as a friend—but only after we have had the association. This is a good example of the importance of the will to believe.

James elaborates this idea by another example of a man lost in the woods who comes to a ravine. He must leap across it if he is to continue on his way, but he does not have the evidence that he can do it. If he believes that he can jump across the ravine, he will take the risk and may succeed. If he hesitates, he may fail. The greater his hesitation, the greater his danger. It is only belief that enables us to overcome our hesitation in such situations. James tells us that this theory is more useful in the fields of morality and religion than in others, because in these fields of experience, one must believe in something on the basis of love, not of evidence. It is only when one believes that he is inspired to look for evidence; the man who refuses to believe anything will not uncover any of the evidence.

This has become the most controversial of all of James' theories, and the object of the most criticism. Some philosophers, not content with merely rejecting James' theory, go to considerable lengths to ridicule him. They say that according to James' theory, a man can believe anything he wishes to believe. A man may believe that he is a millionaire, when, in fact, he is penniless. How absurd! But, of course, this is a misunderstanding. James is an essayist, and he enjoys writing. When he writes about a problem, he uses figurative language, and elaborates his point even to a degree of exaggeration. The fact that James enjoys his use of literary license has made him vulnerable to misinterpretation by unfriendly critics. But it is not necessary for me to defend James at this time. I should prefer to go on to the third point we mentioned that is, James' advocacy of the instrumental determination of the truth or falsity of ideals and principles. And this is the guaranty of his whole theory.

This is the essence of James' Pragmatism. Initially James constructed his Pragmatism as "a theory of truth." There are two traditional theories of truth. The first is that truth is the correspondence between the perception and the external object. If the one does not correspond to the other, there is no truth, only falsity. The other theory was that the external object and its perception by the human mind are two completely different entities, and that there is no warrant for comparing the two to see whether they correspond. According to this theory, truth lies in the consistency of thought itself. When there is no contradiction in our thought, our thought is thereby true. James discredits both these traditional theories of truth, and advances the theory that the truth of all perceptions, ideas, and theories is to be determined by the degree to which the consequences they produce coincide with what they promise or predict. When they work well and produce useful consequences, they are true; otherwise they are false. This is a summary of the pragmatic theory of truth.

Some people believe that every theory has to go through the same three periods: first, a period in which everybody is sure that the theory is ridiculous; second, a period when people concede that there may be some truth in the theory, but that it is not very important; and third, a period when people insist that they have taken the theory for granted all along. James' theory has not yet reached this third stage; but I believe that the development of science will expedite its acceptance. Science itself went through the period when its hypotheses were laughed off as ridiculous; then there was a time when people agreed that "there was probably some truth in it," but that it wasn't particularly important; now everyone takes the laws of science for granted, and their validity is not questioned. This supports the definition of truth as an hypothesis which has been verified in practice.

In brief, James' theory is replacing the traditional concept of absolute truth in philosophy with experimentalism. James recognizes the gradual growth and expansion of truth by means of experimentation and verification. A devotee of informal discourse and a master of literary expression, James has never published any orthodox philosophy; but he has exercised tremendous influence, especially in England and the United States. Since he advanced his theories, the conduct and the nature of philosophy have undergone a radical transformation.

James has consistently opposed absolute dogmatism in philosophy, and at the same time he has repudiated utter skepticism. Even though he recognizes that no truth can be discovered unless there is an inclination to doubt, he eschews absolute skepticism because it is not constructive. Skepticism, according to James, can be justified only when it advances an alternative hypothesis; and if the skeptic's hypothesis is verified, we must accept it in lieu of the earlier one which gave rise to the skeptic's doubt. What is most distasteful to James is a skepticism which brings with it nothing that can contribute constructively to investigation. He advises us to doubt, but he warns us against an attitude of complete skepticism. He asks us to look for new truth in the results of our past experiments at the same time that we continue to experiment and to seek for a growing area of practical belief.

James' theories are valuable not only because they supersede traditional dogmatism and skepticism, but even more so because they have led to greater regard for individuality. His pet aversion is "a block universe," which he compares to the Procrustean bed. The reference, of course, is to Procrustes, a legendary giant of Attica, who seized travellers and forced them into an iron bed, cutting off their feet if they were longer than the bed, stretching them by force if they were shorter, so that every traveller fitted the length of the bed exactly. James sees traditional dogmatic philosophy forcing all truth into a single pattern, as Procrustes forced his victims to fit his bed. James calls, instead, for human life to be a continual process of re-experimenting and re-creating.

Henri Bergson

I

Bergson was born in 1859, the year in which Darwin's *Origin of the Species* was published, and his philosophy has been a major factor in developing the philosophical implications of the theory of evolution.*

Bergson's philosophy resembles James' in that both of them take psychology as their starting point, and that both have utilized the concepts of psychology in constructing their philosophies. They differ, however, in two important respects: first, in contrast to James' emphasis on experimentation, Bergson assigns a major role to introspection, and second, while James denigrates systematization in philosophy, and disclaims any interest in constructing a systematic philosophy, Bergson organizes all philosophical problems into one philosophic system. It is interesting that so many students of philosophy had assumed that Hegel had achieved the ultimate in systematization, and that after him there would be no other systematic philosophers. They did not foresee that Spencer would construct his own

---

* At this point, Dr. Hu Shih, who was interpreting, interjected the remark that Dr. Dewey, himself, was also born in this same year, and that his philosophy, as well as that of Bergson, had been instrumental in developing the philosophical implications of the theory of evolution.

philosophical system, or that a later appearance on the scene would be Bergson's systematic philosophy.

But since Bergson has organized his philosophy in relation to combinations of philosophical problems, we must first identify the problems to which he directs his attention. These problems can be subsumed under three headings.

The first group of problems with which Bergson deals are those which arise out of the relationship between the noumenal world and the phenomenal world; between the existence of reality, or noumenon on the one hand, and the surface manifestations or phenomena, which are the objects of our perception on the other. Both Plato and Kant had advanced the view that human perception is limited to the phenomenal world, and that the noumenal world is unknown and unknowable. Spencer had said essentially the same thing. The problems in this group have been of fundamental importance in Bergson's philosophy. The second group of problems which have concerned Bergson are those having to do with the question of whether the universe is immutable or changing; whether it is free or predetermined. The third group are those problems which deal with the relationship between mind and matter. These have been important problems throughout the history of French philosophy, since the time that Descartes postulated an opposition between mind and matter, basing his view on his observation that the mind is capable of thought, while matter is only extension. Since the time of Descartes this problem has concerned philosophers the world over, and it is not to be wondered at that Bergson devoted particular attention to it.

These three groups of problems were not Bergson's initial concern. He began by examining the view that all man can really know is the experience of his own mind. We can, he concluded, have clear knowledge only of ourselves, and all other experience is merely superficial. Bergson and James hold remarkably similar views of the nature of mind; as we pointed out in an earlier lecture, James views the mind as a "stream of consciousness"; Bergson also takes the view that the mind is a stream which runs without repetition and which is inseparable. "One cannot step twice into the same river." By the same token, one cannot have the same thought or perception twice. This desk which we saw the other day is no longer the same desk today, because our experience has changed, no matter how imperceptibly, since the last time we saw it. Thus, for both philosophers, the experience of the human mind is ever-changing, always transforming, and continually moving forward.

This concept of mind runs counter to the common-sense view of experience. People in general act on the assumption that experience can be separated into its constituent parts, just as we can separate the cup from the teapot, and the teapot from the book; just as we can distinguish the flame of the candle from the fire in the stove. They are thus unable to grasp Bergson's view of experience as an ever-moving stream; for them this is clearly contrary to fact. Both James and Bergson reply to this criticism by pointing out that people have traditionally viewed the human mind as though their concepts of material things could be transferred and applied to it. Just as material objects can be separated into their component parts, they think, mind can be reduced to its constituent elements. But how do people transfer their concepts of material things and try to make them apply to the mind? Bergson and James arrived at different answers to this question.

Why, Bergson asks himself, must people insist that their experience be cut into segments, if the experience of mind is like a flowing stream? He concludes that the reason men do this is that they want to be understood by their fellow men. The need to communicate with others forces them to segment their experience into units which can be dealt with through language. Linguistic symbols can portray only separated segments of experience; the necessity for communication, therefore, requires that men slice reality into innumerable small bits.

Working from this concept of experience, Bergson constructs his unique and fundamental concept of "duration." Duration is, he says, to be distinguished from time. What, then is it? Duration is an endless moving forward which carries all the past within itself. Bergson compares duration to a snowball rolling down the mountainside—a figure of speech which implies first that it incorporated within itself all that is past; and second, that because it becomes bigger and bigger as it rolls, it is continually transformed.

Bergson bases his explanation of internal experience on this concept of duration. In the first place, he notes, existence means change;

there can be no existence without change. In the second place, change means growing and maturing. And in the third place, growing and maturing involve endless self-creation. The first point is easy to grasp; and the second, in relation to which he employs the metaphor of the snowball, is not particularly difficult. But what does the third point imply? Endless self-creation means the continual addition of new meaning to existing experience. For example, my best friend may know all my past, but he cannot know what I am going to do tomorrow; he cannot know even what I am going to do five minutes from now. All experience is a result of continual creation; none of it is predetermined. Even the most intimate knowledge of past experience cannot be a basis for reliably predicting the future. When an artist standing before a blank canvas picks up his brush, no one—not even he, himself—can know ahead of time what the result will be. If he knew before he started to paint what his painting would look like, the result would have been achieved before the effort was undertaken— and this would be a contradiction. Bergson has employed this example a number of times when he expounds the idea that every experience is new, and is thus a result of self-creation.

We must accept this basic concept for the time being, so that we can explore the results which come about when Bergson applies it to the three groups of philosophical problems which we mentioned earlier. When this concept is applied to the third group, those dealing with the relationship of mind and matter, it leads to the conclusion that the two are incompatible and incommensurable. The material world is static, unchanging, fixed, and can be reduced to its component parts, right down to molecules and atoms. The material world is composed of particles; and although a material object can move in space, and although the material world can be re-organized, yet matter remains unchanged. For example, this book can be moved from here to there, but it remains a part of this room. According to the law of conservation of matter in chemistry, when this piece of paper is burned, its atoms remain unchanged, although they may be reorganized into molecules of another structure.

Bergson sees the material world solely in spatial relationships; only mental experience can be explained in terms of duration. Matter is confined within spatial relationships, and even when the element of time appears to be involved, it is only an aspect of or "disguise" for spatial relationship. Duration itself is change; the time which characterizes the material world is not duration, but pseudo-time. When, for example, we say that there will be an eclipse of the sun three months hence, it would appear that these three months represent duration; but, according to Bergson, the period of three months can be divided into any number of segments, and therefore it is pseudo-time, still a disguise of space.

An example which makes explicit the distinction between Bergson's pseudo-time and duration can be found in the clock. Here time is indicated by the hour-hand and the minute-hand; it is not duration, but is merely the spatial relationship between the two hands of the clock. Such "time" is not duration; it is a disguise of space. On the other hand, when one is hungry and waiting for food, or when he is in danger of drowning and calling for help, or when he is waiting in court for trial or sentence, he incorporates all his past experience into the moment, and moves forward to the future. This can be called "duration." We can distinguish between what Bergson means by duration and pseudo-time if we remember these examples—the clock, and the situations we have mentioned.

In brief, Bergson's material world is a matter of spatial relationships, while the spiritual world is composed of living experience, which is what he means by duration. Bergson makes the same distinction between perception and recollection. Perception results from the influence of material things; for example, this glass, when it reflects the flame of the candle, "perceives" the candle-light; a mirror, reflecting everything in front of it, is another case of perception. Thus the effect of matter is limited to the sphere of pure perception.

These examples of the glass and the mirror having perception show us that, for Bergson, perception is entirely an effect of matter. But recollection lies in another sphere; one can sum up all his past experiences and leap into the future through the processes of growth and assimilation. This unique and peculiar aspect of human nature is utterly transcendent of matter. Of course, we have become so accustomed to it that we notice nothing strange about it; but if we could actually grasp the true function and nature of recollection, we should no longer feel any need for a theory of pure materialism.

Let us take this idea to a slightly higher level of abstraction. When one material object perceives the other, as the glass perceives the candle-flame, or the mirror perceives the teapot, we may say that perception takes place, but the process is without life. On the other hand when the human mind perceives, it changes the original nature of the material object. What we perceive is determined by our conscious choice or unconscious selection. The hand held close to the eye blocks out the sight of a distant door; and Bergson tells us that this is because what is near to us is usually more important than something that is far away. The important object blocks out the less important one. But when we walk to the door, the door becomes the imporant object which we perceive clearly.

All of us now know that the earth is spherical; but when this idea was first advanced, people were incredulous. How, they asked, can people live on the other side of the earth when they would be upside down if the earth were truly a sphere? Bergson uses this example to show how inadequately human perception deals with matter. He tells us that man has cut the universe into tiny segments in order to deal with it and meet his needs, when, as a matter of actual fact, the universe is one and indivisible; that in spite of our need to utilize direction and position in the material world, to speak of objects as being "beneath" or "above," "ahead" or "behind," the real universe is continuous, with no part of it separated from any other part. What appear to be separate entities which combine to make up the universe, are man's arbitrary creations—creations necessary to the satisfaction of his needs, but nevertheless unreal and arbitrary.

Application and elaboration of this idea leads Bergson to hypothesize that the dead and immutable material world might well be active, changing, and alive, that is, that there is the possibility that at some time it may become identical with the spiritual world. This is, indeed, a bold assumption. But according to Bergson, there was originally no distinction between the material world and the spiritual world; that the separation of this continuous universe into discontinuous and discrete units, fixed and dead, is the work of man's intelligence—something man has done to it to adapt it to his needs. Bergson indicates that this is a matter of distress to him.

This hypothesis that there is no necessary distinction between the material world and the spiritual world had never been verified until Bergson undertook verification in his *Creative Evolution*, which was published in 1907. But we must skip over this point for the moment, and go on to two cases which lend support to Bergson's concept. First, in science the distinction between mass and energy has been discarded; the scientist interprets this table not in terms of substance, but in terms of the innumerable energies which move in certain velocities and certain patterns. Scientists no longer distinguish between mass and energy, but explain mass in terms of energy. But even in his recollections, man cuts his experience into pieces, as when he takes an examination in a given subject, he concentrates on his experience with that subject to the exclusion of everything else. This is a good case in point, to illustrate how man has cut the material world into segments for his own convenience.

Let us see what happens when we apply this concept to the first group of philosophical problems we mentioned—the problems having to do with the noumenal world and the phenomenal world. Traditionally people have accorded a higher status to the noumenal world than to the phenomenal world, and have assumed that the former transcends the latter. But Bergson holds that the noumenal world is not, in fact, of a higher order than the phenomenal world, and the former really is not difficult to understand. For him, the noumenal world means duration, and this is a continuous process of creation and transformation. When man engages single-mindedly in introspection and does not segment his universe in order to satisfy his needs, he will naturally be able to enter the sphere of duration.

As he deals with this problem of the distinction between the noumenal world and the phenomenal world, Bergson utilizes two important concepts of epistemology: intellect, and intuition. Bergson and James are alike in their recognition of the close relationship which prevails between knowledge and human needs and interests, that is, that the value of knowledge lies in its utility in satisfying these needs and interests. But Bergson parts company with Pragmatism when he denigrates and distrusts knowledge, asserting that it is overshadowed by duration.

Bergson deprecates knowledge and thinks highly of intuition. He insists that when man's introspection reaches a certain level, his intuition will naturally enable him to recognize that the noumenal world is a process of continuous creation. Now obviously this sort of statement smacks of mysticism, but Bergson has always been influenced by traditional mysticism. For all practical purposes we can say that mystical strains in European philosophy all derive from Asia. Bergson is a Jew, and comes from Alexandria, a crossroads for Asia, Africa, and Europe, which has been permeated with mystical thought since the second century before Christ. It is quite interesting for us to note that Bergson, being a scientist, has his thinking shot through with mysticism.

We must not ignore the importance of this combination in Bergson's philosophy of the scientific outlook on the one hand and of a mystical aspect which can meet the religious and metaphysical desires of man on the other. I suppose that this must be the reason why Bergson has become so well-known and has attracted so many disciples. His reputation and the size of his following should not surprise us, since he bases his epistemology in Pragmatism, and combines with it other elements which satisfy needs which some people find that Pragmatism does not meet.

Now let us apply Bergson's concepts to the third and last group in the problems we listed, the problem of whether the universe is predetermined or free. Bergson concludes that the universe of duration cannot be predetermined, for it is in the process of continuous creation, action, and transformation. Even though man can know the past better than ever before, he will never be able to predict the future. But, at the same time, Bergson sees the material world within the framework of space as fixed, disjunctive, and predetermined.

Bergson's concept of duration as a process of continuous creation is highly poetic. When a poet writes a poem, he used numbers of separate words which might be thought of as units; but the poem taken as a whole creative work of art is a unique entity, not just a succession of verbal symbols. We will not find the same poem anywhere else. The inspiration of the poet is, in a sense, mystical. Thus it is that the real life, life which is creative, introspective and always transforming, is free, while processes which are mechanical and habitual are predetermined.

II

In our last lecture we described some of the important concepts which Bergson employs. We noted that Bergson defines reality as psychological existence, as change which incorporates into itself all of the past as it moves forward into the future. To this process Bergson applies the name "duration." In his philosophy he attaches so much importance to change that he comes to the conclusion that what is changing is change itself. Thus, the only reality which he recognizes is change itself, nothing else.

Bergson regards material objects as remnants, or "leavings," which have been crowded out and left behind in the continuous process of change. He insists that the only reality is the mental existence of such continuous change, and that matter is that which has been cast off, rejected, or frozen out as the process of change continues endlessly. In his book, *Creative Evolution*, he makes use of the evolutionary hypothesis to explain how material things are always undergoing decay. In this book he seeks to resolve the difficulties which confront scientists as they continue to develop the theory of organic evolution. Bergson advances an apparently simple solution. He notes that Darwin had based his hypothesis on three basic points. The first of these is his assumption that the functional organs of creatures have come into existence through the processes of accumulation of minor variations in the primitive organs. The second point is that these changes have occurred automatically and without plan in the environment which they were to deal with. The third point is natural selection, or the theory that creatures which cope successfully with their environment survive and reproduce with favorable variations, while those which fail to make successful adaptations become extinct.

There is one great difficulty with Darwin's theory. If, as Darwin claimed, complex organs come into existence by means of accumulation and accommodation of minor changes, and then serve useful purposes, the question remains of what use these organs could have been before they became complex. Darwin notes that the eye has developed out of the creature's coping with its environment. But the eye does not serve as a means of coping with the environment until it has become a complex organ. When it was still a small part of the primitive organism, it could not function as an eye. How, then, could it have evolved? This question is a difficult one.

People who were baffled by this difficulty in Darwin's theory countered with an alternative explanation—that the change was not mechanical accumulation, as Darwin had claimed, but that there had to be a Creator, who created the universe with a purpose and a plan in mind, and then constructed it step by step. They compare this with building a house, for which we must first draw plans, and then construct the foundations, the floors, walls, roof, and finally add architectural embellishments: Each of these activities proceeds on the basis of the earlier one, so the whole thing together can be viewed as a cumulative endeavor. The advocates of this theory argue that the evolution of creatures is a comparable process; that the evolution of the eye is a change, planned with reference to a prior purpose. To this view we apply the name "teleology."

In the early chapters of his book, *Creative Evolution*, Bergson is critical of both mechanistic and teleogical views of evolution. We will note his criticisms before we talk about his own theory. He attributes a common mistake to Darwinian mechanism and to teleology, this being that both recognize only elements which already exist, and ignore the possibility that new elements can be created. Darwin's view is that evolution resulted from the mechanical accumulation of minor variations, and that when such accumulation took place smoothly, the organism or the species survived, and that otherwise the creature perished or the species became extinct. All these variations and the mechanical laws which governed them had always existed; there had never been and could not have been any new elements, only reconstitution of the already existing. The teleologist, with his insistence on a plan comparable to that used in building a house, failed fully as completely to take account of the possibility of newly created elements.

Bergson blames both these theories for depending on intelligence and for ignoring the fact that intelligence can deal only with matter, but that it cannot serve to provide an understanding of life. The life of creatures in the process of evolution is, for Bergson, duration; and since intelligence can deal only with those things which have been sloughed off or divided into segments, it cannot enable man to

understand life, which is a process of continuous change and creation. He offers the comparison of the little rock on the beach which is
hit by the tide, and asks how the stone, which is dead and inert, can
possibly understand the nature of the tide which engulfs it. He says
that this is comparable to man's effort to use intelligence in order to
understand life.

Insisting that life can not be understood through the medium of
intelligence, Bergson goes on to say that since life is a function of will
it can be understood only by action of the will. Man can employ
intelligence when he dissects an organism and analyzes it in relation
to its arteries and veins, its skin and muscle, and even its molecules
and atoms. But no matter how minutely intelligence enables us to
analyze the body of the creature, it cannot provide us with understanding of life, for life is a totality, and the more we try to analyze it
the more difficult it becomes to understand. For an understanding of
life, we must resort to will. When will is the most active, that is, when
we are most excited and moving forward most enthusiastically, we
are best able to understand the meaning of life.

Bergson sees life as a function of will; and will is without either plan
or consciousness; it is the impulse which moves life forward, and
which enables it to overcome obstacles which stand in the way of its
continual forward movement. This experience of the will is the true
phenomenon of life; the only way to grasp the true meaning of life is
to recognize that it is essentially impulse. No other theory can explain
the facts of evolution.

Bergson believes that this is the only way in which we can satisfac-
torily explain the changes which occur in the organs of creatures in
the process of evolution. He uses the term *élan vital* to designate a
continuous movement toward the future. He insists that both mechanism and teleology have failed to provide a satisfactory explanation
for the origins of complex organs. Bergson himself says that these
complex organs have come into existence simply as a result of the will
to live which exists within the organism. When *élan vital* encounters
difficulty, it overcomes it and continues to move forward without
plan or consideration. Our eye, Bergson says, is the result of our will
to see; and as time has gone on, it has become the most satisfactory
organ for dealing with our environment.

Bergson speaks of the eye as a vestige of life's constant movement into the future. Because life, by its own nature, overcomes any difficulty it encounters in its forward movement, the eye is the result of our internalized will to see. Or, to take another example, if we scatter iron filings on the table and then run our fingers along the surface of the table, our fingers will leave tracings. The mechanist would say that these traces are the result of accident, while the teleologist would say that the pattern left in the iron filings accords with a preexistent plan. Neither outlook takes account of the view that life is impulse, moving always into the future, overcoming the obstacles it meets, and leaving vestiges of the will in its wake.

We have been talking about one aspect of Darwin's theory of evolution. Now let us look at the second, which is the origin of species. Bergson is convinced that evolutionists are mistaken when they assume that plants, lower animals, and then man constitute a straight line of evolution. He insists that evolution does not occur in a straight line; that when life moves forward, it seeks the channels which allow the most satisfactory and rapid movement. It may be temporarily halted by an obstacle, but then it overcomes the obstacle and moves forward again. This is his reason for saying that the species have evolved out of a move-and-stop-and-then-move-again pattern, and for looking upon different species of plants and animals as the products of this stop-move-stop process, or as different stages in the development of life.

As life has moved forward from its beginning, it has not followed a straight-line direction. It undertakes to conquer obstacles it encounters in its progress, doing this by one experiment after another; but when no means avails to overcome the obstacle, life is halted at that point and no longer moves forward. Bergson's *élan vital* explains that some life was stopped at the stage of insects, other life continued its forward movement to become reptiles, and still other life continued its forward movement until it eventuated in man.

Bergson recognizes Spencer as the philosopher who has contributed most to the philosophical implications of the theory of evolution. Spencer explains the forms of various creatures in terms of the environment within which they live—fish are what they are because they live in the water, birds what they are because they have to fly in the air. Each species is a response to the environment in which it exists. Bergson disagrees with Spencer on this point, reversing him to say that the environment itself results from life's will to live. For example, he says, the bridges, the tunnels, and the fills on the highway which connects the city with a village are not so much a part of the environment as a result of it; their very existence results, Bergson tells us, from the will to build the highway, and the bridges, tunnels, and fills are contingent upon and derived from this will. By the same token, he argues, that species of plant and animal life cannot be determined by the environment in which they live. The only reason why a creature or species would adapt itself to a given environment, he says, is that it has the will to live.

So much for Darwin's second point; now let us look at the third, his comparison of the plant, the animal, and man. We must skip over, for the moment, what Bergson has to say about plants; but note that the distinction he makes between man and lower animals is that the latter have developed their instincts, while man has developed his intelligence. Insects, such as ants and bees, do not have intelligence, but following the impulse of life to move forward and to overcome obstacles, they have developed their instincts to the greatest possible degree.

Bergson points out three differences between the instincts of lower animals and the intelligence of man. The first difference to which he calls attention is that man uses his intelligence to deal with matter, and the lower animals use their instinct to deal with life. He supports his view with a vivid illustration of a certain species of wasp which lays her eggs inside the bodies of other animals. She stings the host animal in seven places, each of these being a vital nerve center, so that the animal is numbed and unable to move, and so that the larvae which hatch from the eggs she has laid inside the animal can be nourished on the animal's tissues until they pupate. This is a feat quite beyond man's abilities; but the animal operates with unfailing exactitude because of the degree of development of her instincts. Bergson sees this as the most important of the three differences between man and the lower animals. Because man is inferior to other animals in the development of his instincts, he compensates by developing his intelligence.

The second difference is that man is a tool-making animal. Of course some animals also have "tools" such as their claws, their fangs, or their beaks—but these are all parts of their bodies, and they are unable to make tools which are separate from themselves. But man is different; when he wants to see more than the naked eye can compass, he makes microscopes and telescopes. The animal is warmed only by his own fur, but man makes fire—first by striking flint on metal, then in an open hearth, and now in stoves. These are examples of the ways in which man supplements his instincts by using his intelligence.

In the third place, both man and the lower animal have both strengths and weaknesses. The strength of the lower animals lies in the development of their instincts, their weakness in the absence of intelligence and in their inability to make tools. On the other hand, man can use his intelligence to make such tools as microscopes and telescopes, as we have just mentioned, but, since he cannot develop his instincts to the extent that the lower animals do, he is incapable of understanding the real meaning of life.

Bergson believes that the major problem of philosophy is that of combining the instincts of the lower animals with the intelligence of man. He notes that although man has not developed his instincts fully, he fortunately retains some of them, such as sleep, which is a heritage from the plant, and dreams, a heritage from animals. The fact that man retains these vestiges of instinct is the basis for holding out some hope for him. But it is only as he returns to the use of intuition that man can combine his instincts with his intelligence. We can see evidence that man does still have remnants of instincts when we see lower animals finding what they are seeking even though they know nothing about method, while man sometimes cannot find what he wants, even when he has developed an appropriate method. This weakness will be remedied only when man learns to combine his intelligence with intuition.

In our discussion thus far, we have assumed that matter exists. But Bergson defines reality as a psychological existence which he equates with change. Where, then, does matter come into the picture? Using his great skill with words, and appealing to his concept of evolution, Bergson has yielded to the demand that he explain the origin of matter. I shall not say much about this here, partly because we don't have much time, and partly because I, myself, do not understand it very clearly. Bergson tells us that matter originates from psychological existence. But how? He uses the example of a great poet reading one of his poems aloud. When his audience concentrates on the poem—on its meaning, its rhythm, and its over all excellence—they do not pay attention to the separate words, or to the structure of the sentences, the spelling, and so on. This is because they are concentrating on the poem, as a poem; when they get tired or their attention wanders, they hear only the separate words, and lose sight of the fact and the meaning of the poem. But when they again concentrate on the poem as a poem, they combine all the elements, and what they hear is the poem.

The implication of this example seems to be that when we concentrate, we are in the spiritual world, and that when our attention is diverted, we immediately revert to the material world. Bergson explains the origin of matter in the same way: in the beginning there is only duration, or enthusiastic forward movement. Sometimes, though, we allow ourselves to relax. Life itself is duration without matter; but as we relax, we become part of the material world. He also uses the example of the sky-rocket. As it soars higher and higher, it is full of spirit; but when it falls to the earth, its burned-out shell becomes matter.

Time is running out, so I cannot give you a detailed criticism of Bergson's philosophy, but there are a few things that I do want to say. Bergson's manner of dealing with various philosophical problems is a tribute to his intellectual stature. An accomplished artist, he has performed with excellence in other fields of endeavor. The most important of his contributions is his argument that the meaning of life cannot be grasped through knowledge, that we can understand life only by living it. Behaviors cannot be the objects of knowledge; they can be understood only through behaving or acting. It is true that this concept is not original with Bergson, but he has developed it more fully and more explicitly than has anyone else.

Another important contribution is Bergson's concept of continuous creation and continuous evolution, with the ever-present possibility of adding new elements. Again, although Bergson did not originate this idea, he has developed and explicated it in competent fashion. Also we must give Bergson credit for his development of the thesis that truth can never be reached through pure reason, but only when an inner intuition is exercised.

But, because of his insistence on organizing all his ideas—many of which, in themselves, have great value, as we have seen—into one consistent system, and because of his liberal use of examples, as well as his literary style, Bergson goes to extremes and has failed in his desire to construct a philosophical system. All I can say here is that he has not succeeded in avoiding the trap into which so many of the great traditional philosophers fell—the overwhelming desire to arrange all his insights into one coherent system, and to refer everything in it to one central idea. For this reason Bergson has encountered many difficulties, and has fallen into many inconsistencies. In this particular aspect, James is more sophisticated than Bergson. Although James develops his philosophical insights along many lines, he has no wish to organize them into one coherent philosophical system. We can say that Bergson's preoccupation with building a philosophical system is his greatest weakness, and is a contributing cause to the fact that he does not enjoy the preeminence that might have been his.

Bertrand Russell

I

This evening we will talk about the third of the philosophers with whom we are dealing in this series of lectures, Bertrand Russell, a young Englishman. A few years ago Russell was a professor of mathematics at Cambridge University, but because of his outstpoken pacifism he incurred the displeasure of the British government when the European War broke out, and he resigned his professorship until the end of the war. Today we will talk about the theoretical aspects of Russell's philosophy, leaving consideration of his ethics and political philosophy for our next lecture.

It would be difficult to find another philosopher so entirely different from both James and Bergson as Russell is. As we have seen, James and Bergson share many points in common, but as far as the theoretical aspects of philosophy are concerned, Russell does not share a single point with either of them. Both James and Bergson base their philosophy in psychology, and begin their inquiries with consideration of human affairs, with the concerns of conscious, living human beings. Russell, on the other hand, starts with mathematics, the most abstract and formal of the sciences. He distrusts psychology, deeming it to be not only irrelevant to philosophy, but a source of confusion which impedes the systematization of philosophy.

Because Russell insists that knowledge must be universal, and that it can never be purely personal, he abjures psychology on the ground that its utilization in philosophy would obviate universality. Russell tells us that the reason mathematics has not earlier been used as a basis for philosophy is that it was not until recent years that mathematics was sufficiently developed to serve this purpose. But he is sure that now man has developed mathematics to a sufficiently high degree to warrant its employment as the foundation of philosophical method.

There is one point at which the philosophy of Russell resembles that of James, although this may not be particularly significant, and this is that both are pluralists. I'm sure that you know that some philosophies are pluralistic, and others monistic. A pluralistic philosopher refuses to try to embrace all reality under a single principle, while on the other hand the monistic philosopher does. James, with his great emphasis on individuality, takes the individual as the central point from which experience is to be considered, and he is thus a pluralistic philosopher. In this particular respect, Russell's basic position is like that of James, and we can also call him a pluralist.

In his writings Russell designates his philosophy "logical atomism" or "absolute pluralism." In espousing a pluralistic view, Russell points out that pluralism does not admit of the concept of a single, unitary universe, a concept which was generally accepted prior to the development of modern astronomy. For centuries people had thought of the earth as the center of the universe, with the sun, moon, and stars revolving about it. But the work of Copernicus rendered this concept untenable, and now astronomy has developed to the point at which it is no longer possible to think in terms of a single universe.

At this point I must make one thing clear: since Russell's philosophy is so completely founded in mathematics, which is a highly specialized area of inquiry, it would be impossible for me to give anything like an adequate introduction to it, or even a coherent outline of it, within the scope of these two popular lectures. This evening I am not going to talk about the content of Russell's philosophy at all; instead, I have chosen to discuss with you some of Russell's criticisms of other schools of philosophy, in the hope that this somewhat negative approach will suggest to you the general outlines of his own position.

Russell sees two fundamental mistakes in traditional philosophy: first, it undertook to establish the existance of a unified universe, and to subsume all reality under one principle; and second, it has been unduly influenced by religion and ethics, and has undertaken to explain the universe by use of religious and ethical terminologies. Most such philosophies have attributed inherent goodness to the universe, and have assumed that this goodness is an aspect of reality.

Many religiously oriented philosophers have utilized their religious beliefs as they have dealt with the universe or with reality; they have worked from the assumption that the universe is basically good, and that life is worth living. Even those philosophers who have rejected religion have been, at times without being aware of it, influenced by ethical and moral considerations. For example, even the evolutionists have interpreted the evolution of the universe in terms of moral concepts, presenting evolution as a process of transforming evil into good, and good into better. Russell rebukes both Spencer and Bergson for their resort to moral concepts in their explanations of evolution, and blames both for trying to explain reality in terms of what they consider to be "the better."

According to Russell not only has the progress of astronomy undermined the concept of a single, unified universe; it has also vitiated all attempts to explain the universe in terms of ethical concepts. In the past, when people thought that the earth was the center of the universe, and that man was the center of the earth, and when they regarded religion and ethics as central to human existence, it was no more than natural for them to conclude that religion and ethics were of equally central importance to the entire universe. What men did was to take the criteria by which they judged their own lives, and extend these to apply to the universe as they conceived it. But now modern astronomy has made us aware of the fact that the earth is no more than a small point in the solar system, and that man is only a trivial object on the earth. How, then, Russell asks, can man's religion and his ethical systems hold any status in the universe?

After the outbreak of the European War, Russell became greatly discouraged about the prospects for world culture. In one of his articles he develops the idea of the unimportance of man in reference to the universe. He notes that the Milky Way is only a small portion of the universe; that in this small portion, the solar system is no more than a small black point, and that in this small point, the earth and the other planets could not be seen except through a microscope, and even under the microscope they would still be infinitesimal. On one of these infinitesimal points, the earth, incredibly tiny beings, composed of gas and water, busily and continually dart hither and yon, trying to extend the brief period of their lives, and killing other similar beings in their efforts to do so. Compared with the sun, man's life is brief indeed. But if they could be observed by beings on other worlds, those beings would hope that men could hasten their own destruction by killing each other.

Russell insists that men must discard their prejudices and biases before they can develop a worthwhile philosophy. For him, philosophy is a matter of pure reason; it is speculative and is not related in any way with behavior, but is concerned only with a true knowledge of the universe. Among the sciences, only mathematics is sufficiently detached from mundane concerns, sufficiently close to pure reason, to serve as the foundation for a rational philosophy. Russell says that philosophy cannot start with the results obtained by science, but that it must utilize scientific methodology. The purest and most accurate of the sciences is mathematics; hence the method of mathematics must become the method of philosophy. The objects of psychology and physics and the other sciences are existential, that is, they each exist as an object; but mathematics has nothing to do with existence. Dealing with the most abstract and universal formulae, it transcends existence. This is why the method of mathematics must be the method of philosophy.

Russell sees psychology and physics and the other sciences as being concerned with individual objects, not with universal and abstract common principles. Mathematics, on the other hand, is concerned only with the most universal and the most abstract formulae, with principles which can be applied in all fields of inquiry independently of the restrictions imposed by concrete individual objects. True knowledge can be sought only through application of the most universal and most abstract common principles—principles which apply only to the existence of truth, even without reference to their own existence as principles. Since philosophy is to be applied to the universals, its principles cannot be either verified or disproved by empirical experience. Empirical experience is materialistic; but the laws of philosophy are universal in character. These principles are eternal, no matter how much or how often the world changes. Thus only the principles of mathematics and logic can be the foundations of philosophy.

Russell takes this concept to an extreme. He even equates "love" and "hate." What he really means, of course, is that these two concepts seem to have important differences in our experience of them, but when they are subjected to logical or philosophical examination, they turn out to be relative to, rather than opposed to, each other.

There is one thing about Russell's philosophy which is strange. In its ethical and social aspects it is quite radical, and fairly consistent with democracy; while in its theoretical aspects it smacks of authoritarianism appropriate to an aristocracy. Russell exalts reason and ignores perception; he emphasizes common principles and depreciates the individual object; he assigns to reason a much higher status than he accords to experience. His philosophy in this respect resembles rationalism. This is a strange phenomenon; there is no other philosopher whose theoretical considerations reflect the outlook of aristocracy while at the same time his practical considerations are so close to the democratic ideal.

Why do we compare this attitude with that of the aristocracy? It is simply that some people are impatient with the practical affairs of life, and seek to raise themselves above mundane considerations and enter a sphere of pure reflection. Such people feel that they are "artistic," and that they belong to a higher order of being than the run of common man. It is not difficult to see that the theoretical aspects of Russell's philosophy are characterized by this tendency.

In one of his articles in which he extols the merit of pure mathematics, and deals with the distinction between the practical life of man and his ideal life, Russell avers that the most one can hope for in practical life is some sort of adjustment between the ideal on the one hand, and what is possible on the other. But in the world of pure reason, no such adjustment is needed; there is nothing to limit development or to stand in the way of continuing increment of creative activity and noble aspiration. This world of pure reason is far above all human desiring; it is immeasurably beyond the impoverished phenomena of nature; there man can construct a systematic universe for himself and dwell therein in perfect peace. There human freedom can be realized, and the sufferings of practical existence be known no more.

In Russell's more popular works we see evidence of his pessimism, amounting at times to anguish. He compares human life to a long journey in the dark, during which the traveller is beset on all sides with perils. Fatigued and tortured, man strives forward toward a destination which he knows not, and has small hope of reaching; and should he reach it, he can pause only a short time before having to resume his travels. This sort of pessimism is not infrequent in philosophy, particularly in philosophies formulated by philosophers who insist that the world of common principles must necessarily transcend the world of individual experience.

In an earlier lecture I noted that James takes the individual object as the most important and precious aspect of existence, and we may wonder why so many other philosophers accord priority to common principles. Russell's disposition is just the opposite of James'. Russell sees the universal principle as a haven of safety for man, as the ultimate and noblest goal toward which man may strive. At the same time that he acquiesces in the mystic's concept of time as an unimportant and superficial aspect of the reality, he tells us that man's first step through the door of wisdom is just to learn to find truth in the consideration of time as unimportant and superficial.

I cannot at this time deal with the details of Russell's philosophy. I have been talking chiefly about his attitude toward and his criticisms of other philosophies. It has been said that no more than twenty people in the whole world really understand mathematical philosophy—and I readily admit that I am not one of those twenty! There is one point, though, that can be discussed here. The natural sciences are means of dealing with individual objects through reference to common principles. By "common principle" in this connection we mean the scientific laws and principles by means of which we gain an understanding and grasp of our environment, even though the laws themselves are abstract and universal. The object toward which scientific endeavor is directed is the individual fact. How can science relate the two—interpret the individual fact in accordance with universal principle?

One answer to this problem is offered in modern idealism (which is to be distinguished from classic idealism). The Irish philosopher, Berkeley, held that true knowledge of the external world is nothing more than perception, and that what perception consists of is no more than sensation. For example, we see the candle as having a white light and a black wick, and when we touch it, we can tell that it is soft and greasy. A combination of these perceptions becomes our sensation, and constitutes our whole knowledge of the candle. Over and above this, there may exist a "reality" of the candle, but this is not to be known to the human intelligence; and even if it is there, it is of no concern to us. Knowledge is the combination of our various sensations; there is no call for us to concern ourselves with the problem of whether reality exists or whether it doesn't.

In one sense it seems that the progress of the natural sciences lends support to this concept. We now say that the reality of material things is actually the motion of the atoms and molecules which constitute them, and that all their characteristics are the results of such motion. But the idealist denies the reality of the material object, arguing that atoms and molecules are constructs of the human mind, and that as effects produced by our intentional and psychological assumptions, they are wholly subjective. In making these remarks, I have no intention of raising the old problem of mind and matter; my purpose is only to locate the point of dispute. Russell also explains the relationship between the scientist's atoms and molecules on the one hand, and the existence of the individual object on the other, telling us that this relationship is subject to mathematical formulation.

Russell recognizes that the object of perception is only the beginning point of our knowledge, but he is not an idealist. His approach to the problem is similar to that of Leibnitz (1646-1716) who devised the concept of the monad. The sensation of each person is a matter of that person's point of view, and each such sensation has its own reality. With each monad having its own point of view, each person has his own private universe.

Russell holds that since the object of perception is dependent upon the point of view of the individual, and since no two persons ever have identical points of view, their perceptions may be quite different, the one from the other. But Russell permits perception to indicate real existence. For example, when we look at the table from the top, we get a perception which differs from the one we get when we look at it from underneath; but still, no two persons ever have exactly the same perception of the table. Russell would say that there is not just one table, but as many tables as there are persons perceiving it. Each person has his own table, so to speak. As with Leibnitz's monad, since each person has his own point of view, each also has his own universe. Mathematics and science function as means of communication. Insofar as your table can be demonstrated to be the same as his, a systematic universe can begin to be organized. In fact, since each person does have his own universe, the only means of communication possible to us come from logic, the sciences, and mathematics.

Bergson wrote an article in which he contends that it is not possible for human intelligence to encompass reality, change, and duration. He insists that intelligence cuts reality into segments, as the motion picture camera takes pictures of objects in movement in separate "frames," each of which is actually a still photograph. When Bergson drew this analogy, Russell had never seen a motion picture; but after reading Bergson's article, he did go to see one, and came away agreeing with Bergson that the motion picture camera had indeed divided reality into segments.

But we must also note that although Russell agrees that Bergson's description is accurate, what he means by "dividing into segments" is just the opposite of what Bergson means. Bergson insists that reality is continuous and changing, and that the separated segments are unreal; Russell, on the other hand, sees the movement as misleading, and the segments as real. Each individual object has its own existence; each individual has his own world. This is why Russell calls himself an "absolute pluralist." Reality is segmented, not continuous as Bergson contends. It is only through application of abstract laws that man can organize these segments of reality into a continuous universe. The construction of a universe is the function of science; the universe was not originally continuous. This is rugged individualism with a vengeance!

In our next and final lecture, we will talk about Russell's ethics and his political philosophy.

II

We mentioned in our last lecture that the theoretical aspects of Russell's philosophy differ markedly from the practical aspects. This difference is accounted for by the rigid distinctions which Russell draws between reason and experience, between knowledge and activity, and between the common principle and the individual fact. These distinctions are responsible for the sharp divergence between the theoretical aspects of his philosophy and the social aspects.

These distinctions have led Russell to apply sharply different emphases to the theoretical aspects of his philosophy on the one hand, and to the practical and social aspects on the other. When dealing with the theoretical aspect, Russell subjects human knowledge to fact, and argues that man can have only a speculative view of and a spectator's attitude toward fact—something comparable to the mirror which reflects objects as though the reflected objects were real. But when he deals with practical and social matters, Russell's philosophy is of quite another sort; he depreciates the existent individual fact, and emphasizes such concepts as creation, growth, change, and transformation.

When he deals with theoretical matters, Russell takes a dim view of impulse; but impulse takes on considerable importance when he directs his philosophical inquiry toward human behavior—an importance comparable to that of *élan vital* in Bergson's philosophy. Russell is not willing to let impulse intrude where knowledge is concerned for fear that it might disturb the quietude of knowledge; but he recognizes the importance of impulse when he deals with practical concerns. In fact, he makes it the basis of human behavior.

We cannot at this moment enter into a detailed discussion of the question of whether these such sharply divergent positions on theoretical matters and on practical matters constitute a logical contradiction; nor can we go into detail about the question of whether, or how, his theoretical philosophy has influenced his practical philosophy. We can only summarize the main points of his social philosophy. The difference between Russell's theoretical philosophy and his social and practical philosophy is not merely a matter of differing content, but is reflected in vastly different styles of writing. His writing in theoretical philosophy, with its style drawn from mathematics, is very difficult to understand; but when he deals with practical philosophy, he employs a popular style which great numbers of readers find most attractive.

The three basic works in which Russell presents his social philosophy are *Principles of Social Reconstruction, Political Ideals,* and *Roads to Freedom.* All three of these books were written after the outbreak of the European War, and it can be said that all of them are, directly or indirectly, influenced by the war. When the war broke out, Russell was aghast, and viewed the war as a result of the combined evil powers of man—his power to destroy, his power to detract from the meaning of life, and his power to obstruct the development and creation of life. To combat such evil powers, Russell pleads for the rapid development of man's creative and progressive abilities. This advocacy is the central theme of his social philosophy.

A word must be added here: twenty-four years ago, in 1896, Russell published his *German Social Democracy*, at a time when interest ran high in the work of Karl Marx, and in the development of social democratic theory. Russell's book was chiefly factual and historical, but it affords evidence that even that long ago he was vitally interested in social problems.

When we compare the theoretical aspects of Russell's philosophy with what he has to say about social and practical problems, we note that the theoretical aspect is based on mathematics as a universal science, and that it depreciates individual psychology as being irrelevant; but when he deals with practical matters, psychology assumes a basic and important role. In fact, Russell holds that all institutions have originated to meet psychological needs, and, even further, that these institutions cannot be adequately explained without reference to instincts. He not only erects his theories on psychological bases, but resorts to psychology as the criterion by which institutions are to be criticized, to determine which arouse higher impulses and which suppress the higher impulses and encourage the baser ones.

Russell sees human psychology as having three components: first, instinct; second, mind; and third, spirit. The parts of life which fall in the sphere of instinct include all natural impulses such as self-defense, hunger, thirst, and sex; and when we extend the concept of reproduction, the family and the state. In short, instinct is the sphere in which is determined the success or failure of the individual career, and of the family and the state. It is the part of life which we inherit from the lower animals. The life of the mind is different from the life of instinct, in that the latter is personal, while the former is impersonal. Through the life of the mind, man disregards his own benefits or sufferings, and strives to attain universal knowledge.

Russell's concept of spirit somewhat resembles his concept of mind, in that both transcend the individual aspects of life. But he has the life of the mind transcending individual knowledge, while life of the spirit transcends individual feeling. The life which has feeling at its center finds fruition in the fine arts and in religion. The fine arts begin in instinct and ascend to feeling, while religion, arising in feeling, gradually seeps down to permeate the life of instinct.

For Russell, the ideal development is one in which these three elements are in balance. Instinct infuses us with energy; knowledge provides us with method; and spirit directs us toward purpose. When energy, method, and purpose are coordinate, a man is at his best. But such a condition is rare in ordinary life; all too often we sacrifice two of the elements in our efforts to develop a third. When we sacrifice mind and spirit for excessive development of the life of instinct, we live the life of savages. When our effort to satisfy desire is not sufficiently informed by knowledge, we are barbarians, not civilized people. And when the life of the mind becomes too critical of the life of instinct, we become skeptics; we distrust the world; we lose the enthusiasm which only instinct can generate, become coldly critical and detached, and eventually withdraw from the world of action.

Russell tells us that man has developed the life of the mind to such an extreme that the necessity has arisen for schools of philosophy which might come to the rescue and help him coordinate the parts that make up the whole. Among such schools of philosophy Russell includes James' Pragmatism and Bergson's Vitalism, both of which we have discussed in earlier lectures in this series. But Russell rejects both approaches, because he says that they are merely trying to adjust mind to instinct. He accuses them of having tried to make knowledge subordinate to instinct.

Russell holds that man should be characterized by universal feeling, so that he will not be confined and restricted by consideration of his own welfare, or the welfare of his family or his state. Instead, a man should be concerned with the welfare of all mankind, and direct all his efforts toward the promotion of this general welfare.

Russell lays upon social institutions the onus of individual man's inability to develop himself to the fullest. Such obstruction and suppression of individual development, however, is not of fundamental importance; no matter how great influence social institutions can wield, they cannot take away a man's internal freedom. Far more dreadful is social temptation and bribery. For example, an artist may have tremendous potential for artistic creation, but society subjects him to its control with money and the promise of fame, so that he dare not create according to his own vision, but succumbs, and ends up by pandering to the prevailing tastes of his society—and, in so doing, is less than he might have been. The case is no different with the writer, or with the politician. Russell seems to distrust the politician most of all; in his opinion there is no politician who does not prostitute himself to the whims of his constituency, and who, even after he surrenders his integrity, does not continue to subordinate his principles to the wishes of those whom he serves. Because these tactics of temptation and bribery, of buying men's souls, can and do stifle internal freedom beyond the possibility of resuscitation, they are more to be dreaded than forces which merely oppose or seek to suppress individual freedom.

But how, Russell asks, do such temptations and bribery, such purchase of man's soul, manage to obstruct the development of his individual freedom? Because social organization impairs the creative impulse and fosters the possessive impulse. Human activities fall into two categories, the creative and the possessive; and each is the manifestation of impulses which are creative or possessive. One cannot have such material goods as clothing, food, and other objects, and at the same time allow others to possess them. The impulse to ownership of such goods is possessive. The scientist, on the other hand, when he discovers a new scientific law, or discerns a hitherto undiscovered relationship, has no concern with the way the discovery may affect him as an individual, but immediately shares his discovery through publication. His impulse is creative. But social organizations encourage man's possessive impulse, and stifle his creative impulse.

This categorization of human impulses into the creative and the possessive is basic in Russell's social philosophy. In fact, we can say that his whole social philosophy is no more than the elaboration and application of this concept. He uses it as a criterion against which to judge social institutions, and by means of which to determine which should be cultivated and which controlled. He takes exception both to state ownership of property and to private ownership. Both these institutions are indispensable to the operation of our society as it now exists, but Russell objects that both foster the possessive impulse. To put it simply, Russell takes the central ideas of socialism and anarchism, and combines them into one concept which forms the basis of his advocacies. He says, for example, that when the possession of property is accorded central importance, the state, in protecting private ownership, helps the rich to become richer, and suppresses the poor. Extending this principle from its internal affairs to its international relations, the state lends its power to the suppression of small states, and thus contributes to the growth of imperialism.

As we have already said, the European War convinced Russell that war is an evil, a manifestation of the power to destroy. For him, war demonstrates the bankruptcy of both institutions, state ownership of property and private ownership. Private ownership, with its inherent competition in both industry and commerce, has promoted colonialism and fostered the development of imperialism. Further, the state as an institution, by protecting private ownership, vitiates individual freedom and reason, and subjects the individual to the control of and suppression by national power. As far as Russell is concerned, the European war was an irrefutable demonstration of the deficiencies inherent in both state and private ownership of property.

Aside from these two institutions, Russell says that the institutions of education, the family, and religion should have fostered the development of creative impulses, but that, in cold fact, they have failed to do so. It is not so much that such institutions are not by nature capable of fostering creative impulses as it is that they have become contaminated with possessive impulses, and have come so completely under their sway that they have fallen into decadence. Education should be a process of adventure and invention. It should be creative. But, instead, it has become an agent for possessiveness. Infiltration of the educative process by the institution of property has imposed shackles which prevent the free development of education. Thus education has degenerated into preservation of the status quo. The aim of the school as it now exists has become that of making the individual obedient and complaisant, of rendering him unquestioningly subject to the controls and regulations which surround him. Education is no longer concerned, as it ought to be, with the free development of creative impulses.

Russell charges that existing educational institutions aim not at the cultivation of thought, but rather at the cultivation of belief. Why should this be? Because education, as an institution, has been subordinated to the institution of property, and the educator is afraid that independent thought might create disturbances which would threaten property rights. Creative education should be a matter of adventure; but Russell claims that man fears thought more than anything else in the world, even more than he fears death and destruction. Thought is persistent; it is reforming; it is destructive; critical thought ignores privilege, power, existing institutions and comfortable habits; it is anarchic; it recognizes no authority and fears no law; it is great; it is quick; it is free; it enlightens the world; it is the ultimate honor of man. Creative education should not limit itself to the preservation of the past; it should aim at the creation of a better future.

Russell brings his fundamental concept of creative and possessive impulses to bear not only on existing institutions, but on programs of social reconstruction as well. He has commented critically on all such programs that he has been able to find, and finds fatal flaws in all of them. His criticism of socialism is that it is primarily a philosophy of economics. He sets forth four criteria by which we should measure any industrial institution: first, does it provide a maximum of production?; second, does it foster a fair system of distribution?; third, does it accord workers reasonable treatment?; and fourth (the most important), does it accelerate material and spiritual development, and bring about progress and enrichment? If an industrial institution satisfies only the first criterion, then we have over-production and our economy goes out of kilter. Socialism satisfies this criterion, and the second and third as well, but it has not yet progressed to the point of satisfying the fourth.

For another thing, when socialism is put into practice, the state as an institution must be strengthened. Russell derogates the institution of the state, blaming it for suppressing the individual and impeding his free development.

We have already talked about the negative aspects of Russell's philosophy in general. The constructive elements of his philosophy are not so much ideas which he has developed independently as they are combinations of ideas drawn from various schools of socialism. For example, he favors public ownership of the land, of mining, and of transportation facilities, and strongly supports cooperatives both for producers and for consumers. He has written in support of the guild system in industry and commerce, and in advocacy of full autonomy for professional groups. For Russell the state is no more than a judge which safeguards the rights of the people; and he says that there should be a federal government above the state to restrain it from using its power in ways contrary to the general good.

These three contemporary philosophers, James, Bergson, and Russell represent the spirit of our time, both in their books and in the influence they have had on public opinion. Russell appears to differ from the other two, but when we examine matters closely we find that the difference is quite superficial. We find that Russell's philosophy about the state and about society is not essentially different from that of James and Bergson. Russell joins forces with them in the importance he attaches to creation, growth, change, and transformation. Even though Russell criticizes James for subordinating the life of instinct to the affairs of practical living, he himself incorporates universal feeling into knowledge. But James is more sophisticated than Russell, for while Russell takes mankind as a whole as the subject of his observations, James gives his attention to the individual person. James has consistently refused to concern himself with the concept of mankind in the abstract, and has devoted himself entirely to the life of the individual as an individual.

To conclude, each of these three philosophers has made his own contribution. James develops the concept of a dependable future which is active and flexible, and which can be freely created by those who live in it; his radical liberalism is a philosophy which invites each man to create his own future world. This is James' contribution. Bergson's emphasis on intuition adds an element of freshness to this creation of one's own future, especially when he insists that it is not a matter of rationalizing or calculating, but comes as a result of our innate impulse to forward striving. This is Bergson's contribution. Russell develops the idea of broad and universal knowledge which is not subject to the limitations of the thinking of individuals; and tells us how such knowledge can supplement intuition, so that man can give direction to his forward striving. This is Russell's contribution.

A SURVEY OF GREEK PHILOSOPHY

INTRODUCTION

About 1000 B.C. the eastern seaboard of Asia Minor was settled by emigrants from mainland Greece. In the central region Greeks speaking the Ionic dialect were established. Almost the entire group of thinkers known as Pre-Socratic were Ionians. The Scythians, Assyrians, Babylonians and Persians rose and stimulated but did not absorb the exiled Greeks. They created their own culture—the Iliad and the Odyssey, the alphabet and the city-states. The Greek alphabet was adapted from the semitic Phenicians in regular commercial transactions. There was a rise of monotheism influenced by the Hebrew religion.[1]

It is clear that Greek thought was a product of intermingling of great cultures with the opportunity of sufficient peace to make powerful and original contributions of permanent value to civilized thought. Aristotle provides reliable information about the Pre-Socratics by his theory of scientific method. He preserved the discoveries of the scientists and mathematicians as well as the method of investigation.

Socrates condemned natural philosophy (the inductive science of his predecessors) as inferior to the search for morality and the good life. He deplored the search for origins rather than final ends.

"Plato," confessed Dewey, "still provides my favorite philosophical reading. For I am unable to find in him that all-comprehensive and overriding system which later interpretation has—conferred upon him as a dubious boon. I am dubious of my own ability to reach inclusive systematic unity. Nothing could be more helpful to present philosophizing than a "Back to Plato" movement; but it would have to be back to the dramatic, restless, cooperative inquiring Plato of the Dialogues."[2]

Plato sought wisdom in the whole of truth. He had no thought of barriers between different fields of inquiry. All knowledge was his province and this included mathematics, physics, ethics, politics, religion and metaphysics. His writings are valid for their meaning as well as drama.

Using Plato's love of geometry as a tool for understanding his ideas one can say that one leg of his triangle is that the philosopher seeks what is absolute and permanent behind appearances. The second leg is that the philosopher should rule the community; and the apex is Plato's belief in reality as timeless essences. Before he reaches the apex of final metaphysical ideas, he abandons logic and soars into the myths that are the legacy of Pythagoris. Plato's dialogues reveal thought in process—man thinking—a phrase which students of Dewey ascribed to his own lectures. We can follow the processes which point to a conclusion among the hesitations, doubts, and contradictions.

Dewey adequately deals with Plato's theory of reality, his metaphysics and his ethics. He lacks the time to deal with the complex dialogues of Plato's later period: Parmenides, Timaeus and the Laws, where the tone becomes increasingly religious.

Universals are primary while particulars are real only insofar as they participate in universals. As particulars they have no being at all. Common sense would say this was thinking backward. We see a woman who is beautiful and a man who is just. The man and woman are not abstract. They are living, human, precious beings. Beauty in the abstract is just a name. "Words, words, words," as Hamlet said. We have facts and need not explain them by fictions.

But Plato's universal is not a "thing"—it is a new category of reality. He believes that to every ordinary thing there corresponds a perfect thing which does not change or decay. It is an arrested state of a Golden Age which knows no change. This belief in perfect and unchanging things—the Theory of Ideas, became the central doctrine of his philosophy. Forms or Ideas do not exist in time and space. If they did they would decay and change. However, they must be in contact with time and space, for the philosopher who has grasped the Ideal must return, like the Buddha or the Messiah, to Plato's famous allegorical cavern whose inhabitants mistake the shadows cast on the wall of the cave for the objects of the real world outside the cave, to instruct the unliberated.[3]

Zeno's paradox has puzzled and amused philosophers for eons. It is a problem of mathematics and the difference between large numbers and infinity. The subject has been treated by Edward Kasner and James Newman. It seems the problem arises from trying to measure a finite distance with an infinite measuring rod.[4]

The subject is also treated by Launcelot Hogben.[5] He notes:

> Plato's exaltation of mathematics as an august and mysterious ritual had its roots in dark superstitions which troubled, and fanciful puerileties which entranced people who were living through the childhood of civilization.... Plato placed animism beyond the reach of experimental exposure by inventing a world of 'universals.' This world of universals was the world as God knows it, the 'real' world of which our own is but the shadow.
>
> His *Timaeus* is a fascinating anthology of the queer perversities to which this magic of symbolism could be pushed. Real earth, as opposed to the solid earth on which we build houses, is an equalateral triangle. Real fire, as opposed to fire against which you insure, is an isosceles triangle. Real air, as opposed to the air which you pump into a tire, is a scalene triangle. God, he tells us, "imitating the spherical shape of the universe, enclosed the two divine courses into a spherical body, that namely, which we now term the head." In order that the head "might not tumble about among the deep and high places of the earth—it was provided with the body to be a vehicle and means of locomotion."
>
> The supremacy of the head is very flattering to intellectuals who have no practical problems to occupy them—an educational system which was based on Plato's teaching is apt to put the head before the stomach.[6]

"The rules of ordinary grammar are not obvious. They have to be learned. They are conveniences. So it is with mathematics, the grammar of size. The rules of mathematics are rules to be learned."[7]

Two views are commonly held about mathematics. One, that of Plato, is that mathematical statements represent eternal truths. Plato's doctrine was used by the German philosopher Kant, as a stick with which to beat the materialists of his time. Kant thought that the principles of geometry were eternal, and that they were totally independent of our sense organs. It happened that Kant wrote just before biologists discovered that we have a sense organ, part of what is called the internal ear, sensitive to the pull of gravitation. Since that discovery—the geometry which Kant knew has been brought down to earth by Einstein. It no longer dwells in the sky where Plato put it.[8]

In the Greek slave civilization there was little cooperation between theoretical speculation and the practical application to which discoveries could be put to ease the strain of human musculature to the bedrock of earth against which it was pitted.

Aristotle is generally regarded as being in opposition to Plato. But for twenty of his formative years he was a student in Plato's academy and Plato's assistant. On Plato's death in 347, he was succeeded by a nephew (Speusippus) who represented a trend Aristotle could not follow. In fact Aristotle's thought was closer to Plato than Plato's successor at the Academy.

Aristotle's thought is entirely dominated by Plato. He endorsed and systematized Plato's theory of slavery. We owe to Aristotle's denunciations our knowledge of the Athenian opposition to slavery. He preserved the arguments of those who fought for freedom. Aristotle's theory of the state is founded on the *Republic* and the *Laws*. Slaves and manual workers do not participate in government. The rulers must not work. Only hunting and war are permitted. Aristotle urged a liberal (freeman's) education as opposed to slave, servant or professional work. The first principle of all action is leisure.

One of the main points in Plato's theory is that he must consider forms or essences as existing prior to and apart from, sensible things. Aristotle makes sensible things move towards their final causes or

ends and identifies them with their forms or essences. These changes
show only minor alterations of Plato's essentials. For Aristotle all
movement or change means the actualization of the potentialities
inherent in the essence of a thing. We find ourselves back at Plato's
original point of view.

Had we progressed from the Pre-Socratics who speculated about
atoms, observed the properties of the magnet, dissected animals and
catalogued plants three centuries before Aristotle and Plato to the
17th Century, which Whitehead dubbed "The Century of Genius," we
would have avoided the soul-numbing, mind-freezing centuries of
darkness, oppression, pain and intolerance that blanketed the West
for a millenium and a half.

Even so conciliatory a thinker a Leo Baeck concedes that:

> Plato is the founder of every system based on the idea of hier-
> archy and the omnipotence of the state. Every secular, every eccle-
> siastical, as well as every ideological dictatorship, even to the
> Bolshevism of our own day, has derived from and been nourished
> by Plato's social ideas and philosophy of the state.[9]

Plato's "Allegory of the Cave" is universally praised for its insight
into the nature of reality. Has it occurred to the philosophers to
consider this allegory as an instance of the degradation and dehuman-
ization of man? What justification is there for men having their legs
and necks chained from childhood, so they remain in the same spot,
able to look forward only, and prevented by chains from turning their
heads? All they see is a screen on which marionette players show
puppets. Thus truth would be nothing but the shadows of the images.
The enchantment of this allegory seems to conceal the great paradox
of these philosopher-kings thinking of the nature of being by an
experiment worthy of Himmler and Eichmann.

Whitehead notes: "The safest general characterization of the
European philosophical tradition is that it consists of a series of
footnotes to Plato."[10] If this is the case, and I find no evidence to
contradict it, then it is time to turn to what may well be the heart of
Dewey's philosophy when he writes: "Philosophy recovers itself when
it ceases to be a device for dealing with the problems of philosophers

and becomes a method cultivated by philosophers for dealing with the problems of men."[11]

Dewey's attitude to Greek philosophy is ambivalent. Plato is his favorite reading matter. Yet no one is more critical of the Christian scholastic use of Greek authority as a return to the supernatural, of what Gilbert Murray has termed "the failure of nerve."

Yet the rediscovery of Greek thought as an art of control based on the study of nature "marks what we call the modern era."[12]

> That the sciences were born of the arts, the physical sciences of the crafts and technologies of healing—is I suppose an admitted fact.[13]

Here Dewey sharply distinguishes art and science:

> The first step away from oppression by immediate things and events was taken when man employed tools and appliances for manipulating things so as to render them contributory to desired objects. In responding to things not in their immediate qualities but for the sake of ulterior results, immediate qualities are dimmed while those features which are signs, indices of something else, are distinguished. A thing is more significantly what it makes possible than what it immediately is.[14]

Greek thinkers disparaged experience. It was an inferior portion of nature, infected with chance and change. Experience meant art, the contingencies of nature, while reason, theory, exhibited its universalities. Art was born of deprivation, incompleteness, while reason manifested totality of Being. The community in which Greek art was produced had a servile status. The artist was an artisan and occupied an inferior position. "Objects of rational thought—were the only things that met the specification of freedom."[15]

> Values are values, things immediately having certain intrinsic qualities. Of them as values there is accordingly nothing to be said; they are what they are.
>
> Things that are means and things that are fulfillments have different qualities; but so do symphonies, operas and oratorios.

When thought and discussion enter, when theorizing sets in, when there is anything beyond bare immediate enjoyment and suffering, it is the means-consequence relationship that is considered. Thought goes beyond immediate existence to its relationships the conditions which mediate it and the things to which it is in turn mediatory.[16]

Values as such, cannot be reflected upon; they either are or are not enjoyed.[17]

When criticism and the critical attitude are legitimately distinguished from appreciation and taste, we are in the presence of one case of the constant rhythm of "perchings and flights" (to borrow James' terms), characteristic of alternate emphasis upon the immediate and mediate, the consummatory and the instrumental, phases of all conscious experience.[18]

Greek science imputed efficacy to qualities. The world was formulated and explained on the basis of the causal efficacy of these qualities (wet and dry, hot and cold). The scientific revolution of the seventeenth century took its departure from a denial of causal status (and hence of significance for science) of these and all other direct qualities. The error of Greek science lay not in assigning qualities to natural existence, but in misconceiving the locus of their efficacy. It attributed to qualities apart from organic action efficiencies which qualities possess only through the medium of an organized activity of life and mind.[19]

Plato felt that existing evils were due to the absence of such fixed patterns as controlled the productions of artisans. The ethical purport of philosophy was to furnish them, and when once they were instituted, they were to be consecrated by religion, adorned by art, inculcated by education and enforced by magistrates so that alteration of them would be impossible.[20]

The very fitness of the Aristotelian logical organon in respect to the culture and common sense of a certain group in the period in which it was formulated unfits it to be a logical formulation of not only the science but even of the common sense of the present cultural epoch.[21]

The division of the world into two kinds of Being, one superior, accessible only to reason and ideal in nature, the other inferior, material, changeable, empirical, accessible to sense-observation, turns inevitably into the idea that knowledge is contemplative in nature. When the practice of knowledge ceased to be dialectical and became experimental, knowing became preoccupied with changes and the test of knowledge became the ability to bring about certain changes.[22]

For things are objects to be treated, used, acted upon and with, enjoyed and endured even more than things to be known. They are things *had* before they are things cognized.

It is important for philosophic theory to be aware that the distinct and evident are prized and why they are. But it is equally important to note that the dark and twilight abound. For in any object of primary experience there are always potentialities which are not explicit; any object that is overt is charged with possible consequences that are hidden; the most overt act has factors which are not explicit.[23]

Compare:

The thesis of the essays is that thinking is instrumental to a control of the environment, a control affected through acts which would not be undertaken without the prior resolution of a complex situation into assured elements and the accompanying projection of possibilities.[24]

Anything that may be called knowledge, or a known object, marks a question answered, a difficulty disposed of, confusion cleared up, an inconsistency reduced to coherence, a perplexity mastered. Without reference to this mediating element, what is called knowledge is but direct and unswerving action, or else a possessive enjoyment. Similarly, thinking is the actual transition from the problematic to the secure. There is no separate "mind" gifted with a faculty of thought; such a conception of thought ends in postulating the mystery of a power outside of nature and yet able to intervene within it. Thinking is objectively discoverable as that mode of serial responsive behavior to a problematic situation in which transition to the relatively settled and clear is effected.[25]

The things of primary experience are so arresting and engrossing that we tend to accept them just as they are—the flat earth, the march of the sun from east to west and its sinking under the earth. Current beliefs in morals, religion and politics similarly reflect the social conditions which present themselves. Only analysis shows that the *ways* in which we believe and expect have a tremendous affect upon *what* we believe and expect.

In spite of the acute and penetrating powers of observation among the Greeks, their "science" is a monument of the extent to which the effects of acquired social habits as well as of organic constitution were attributed directly to natural events.[26]

Note that "science" in this context refers to Plato-Aristotle and not the Ionic pre-Socratic atomists.

The Aristotelian conception of four-fold "causation" is openly borrowed from the arts, which for the artisan are utilitarian and menial, and are "fine" or liberal only for the cultivated spectator who is possessed of leisure—that is, is relieved from the necessity of partaking laborously in change and matter.[27]

The body is decked before it is clothed. While homes are still hovels, temples and palaces are embellished. Luxuries prevail over necessities. The history of man shows that man takes his enjoyment neat, and at as short range as possible.[28]

The Greeks were more naive than we are. Their thinkers were as much dominated by the esthetic characters of experienced objects as modern thinkers are by their scientific and economic (or relational) traits. Consequently they had no difficulty in recognizing the importance of qualities and things inherently closed or final.[29]

Many modern thinkers, influenced by the notion that knowledge is the only mode of experience that grasps things, assuming the ubiquity of cognition, and noting that immediacy or qualitative existence has no place in authentic science, have asserted that qualities are always and only states of consciousness.[30]

Resort to esthetic objects is the spontaneous human escape and consolation in a trying and difficult world. A world that consisted entirely of stable objects directly presented and possessed would have no esthetic qualities; it would just be. Objects are actually esthetic when they turn hazard and defeat to an issue which is above and beyond trouble and vicissitude. Festal celebration and consummatory delights belong only in a world that knows risk and hardship.[31]

Greek philosophy as well as Greek art is a memorial of the joy in what is finished when it is found amid a world of unrest, struggle, and uncertainty in what, since it is ended, does not commit us to the uncertain hazards of what is still going on. Without such experiences as those of Greek art it is hardly conceivable that the craving for the passage of change into rest, of the contingent, mixed and wandering into the composed and total, would have found a model after which to design a universe like the cosmos of Platonic and Aristotelian tradition. Form was the first and last word of philosophy because it had been that of art; form is change arrested in a prerogative object. It conveys an intimation of potentialities completely actualized in a happier realm, where events are not events, but are arrested and brought to a close in an eternal self-sustaining activity.[32]

Even with Aristotle, a coldly defining theory called metaphysics, of the traits of Being, becomes a theology, or science of ultimate and eternal reality. Forms are ideal and the ideal is the rational apprehended by reason. The material for this point of view was found empirically in what is consummatory and final; and the dominion exercised by art in Greek culture fostered and enhanced attention to objects of this immediately enjoyed kind.[33]

Is there an ingredient of truth in ancient metaphysics which may be extracted and re-affirmed? *Any* quality as such is final. If experienced things are valid evidence, then nature in having qualities within itself has what in the literal sense must be called ends, terminals, arrests, enclosures.

It is but another way of saying that nature is an affair *of* affairs, wherein each one, no matter how linked up it may be with others, has its *own* quality.[34]

That Plato and Aristotle should have borrowed from the communal objects of the fine arts, from ceremonies, worship and the consummatory objects of Greek culture and should have idealized their borrowings into new objects of art is something to be thankful for.[35]

In existence, or metaphysically, cause and effect are on the same level; they are portions of one and the same historic process, each having immediate or esthetic quality and each having efficacy, or serial connection. Since existence is historic it can be known or understood only as each portion is distinguished and related. For knowledge "cause" and "effect" alike have a partial and truncated being. It is as much a part of the real being of atoms that they give rise in time, under increasing complication of relationships, to the qualities of blue and sweet, pain and beauty, as that they have at a cross-section of time extension, mass or weight.[36]

Aristotle could draw his account of the four fundamental affairs of nature from analysis of the procedure of the artisan, with no suspicion that he was thereby subjecting his metaphysics to an anthropomorphic rendering of nature. Greek philosophy converted no psychological conditions but positive institutional affairs into cosmic realities.[37]

To Aristotle the universal was more real, metaphysically, than the particular. The gist of his theory is at least suggested by the reason he gives for regarding poetry as more *philosophical* than history. "It is not the business of the poet to tell what has happened but the kind of thing that might happen—what is possible, whether necessary or probable."... For poetry tells us, rather, the universals, history the particulars.[38]

Sense seems, as to Plato, to be a seduction that leads man away from the spiritual. It is tolerated only as a vehicle through which man may be brought to an intuition of immaterial and non-sensuous essence. In view of the fact that the work of art is the impregnation of sensuous material with imaginative values, I know of no way to criticize the theory save to say that it is a ghostly metaphysics irrelevant to actual esthetic experience.[39]

The forms or Ideas which Plato thought were models and patterns of existing things actually had their source in Greek art, so that his treatment of artists is a supreme instance of intellectual ingratitude.[40]

Even a casual reading of these writings of Dewey, widely separated in time and place cannot fail to reveal irreconcilable conflicts. "Nothing could be more helpful to present philosophizing than a 'Back to Plato' movement."[41] And he says that Plato still provides his favorite philosophic reading.[42]

It would be unfair to fasten on Dewey's self-criticism: "I seem to be unstable, chameleon-like, yielding one after another to many diverse and even incompatible influences: struggling to assimilate something from each and yet striving to carry it forward in a way that is logically consistent with what has been learned from its predecessors."[43] In the same article Dewey underscores that the book in which his philosophy has been most fully expounded is *Democracy and Education*. "At all events this handle is offered to any subsequent critic who may wish to lay hold of it."[44]

Dewey's fundamental purpose is to transmute the raw material of experience into refined new objects. If the purpose of the refined object is prediction and control, we are dealing with the methods of science and the logic of problem solving. If the purpose is to crystalize and enhance the having of direct experience, we are dealing with art. His enchantment with classic Greek thought is based on his heroic efforts to derive the basic material of both science and art from the same interaction of the organism with its environment. It is well worth our while to repeat a thought from Dewey's masterpiece, *Experience and Nature:*

> In existence, or metaphysically, cause and effect are on the same level; they are portions of one and the same historic process, each having immediate or esthetic quality and each having efficacy, or serial connection. Since existence is historic it can be known or understood only as each portion is distinguished and related. For knowledge "cause" and "effect" alike have a partial and truncated being. It is as much a part of the real being of atoms that they give rise in time, under increasing complication of relationships, to the qualities of blue and sweet, pain and beauty, as that they have at a cross-section of time extension, mass or weight.[45]
>
> Yet Greek science, mathematics and art are static, immobile, universal, ideal. Dewey's philosophy is a tool of process, change, dynamics, and his goal of education is to prepare the student to face the problems of the present day. Prior thought, even its mistakes, have an intellectual continuity which must be kept alive and its wisdom is fraught with significance, not as an end, but a sign, a guide post to increasingly complex situations. It is a philosophy of emancipation as well as continuity. It advocates the scientific method, without worshiping the objects of science.[46]
>
> "A choice which intelligently manifests individuality enlarges the range of action, and this enlargement in turn confers upon our desires greater insight and foresight, and makes choice more intelligent."[47]

Success, power, freedom in *special* fields is in a maximum degree relatively at the mercy of external conditions. But against kindness and justice there is no law: that is, no counter-acting grain of things nor run of affairs. With respect to such choices, there may be freedom and power, no matter what the frustrations and failures in other modes of action. Such is the virtual claim of moral prophets.[48]

Dewey's own position becomes clarified and reinforced against the background of his predecessors and contemporaries; the traditions of our civilization are unified with his experimental thought. The historical background of his thought becomes acutely important for the extension of his scientific method. Our traditions took form in Greek thought and Judeo-Christian morality. It was particularly to Athens that Dewey looked, not the Ionic pre-Socratic school.

Samuel Meyer

NOTES

[1] See Cyrus H. Gordon, *The Common Background of Greek and Hebrew Civilizations* (New York; W.W. Norton & Co., Inc. 1965); also *The Ancient Near East* (New York: W.W. Norton & Co., Inc. 1965). In ancient culture the general progression was from east to west. The Ionians were an important exception having invaded the Asiatic mainland from the west, although the writing ascribed to Homer was part of the tradition passed to the Ionians by the Hittites and other clans of Asia Minor.

[2] *On Experience, Nature and Freedom*, ed. Richard J. Bernstein (Indianapolis: The Bobbs-Merrill Co., Inc. 1960) pp. 12-13.

[3] For a critique of Plato's historicity, see Karl R. Popper, *The Open Society and its Enemies* (Princeton: Princeton University Press, 1966) Vol. I.

[4] *Mathematics and the Imagination* (New York: Simon & Schuster, 1940) pp. 37-61.

[5] *Mathematics for the Million* (New York: W.W. Norton & Co., Inc. 1968), pp. 10-13.

[6] *Ibid.*, p. 16-18.

[7] *Ibid.*, p. 22.

[8] *Ibid.*, p. 21.

[9] Leo Baeck, *The Pharisees And Other Essays* (New York:

Schocken Books, 1966), p. 71.

10 A.N. Whitehead, *Process and Reality* (New York: The Macmillan Co., 1929) p. 63.

11 *On Experience, Nature and Freedom*, ed. Richard J. Bernstein. Indianapolis: The Bobbs-Merrill Company, Liberal Arts Press, Inc. 1960 pp. 66-67.

12 John Dewey, *Experience and Nature* (La Salle: Open Court Publishing Co., 1925) p. 127.

13 *Ibid.*, p. 128.

14 *Ibid.*

15 *Ibid.*, p. 356.

16 *Ibid.*, pp. 396, 397.

17 *Ibid.*, p. 398.

18 *Ibid.*, pp. 399, 400.

19 *Ibid.*, p. 265.

20 John Dewey, *Reconstruction in Philosophy*, (Boston: Beacon Press, 1957) p. 94.

21 John Dewey, *Logic The Theory of Inquiry*, (New York: Holt, Rinehart and Winston, 1938) p. 65.

22 *Reconstruction in Philosophy*, p. 121.

23 *Experience and Nature*, p. 20-21.

24 John Dewey, *Essays in Experimental Logic*, (Chicago: The Uni-

versity of Chicago Press, 1916) p. 30.

[25] John Dewey, *The Quest for Certainty*, (New York: Capricorn Books, 1960) pp. 226-227.

[26] *Experience and Nature*, p. 14.

[27] *Ibid.*, p. 92.

[28] *Ibid.*, p. 78.

[29] *Ibid.*, p. 87.

[30] *Ibid.*, p. 86.

[31] *Ibid.*, pp. 89-90.

[32] *Ibid.*, p. 90.

[33] *Ibid..* p. 91.

[34] *Ibid.*, pp. 96, 97.

[35] *Ibid.*, p. 108.

[36] *Ibid.*, pp. 109, 110.

[37] *Ibid.*, pp. 214, 215.

[38] John Dewey, *Art As Experience*, (New York: Minton Balch & Company, 1934) p. 284.

[39] *Ibid.*, p. 293.

[40] *Ibid.*, p. 294.

[41] Supra, Note 3.

42 *Ibid.*

43 *On Experience, Nature and Freedom*, op. cit. p. 13.

44 *Ibid.*, p. 14.

45 Supra, note 36.

46 Dewey in his *Logic The Theory of Inquiry*, op. cit. p. 81, lets his admiration for Aristotle go to the point where he states: "For Aristotelian logic enters so vitally into present theories that consideration of it, instead of being historical in import, is a consideration of the contemporary scene." He corrects this by adding: "The need is for logic to do for present science and culture what Aristotle did for the science and culture of his time." See also *John Dewey and Arthur F. Bentley, A Philosophical Correspondence 1933-1951*, ed. Sidney Ratner et al, (New Brunswick: Rutgers University Press, 1964) p. 497: "Galileo's work was definitely directed against the 'science' that had been taken over from Aristotle." Ibid., pp. 554-555: "On the metaphysical logic of Aristotle, all scientific knowledge took the form of definition. This view was derived from his cosmological doctrine that scientific knowledge is always of fixed *forms, essences* or *natures*, which identify and distinguish things as of species."

47 John Dewey, *Philosophy and Civilization*, (New York: Capricorn Books, 1963) p. 286.

48 *Ibid.*, pp. 288, 289.

A SURVEY OF GREEK PHILOSOPHY*

The Origins of Philosophy

European philosophical ideas began to take shape roughly twenty-five hundred years ago, at a time when whole populations were seeking emancipation from old established habits of thinking. Within the compass of a few centuries intellectual ferment occurred throughout the civilized world. In India, Gautama Buddha initiated a revolution in thinking which was ultimately to affect much of Asia. Confucius and Lao-tze formulated philosophical systems which persist into the present. Somewhat later a prophet was born in Judea, who turned men's attention to the worth of the individual human being, and whose teachings ran counter to the legalistic traditions of his day. All these men developed systems of thought which enabled men to live better lives.

Many of the earlier philosophers lived in Greek colonies around the shores of the Mediterranean Sea. The movement which they initiated continued on into Italy, several centuries later. This was the

---

* A series of nineteen lectures delivered at Nanking Teachers College, April-June 1920.—"These lectures constitute a coverage of the subject probably not equaled in a similar compass elsewhere."

—Robert W. Clopton, Dr. Tsuin-chen Ou "John Dewey Lectures in China, 1919-1920" (Honolulu: University Press of Hawaii, 1973), p. 325.

period when the human race began to substitute rational thought for blind adherence to tradition. Philosophy, as such, is born of confusion. When custom and tradition prove to be inadequate means of dealing with disturbed situations, men are forced to think, to organize their thought into patterns, and thus philosophy comes into being.

At the time we are talking about, roughly twenty-five hundred years ago, drastic changes in man's outlook on his world were already taking place, especially in Greece. In the classic tradition of Greece, religious concepts, embodied in myths, had guided the behavior and controlled the thought of the people, but a number of developments about this time combined to vitiate these controls.

It is interesting to note some of the reasons why the earlier Greek philosophers were citizens of Greek city-states located on the rim of the Mediterranean rather than of Athens, the leading city of Greece. For one thing, the Greeks who moved out and established these new city-states must have been more venturesome than their fellow Greeks who were content to remain in Attica—and being more venturesome, were probably more ready to break with tradition. In their new homes they were less subject to the customs, traditions, and ways of thinking handed down from antiquity than were the Athenians, and therefore better able to experiment with new modes of thinking.

In addition, the outlying city-states, especially those in Asia Minor, were inevitably influenced by their contact with the highly developed civilizations of Babylon and Egypt, which were markedly different from the Greek pattern of civilization. Whenever different cultures meet—and it does not seem to matter whether they are advanced or primitive—differences in the approach to common human problems and variations in customs naturally raise questions in both groups. People are curious about the reasons behind the differences they observe, and some of them try to satisfy this curiosity by study. Many of the citizens of the city-states in Asia Minor visited, studied in, and were influenced by Babylon and Egypt, and this is probably one of the reasons why philosophy developed in the outlying states earlier than it did in Athens itself.

Another factor was that these outlying city-states were much more involved in commerce than Athens was, and through their merchants and seamen were in closer and more constant contact with other civilizations. When these people saw people of other countries behaving in ways which were contrary to the customs and traditions of the Greeks, and often living quite successfully, naturally they began to have doubts about things their ancestors had accepted without question. They ventured to try new solutions to old problems, and to strike out into new realms of inquiry—and when men do this, they eventually become philosophers.

We have already said that changes in the social and political situation—especially when these changes are rapid and drastic—create a need which only philosophy can meet, and hence it is in such periods that philosophers get a hearing. I am sure that you know that China's great philosophers formulated their systems of thought at a time when the weaknesses of the "Spring and Autumn" period had resulted in confusion so pronounced that it threatened the very foundations of Chinese culture. The situation was similar in Greece. The country was invaded by the Persians. Commoners displaced the patricians who had held the reins of government for centuries, and political dissension was rife. Beset by troubles from within and from without, people began to recognize the need for reorganization of the bases of their thought, and were ready to listen to philosophers.

Prior to this time, the earlier Greek philosophers had concerned themselves primarily with the phenomena of nature, rather than with the subject-matter which we now regard as that of philosophical speculation. Possibly in the smaller outlying city-states they were closer to nature; in any event they were what we now would call scientists rather than philosophers.

It is important for us to note the difference between the origins of Western philosophy and of Chinese philosophy. Chinese philosophy, from its beginnings, has dealt with man's moral and ethical life, and is immediately applicable to the affairs of living, while Western philosophy originated in inquiry into the phenomena of nature. Even when later Western philosophers concerned themselves with human problems, they tended to treat these in the context of nature, seeing man as a "natural object," and recognizing that his problems are ultimately traceable to his relationships within his natural environment.

The fact that Chinese philosophy is centered on man's conduct, while Western philosophy originated as scientific inquiry, accounts for the remarkable stability of Chinese philosophy which has remained virtually unchanged for centuries, as well as for the developmental and changing character of Western philosophy, which has had to be revised whenever men achieve a clearer understanding of nature. In one sense I suppose we might say that Western philosophy is "less pure" than Chinese philosophy. Western philosophy, both classic and modern, stresses either science or religion, while Chinese philosophy limits its concerns to human conduct. It follows that Chinese philosophy is usually couched in down-to-earth terms; it deals with the concrete and observable actions of men; and it has no need for abstruse speculation. Western philosophy, on the other hand, with all of nature as its realm, of necessity involves speculation and construction of elaborate schemata.

Early Philosophical Problems

The earliest period of Greek philosophy, from around 600 B.C. to 450 B.C. is sometimes referred to as "the colonial period" because of the fact that the philosophers of this period lived in outlying city-states which some people regarded as "colonies." Whatever these philosophers wrote has been lost, except for fragments and quotations included in the writings of philosophers of later periods; but we know from these the nature of the problems with which they dealt, and that they laid the groundwork on which their more famous successors erected their philosophical systems.

Their first problem was "the one and the many," or, as some people prefer to call it, the problem of unity and diversity. Faced with the limitless number and unfathomable complexity of the phenomena of nature, man is impelled to search for some single element or principle which connects and brings order into the complexity of nature. Viewed from the vantage point of such a postulate, the world is one. But nature is stubborn; many phenomena do not lend themselves readily to ordering; and man continues to be confronted with complexity. His search for reconciliation of the view of the world as one and of his experience with the phenomena of nature as many is the problem of unity and plurality with which these early Greek philosophers concerned themselves.

The second problem was that of "being and becoming." In life as we know it, things come into being, and then cease to be. Nothing seems to be permanent. But man "feels in his bones" that there *must* be some eternal principle in the universe, *something* that is not subject to change. The nature of the relationship between that which changes and that which is permanent and unchanging constitutes the problem of being and becoming.

These two problems are closely related. Unity, or "the one" goes with being; and in the same way, plurality, or "the many" belongs with becoming. Whatever remains as it is, without movement or change, is permanent, or "the one," while whatever changes is "the many." The two problems are two sides of a coin. When one believes that the world is one, how can he at the same time believe that it is many? When he believes that the world is many how can he also believe that it is one?

Some schools of philosophy resolve the dilemma by asserting that the world is one, and that this one is the only reality. They account for changing phenomena, for things coming into being and ceasing to be, by characterizing these as illusions, and deny that they are any part of reality. Other schools of philosophy accept a plural universe, and search for relationships among the complex and endlessly changing phenomena with which this universe confronts them.

The early Greek philosophers dealt with this problem with some ingenuity. They continued to search for a single principle, a "one," which would allow for the changing phenomena of "many." Some concluded that water was the essential reality, and theorized that everything in the world derived from water. Others made air the essential reality, and still others selected fire. Their speculations were crude by our standards, and since there were no means by which they could put their theories to test, their science remained naive.

Philosophy does not originate in a vacuum. People think only when something bothers them. Wrestling with the ostensibly insoluble problem of the one and the many, Greek philosophers came up with a variety of questions. Sensitive and intelligent men, they attacked the problem from many sides. They faced the evidence that the world was "many," but at the same time they pressed the search for the "one." How to account for the many by the one? Since the phenomena of the world are so obviously many, can there be a "one"? How to deal with this paradox?

The Greeks' pursuit of this problem led them into physics, and subsequently they developed logic as a means of attack. It seemed that the harder they worked at it, the greater and more perplexing the problem became.

The Search for a Universal Principle

Yesterday we gave a brief description of the origins of Greek philosophy; today we will continue our discussion of the problem of being and becoming.

The thinking of the very early philosophers was rather simple and elementary. They did not really investigate the problem, but speculated about it and postulated their explanations. One of the earliest philosophers theorized that water was the essential reality. He used two supporting arguments, the first being that water undergoes all sorts of changes without ceasing to be water or changing its essential nature. When sufficiently cold water freezes and becomes ice, but when the ice melts, the water is still water. When heated, water changes into vapor, but the vapor recondenses into water. He pointed out the similarity of water to blood, and called attention to flowing streams in which water changed its speed and direction. Water is always changing, yet always essentially the same thing. Its "many" was thus "one." Might this not be true of all the world? His second argument was that all animate beings, men, animals, plants, depend on water to stay alive.

A later philosopher proposed air, rather than water, as the essential reality, the basic substance from which all the "many" derived. Man cannot live without air; this theory equated man's soul with air; air is boundless and infinite, filling, as was supposed at that time, the entire universe. This theory was somewhat more sophisticated than the earlier one which had postulated water as the essential reality.

Still another philosopher advanced the idea that fire is essential reality. Fire produces heat, and all living creatures are in a constant state of combustion, growing cold only when they die. Thus he concluded that life and death can be more readily accounted for by fire than by air. If such phenomena as vapor, smoke, clouds, and so on are the action of heat, then why not suppose that all other phenomena derive ultimately from fire, and that indeed it is the essential reality?

Even though these three theories which posit Water, Air, and Fire respectively as the basic "one" of the universe appear ridiculous to us, they did pave the way for sound and important modern theories, and are thus not to be disparaged. The current theory that the entire universe is in a constant state of becoming, and therefore always changing, certainly bears some relationship to the early naive attempts to explain the world in terms of water or of fire.

Water, Air, and Fire were chosen by these early philosophers because the changes they undergo suggest the multitudinous changes in a pluralistic world. Take fire: when a log is heated, it burns; and after it has burned, it is ashes. Fire itself, with its flickering flame, is always changing. It really isn't too strange, then, for a philosopher to compare the endlessly changing world which he observes to a candle, which, once lighted, burns right down to the end. Change is also characteristic of air, and to a lesser extent, of water. Water runs downhill till it reaches the ocean. "You can not step a second time into the same river, for fresh waters are ever flowing in upon you."

Isn't everything in a state of flux? Is there anything which does not change? These philosophers eventually concluded that the only thing that doesn't change is change itself. They saw all things as being characterized by the inseparability of opposites: wet and dry, heat and cold, suffering and happiness, goodness and badness, loyalty and treachery. Thesis and antithesis bear to each other an inseparable, reciprocal relationship.

This concept of the necessary complementarity of opposites has led to a determinism which holds that man's destiny, his happiness, the goodness of his nature, are inevitable concomitants of changes which occur in the universe. This kind of determination is similar to the philosophy of Lao-tze and Chuang-tsu, both of whom asserted that only a fool could regard the world as unchanging, or suppose that either his happiness or his misery would continue forever.

Being and Becoming

Another Greek philosopher rejected the theories we talked about yesterday, and asserted that reality is eternal and unchanging. For him the phenomena of change, life and death, glory and shame, are mere human illusions and not part of the real world. Being is, he said, and not-being is not. All being is one, self-identical, permanent, harmonious, and indivisible. The entire universe is unchanging, indivisible being. If anything could change, it would have to change from a state of being to not-being; but since everything is being, and since there can be no such state as not-being, change is impossible, and must of necessity be regarded as illusion.

Among the philosophers who asserted that the universe is unchanging* one extended his theory to the religious concept of monotheism; there can be only one God, and all other gods are constructs of the human mind. Just as a painter may paint a horse which does not actually exist, or a non-existent lion, so man may and does use his imagination to create gods. But for this philosopher there could be only the One God.

From the modern point of view this theory seems to be a somewhat unsophisticted derivation from the factual phenomena of physics, but it becomes legitimately a philosophical conception when philosophers use it in their attack on the problem of the one and the many, of being and not-being, and of being and becoming. The conception developed into a standard instrument of Western philosophy, a tool with which philosophers hewed out their views of the universe, anala-

---

* The Chinese text at this point contains the character for "changing," but since this is so obviously a misprint, we have chosen the word which fits the context.

gous to the axe with which a builder hews out beams for the house he is building.

Philosophers continued to cope with the problem of the one and the many, and the problem of being and becoming. Among these was one who took the old Fire, Water, and Air approach, and added a fourth "element," Earth. In his view the world was composed of these four unchanging and eternal elements, and the phenomena of apparent change were to be explained as processes in which the original elements combined and separated in varying mixtures and degrees of mixture. This theory provided a sort of reconciliation between the view that on the one hand reality does change, and on the other hand, that it is changeless and eternal. In this theory the two aspects of the universe complement each other, with a reality which is one, and being behaving in a way which accounted for the many and for becoming.

Still another school of philosophy would not accept the concept of there being merely four elements which made up the whole world, and approached the problem of being and not-being by postulating the existence of innumerable atoms, which collectively constituted being, and of unoccupied space, which they equated with not-being. The universe, according to these philosophers, was made up of the limitless numbers of combinations of atoms and space, of being and not-being.

The atoms postulated by these men (who came to be known as Atomists, or as members of the Atomistic School) differed in size and shape; and their conceptions really were not as close to the idea of atoms which we have today as people sometimes seem to think. But their concept did afford a fruitful approach to the problem of the one and the many; and it did furnish a ground for consideration of quantity and quality. Out of it developed a new distinction between matter and energy, matter being material substance which is inert of itself, and energy being the active force which acts upon matter.

The view that the world is made up of atoms and space gave rise to two other concepts with which Western philosophy still has to deal: the first, that the world is a mechanical and accidental combination of atoms, and the second, diametrically opposed idea, that the mechanical perfection of the universe requires recognition of an ideal intelligence which purposefully realizes itself through control of the atoms which make up the material world. The one view gives us mechanism, the other some form of teleology.

These early developments in Greek philosophy which we have been talking about undoubtedly strike you as elementary, and even disingenuous when judged by our own philosophical standards. But we will see that the development of the more sophisticated, more complicated, and more elaborate systems of later philosophers for the most part have their roots in these fumblings of the earliest Greek philosophers. We must not dismiss a development as unimportant merely because it looks simple to us.

Facts and Theories

In the last few lectures we have seen that consideration of the companion problems of the one and the many, and of being and becoming, gave rise to two schools of philosophical thought, one of which asserted that the universe is one, unchanging, and eternal, the other that change is the central characteristic of the world. These early philosophers hammered out concepts about nature which, despite their elementary structure and their simplicity, have been developed by later philosophers into powerful tools, and on which have been constructed the basic concepts of logic. The work of these early men deserves our respect.

Our topic for today was supposed to be the sophists and the period of enlightenment; but before beginning to speak of the sophists, I think it might be helpful if I would make the kind of quick review of the problems of philosophy that we have been talking about which will highlight the significance of the work of these earlier philosophers. For, after all, the sophists did not so much build a new philosophical outlook as they set themselves the task of interpreting what older philosophers had said, and to applying their theories to the problems of daily living.

First of all we must ask ourselves why people are motivated to search for a principle or a set of principles which will explain their world. When we look at men who are impelled to conduct this kind of inquiry, we find them generally motivated by intellectual interests, moral interests, or religious interests.

The man motivated by intellectual questioning searches for some principle which is fundamental and eternal, which will enable him to bring into some sort of comprehensible relationship the complex phenomena which he observes in his world. He calls the principles for which he searches "laws," and when he discovers them, they enable him to systematize and organize the facts which he observes, so that "the facts of nature" are transmuted into "objects of knowledge." If the ultimate goal of the unity of all knowledge is ever to be reached, it will be by discovery of a principle or the formulation of a law which will enable man to take proper account of any phenomenon he encounters, and to know what its natural relationship is to all other phenomena.

In morals, the case is much the same. Man wants a universal principle, an over-all criterion, because he has an inborn aversion to moral disunity; he finds random activity unsatisfying; and he notes that suffering and injustice are the normal results of recklessness, cruelty, and rebellion. Seeing that law, order, obedience come about when there is unity of outlook, men look for an always more embracing unity which will ultimately enable them to live in peace and social order.

The philosophers who are the most assiduous in prosecuting their search for unifying principles are those whose interests are primarily religious, since the unity of the universe is a fundamental concern of religion. People who have reached conviction about the unity of the universe seem to be better able than others to enjoy happiness and to endure suffering, to face with equanimity the vicissitudes of change, and to achieve spiritual certainty and peace. For the most part, popular interest in religion flourishes in times of social stress and stain, when suffering calls for surcease, and when men seek consolation and emancipation from their afflictions in reliance on a divine being. This is one of the reasons why we see religious leaders so greatly emphasizing dignity and peaceful solitude; why they are concerned with such ideas as peace, dedication, eternity; and why they tend to deprecate change and confusion.

Application of the principle of unity in politics produces conservatism. The conservative seeks a societal unity which will conserve social stability; and he is often willing to restrict individual freedom in order that the end of unity may be achieved. When Confucius taught about every man's duty to respect and honor the emperor, he was calling for a kind of conformity which would result in social unity and security.

Now let us glance at the philosophers for whom the world was in constant flux, and see what we can discern about their motives. Generally, we note the same categories of motives. The philosopher in this group recognizes change as an indisputable factor in science; he knows that the fundamental concerns of science are individual concrete facts, not abstract and general principles. He sees that if science were to place its first emphasis on abstract theories and general principles, it would cease to be science and become meditation, without any necessary reference to the facts of existence. This sort of philosopher sees principles and theories as threads which bind smaller facts into larger ones; but the basic things to him are the facts of experience, rather than the threads of theory which combine them into more comprehensive wholes. He knows that the general and permanent principle is a human construct, that it serves as a convenient tool, but that it is nevertheless abstract, and without meaning apart from the facts that it ties together.

People who look at their world from this point of view are more likely than others to oppose rigid training and come out in favor of free activity, because they see free development and unfettered activity as the wellsprings of evolution. They know that evolution, itself being a process of change, can occur only where change is possible. Hence their emphasis on the development of individuality, and their disparagement of rigid moral codes which inhibit individual development, forestall the realization of human potentials, and reduce the glory of life to the status of illusion. In the same way, those who live in a world which they see to be a changing one are the more likely to advocate and work for social and political freedom.

The Sophists

I hope that the last few lectures have helped us understand that the problems of the one and the many, and of being and becoming, with which the early Greek philosophers concerned themselves, are actual problems of living, not just matters for philosophical speculation. When we look at them closely, we can see how closely they are related to vital problems of our own day, such as the problem of conservatism and progressivism, or the problem of control and freedom.

There is a tendency for those who are conservative in their outlook, and who assert the primacy of law and order, to be the same people who are preoccupied with unity, fixity, and permanence. By the same token, those who take a progressive outlook and who attach great value to freedom and individuality, are, more often than not, those who take it for granted that the universe in which they live is a changing one. As different as their style may be, these two groups of people have one thing in common—each is searching for a consistency in viewpoint which will enable them to make some sort of sense out of their world. But the point of view which makes sense for the one group often looks like nonsense to members of the other, and that is where philosophical conflict enters the picture.

The sophists were travelling teachers—or, in the vocabulary of our day, itinerant university professors. As they travelled, they studied the customs and the beliefs of the people with whom they came in contact, and used what they learned as their subject-matter of instruction. They did not teach children; their students were adults, generally young men. The words "sophist" and "sophistry" derive from the Greek word *sophos*, or wisdom; and the sophists were so named because they were generally regarded—by themselves as well as by others—as "wise men."

The sophists purported to teach virtue. Today we use the term "virtue" as though it were synonymous with "morality," but the Greeks attached a much broader meaning to the term. To them, "virtue" embraced all favorable individual characteristics and abilities, physical and mental, as well as spiritual and moral—the ability to manage one's household and rule his slaves with justice, ability to fight bravely on the battlefield, ability to participate with wisdom in the governing of the city-state—in short, the development of all the graces and abilities that became a man. The sophists gave instruction both in theory and in the practical application of the theory in the affairs of daily life. Rather than have fame and prestige result from chance reaction in crisis situations, the sophists tried to simplify and modify the speculations of their predecessors, and to teach them to their disciples in a form which the latter could readily understand and which they could apply in the day-by-day affairs of living. As we view the situation today, the ends sought by the sophists appear to us to be praiseworthy, but they did come into disrepute, so much so that even today the term "sophistry" is a pejorative one. There are three reasons which explain the disdain with which many people began to look on the sophists.

First off, the sophists rejected traditional customs and beliefs. Greek society was undergoing disturbance and disorder; many people were fearful and uncertain; and although social, political and economic changes were proving the old customs and beliefs to be inefficacious, the confusion was held against the sophists because they were most frequently the ones to point out the failure of the old, the tried and true, and to urge their students to strike out boldly in new approaches to unprecedented problems. The sophists extended their inquiry and their advocacy of new approaches beyond statecraft and economics, and introduced revolutionary methods of thinking about the fine arts, about literature, and about religion. They were particularly vehement in their opposition to traditional methods of discipline, and staunch advocates of the application of the method of intelligence to the whole range of human problems. Small wonder, then, that they called down on their heads the opprobrium of the staunch defenders of tradition to whom custom was sacred.

In the second place the sophists called into question the quasi-religious mythology by which the Greeks had traditionally explained the phenomena of nature. In the old myths the sun, the moon, the stars, the clouds, the rain, the thunder, and so on were personified in or attributed to a pantheon of gods. The sophists tended to disparage this sort of mysticism, and to encourage their disciples to take a naturalistic view of the world. In undermining the old mythology they, in a sense, violated the religious unity of Greece, and this fact subjected them to attack by the conservatives.

A third source of trouble for the sophists lay in the fact that some of their disciples did go to extremes, and often put self-seeking ahead of the virtue which the sophists undertook to impart. This was a period of rapid political change, with the oligarchy of a small number of patrician families being replaced with a more broadly based democracy. Young men who aspired to public office learned the arts of persuasion and argument from the sophists who were their teachers, and then used these arts to their own personal and political advantage rather than for the good of the state. It was only natural that the sophists should come under censure because of such developments. The best known case of this sort of thing was when Socrates was held responsible for the actions of his disciple, Alcibiades, when the latter fomented rebellion in Athens.

The sophists were, then, under the triple indictment of corrupting the youth, of teaching obstinate argument, and of making people selfish. We must grant that a minority of the sophists deserved these strictures, but the great majority of them worked to build a better society, to promote knowledge, and to free men's minds from the fetters of tradition and custom. We might well compare the sophists of the fifth century B.C. with the advocates of absolute individualism in eighteenth century Europe, who, dismayed by the corruption of society, called for the overthrow of existing governments and social institutions, advocated atheism, and promoted freedom of thought and inquiry. Ostensibly both groups appeared to be destructive, but in fact what they were doing was clearing the decks for action. Their destructiveness was obvious; the constructive progress which they made possible was only implicit, and could be recognized and appraised only by hindsight in later generations.

Skepticism and Logic

In our last lecture we talked rather generally about the sophists and the intellectual movement in which they were the movers. Today we will look at two of the problems which were at the forefront of concern at this time.

The first of these is the problem of moral standards. The question was whether moral imperatives, social customs, and standards of judgment are human creations, or do they inhere in the natural order of things? If the former, could they have been formulated by a minority of men as a means of keeping the majority in subjection? Or are they the result of one generation after another following blindly the precedents established by their ancestors?

At the beginning of the period of which we are speaking, the evidence pointed to the conclusion that the morals and customs of the Greeks were for the most part an unexamined heritage from their past. But during this period Greek thought was undergoing drastic change. People raised questions about everything, about the nature and proper function of the state, about morality, about law and justice, about institutions in general. They were applying to the life about them the outcomes of the philosophical arguments about being and becoming, and about the one and the many. They were asking whether the criterion by which man distinguishes good from evil derives from human judgment, or does it somehow inhere, as an objective, transcendent, and permanent principle in the natural order of things. And, they asked, if there is such a permanent principle, what is its warrant and how can it be known? You can see that the sophists raised difficult questions.

The second problem was that of epistemology, or the nature of knowledge. Is knowledge universal, objective, and permanent? Or is it the product of the activity of the human mind, influenced by individual emotion and imagination? This is pretty much the same thing as asking what truth is, and where we are to find it. Are there objective criteria by which truth is to be determined? Is it embedded in tradition, or does it come into existence through human inquiry?

Some of the sophists taught that since the world is in flux and all things are changing, truth, too changes with the times, and that each period of history creates its own truths. They disparaged the idea of the eternal verities, and made man the measure of truth.

This concept of truth bred extreme skepticism—a flaw in the philosophical position which insists that change is the essential principle of the universe. But insistence on the opposite view, which holds that being rather than becoming is the essential principle, bred an equally extreme skepticism. If truth is identified with the one, the real, the unchanging, with being itself, and if the phenomenal world which impinges upon our consciousness is all illusion which hides truth and makes it invisible and imperceptible, how can man not be skeptical?

Zeno, a leader of a school of philosophy which looked upon the world as being eternal and unchanging, is credited with developing a dialectic, or method of argument, by which sense observations could be logically proved to run counter to reality. The paradoxes of Zeno are of interest to every student of the history of philosophy. Two of the most familiar are the paradox of the arrow, and that of Achilles and the tortoise.

In the paradox of the arrow, Zeno argues that "everything is at rest when it is a place equal to itself, and the moving object is always (in a place equal to itself) in the present moment (literally 'in the now'), the moving arrow must be motionless."*

Of Achilles and the tortoise he says "let us suppose that Achilles and a tortoise are going to have a race. Since Achilles is a sportsman, he gives the tortoise a start. Now, by the time that Achilles has reached the place from which the tortoise started, the latter has again advanced to another point; and when Achilles reaches that point, then the tortoise will have advanced still another distance, even if very short. Thus Achilles is always coming nearer to the tortoise, but never actually overtakes it—and never can do so, on the supposition that a line is made up of an infinite number of points, for then Achilles would have to traverse an infinite distance."*

These two paradoxes in which Zeno demonstrates the impossibility of motion are important examples of the kind of arguments utilized in discussion about whether the universe is one or many. Some of the sophists cultivated this mode of argument and used it to

---

* For the two paradoxes we have used here versions quoted from standard works in English. The Paradox of the Arrow is taken from Walter Kaufmann, *Philosophic Classics: Thales to St. Thomas*, Prentice-Hall, Inc. 1963, page 40. Achilles and the Tortoise is from Frederick Copleston, *A History of Philosophy*, Volume I, Part 1, page 74. Image Books, 1962.

trip their antagonists into contradictory statements or untenable positions. One man, for example, used the mathematical axiom that things which are equal to the same thing are equal to each other to "prove" that white is the same as black. White is a color, he said; and black is also a color; hence, since black and white are both equal to the same thing, that is, to "color," they are not different from each other.

Although this sort of reasoning was observably false, the process gave the appearance of being correct. It was partly because men were determined to devise more reliable ways of thinking than these that the art of logic, as we know it, was eventually developed.

Socrates

Among all the sophists, or itinerant professors, the greatest and best-known is Socrates. By his time the center of Greek philosophizing had moved from the outlying city-states to Athens; and by this time also the preoccupation of the earlier sophists with striking the shackles of the past from men's minds had been superseded by a concern for working more constructively. Many ideas were developed in this period which were eventually incorporated into the structure of European civilization. Most of the governments operating in Europe today go back less than a hundred years, but the origins of European thought go back into the mists of antiquity. Western culture is a confluence of three streams: the ethico-religious traditions of the Jews, the social and political institutional structure of the Romans, and the ordering of human thought, or the philosophy, of Athens.

In shifting its headquarters, so to speak, Greek philosophy underwent marked change. The earlier philosophers in the outlying city-states had focussed their inquiry on natural phenomena; the philosophical thought that was now coming to maturity in Athens had men as its central concern. The earlier Greeks had regarded man as a phase of nature, but now philosophers approached natural phenomena in terms of human thought. Instead of resorting, as their predecessors had done, to material terms such as earth, fire, air, and water in their efforts to determine the nature of man, the Athenian philosophers put man at the center of the universe, and drew upon human reason for explanations of natural phenomena. It was as though human reason had somehow endowed nature with a sort of rationality; as though the rationality of nature and the rationality of man differed only in degree.

Rationality, or reason, is the ultimate achievement of man, the ability which enables him to make valid inferences about the relationships among the phenomena of his world. The Athenian philosophers extended what they could learn about man and built up a conception of nature patterned upon it. For them the reality of the universe was not some fortuitous combination of matter or atoms, but was the result of the working out of a plan, to which they applied the term "final cause." This final cause is, of necessity, good. The three concepts, "reason," "final cause" and "good" are related—reason leads man to recognition of the final cause, and the operation of the final cause produces good.

The Athenians employed these three ideas to explain natural phenomena; or we might say that they created a natural philosophy and explained natural phenomena within the framework of their concept of life and their notions of logic. In many instances their explanations were deficient or erroneous in light of scientific discoveries of later centuries; and when Greek philosophy was ultimately incorporated into Christianity, Western men held tenaciously onto the explanations of the Greeks, so that the development of modern science was retarded. It was not until well into the eighteenth century that modern science emancipated men from the control of erroneous conclusions about the world which were fed into the stream of medieval thought from Greek sources.

Socrates was the most important link between the older philosophical tradition and the new approach to life which was taking shape in Athens. So far as we know, Socrates did not write any books; he taught by conversation and discussion, and developed these into the art of dialectic. He learned by the same methods he used to teach others. Because he succeeded so well in his efforts to release his disciples from the restrictions of conventional patterns of thinking, he was attacked and charged with corrupting the youth of Athens. Ultimately he was condemned to death.

Although Socrates, as an itinerant professor, was technically a sophist, he differed from his fellow-sophists in a number of important regards. In the first place he was unique in that he would accept no fees from his students. He said that he taught in the hope of improving his disciples' moral behavior and elevating their ethical outlook; that if he failed to do this, he had earned no fee and should not be paid; and that if he succeeded, the improvement in the character of his disciples was in itself as much of a reward as he could desire.

Socrates' lack of interest in nature also differentiated him from his predecessor philosophers. On the one hand, he saw the problems of human living as being immeasurably more significant than the problems posed by the phenomena of nature, and therefore took human problems as his domain. On the other hand, there was widespread contention among the advocates of different schools of natural science, and Socrates had neither the time nor the inclination to get involved in these disputes. His cardinal maxim when people came to him with questions about what they ought to know or believe about nature was "Know thyself."

The most important difference between Socrates and the other sophists was that while they claimed to be wise and to have a great fund of knowledge, he presented himself always as one eager to learn, and conducted his discussions in ways which suggested that he was clarifying his own ideas rather than giving instruction to others. He never gave arbitrary answers, but countered his disciples' questions with other questions.

Since Socrates left no writings of his own, we know him chiefly through the dialogues of Plato, his most eminent disciple. In these dialogues Plato shows us Socrates, travelling hither and yon, seeking knowledge from other sophists, and in so doing making them aware of their own ignorance. The basis of the Socratic method is the conviction that when a man really becomes aware of his ignorance, he will seek to remedy the situation by gaining knowledge. Although Socrates worked to make men wise, he would not let them call him *sophos*, or "wise man," the common form of address toward other sophists. He would say that he was rather a *philos sophou*, or "one who loves wisdom," and, so the story goes, his remark gave us the term we have used ever since, "philosopher," or "lover of wisdom."

Socrates' Postulates

We noted yesterday that Socrates was always conscious of his own ignorance, and that he looked upon himself more as one who was learning than as one who was teaching. We noted also that his fundamental postulate was that awareness of one's ignorance is a requisite condition to learning.

In his dialogues, Plato represents Socrates engaged in interminable discussion with anyone who would stop and talk to him. He never hesitated to challenge conventional definitions or to call into question established traditions and customary beliefs. When this practice brought him into court on the charge of corrupting the youth of Athens, he did admit that he had travelled the length and breadth of Athens, unsuccessfully seeking to locate someone more intelligent than he was. He obviously did not entertain a very high opinion of his fellow-Athenians.

Socrates assigned the people of his time to three classes. His first classification was the poets, men of vivid imagination who had the ability to apprehend truth through intuition. He saw the relatively few poets in the population as knowing the purpose of life, but as not having either the common sense necessary for the realization of this purpose, or the mother wit necessary to communicate it to others. The poets know the purpose of life but are ignorant of the methods required to give effect to what they know.

Socrates' second classification was that of workers, men who had a good command of method, but no insight into purpose. Their activities tend to be confined to the limits of their occupations; they concern themselves with the immediate requirements of their job, and have no perception of the relationship between their own work and that of others. A sailor can manipulate the sails on a ship, but cannot rule his city. A shoemaker makes shoes, but takes no interest in the government. They work mechanically and routinely, and do not concern themselves with the advantages, disadvantages, or values of their activity. They do not think about the oughts and the ought-nots They are like a physician who cures his patient without asking the question of whether it is better for the man to live or to die. Or like a cook who prepares food without asking whether it is what people ought to be eating. As Socrates saw them, workers proceeded more or less blindly without evaluating their work.

Socrates thought that the people in his third classification, the politicians, ought to have a grasp of both end and method; but his pessimistic view was that this was often not the case, and that most of the people who dabbled in politics did so to their own selfish advantage.

With the people in the first classification lacking the techniques necessary for the realization of the purposes they perceive, and with those in the second classification lacking any view of purpose in life, the task which Socrates saw for the philosopher was to enable these two groups to pool their talents, so that the poet would know how to effect his ideal and the worker would be able to infuse his labor with a sense of purpose.

I am afraid that I have been rambling a bit. The time has come for us to devote our attention to three of the major tenets of Socrates' philosophy, as it comes down to us through the writings of his disciples.

The first of the postulates from which Socrates proceeded was the dictum that "Knowledge is virtue, and ignorance is evil." Whether one's work is ruling a country, running a business, or simply directing his household, he must have knowledge. Knowledge guides men's efforts. People commit crimes and do evil only because of their ignorance, for no one would do evil knowingly and willingly. Thus for Socrates, ignorance is the most lamentable of all possible conditions, inasmuch as it is the source from which all evil deeds derive.

Before deprecating Socrates' doctrine that "knowledge is virtue," we must remind ourselves once more that by "virtue" Socrates referred to a state of full development of man's abilities and characteristics. He was not referring to the sort of knowledge one derives from reading books, but to vivid personal experiencing, to a "real, living knowledge." For him, knowing included personal conviction and emotional commitment. It operates naturally in man's everyday conduct, as in man's enjoyment of pleasant odors and his disgust at foul smells.

Knowledge, in the sense in which Socrates used it, involved cultivation of a real moral consciousness, and the development of a sensitiveness of vision which will make a man want to, and be able to, act rightly in any sort of situation with which he may be confronted. The reason that so many people appear to behave in ways which run counter to what they know to be right is that their knowledge is superficial, and has not been developed to the stage of real moral consciousness.

A second thing for us to keep in mind is the distinction which Socrates made between knowledge *about* a thing, and knowledge *of* it. When he speaks of knowledge, Socrates is referring to the second, and for him knowledge *of* something is the only true knowledge that man can have. This is the knowledge that has to do with the end or the function of the thing known. When we say that one has knowledge *of* eyes, we do not mean only that he can describe the structure of each part, but that he knows the function of each part of the eye as well, and the function of the eye as a unitary organ of the body.

In the same way, we cannot have knowledge of a knife merely by ascertaining its weight and its measurements and finding out which is the cutting edge and which is the back of the blade. We have real knowledge of the knife only when we know its function. This is the definition of knowledge which Socrates employed when he criticised philosophers of an earlier period, who had sought to explain the universe in terms of water, air, fire, and earth, devoting their attention solely to the elements which they thought of as composing the world, without even bothering to investigate, or even speculate upon, its functioning. In his view, these older philosophers had no real knowledge of the universe at all.

The third basic postulate which Socrates advanced was his assertion that ignorance is the beginning of knowledge. He concluded that one is willing to learn only after he becomes aware of his own ignorance, and that thus conscious ignorance is the first step toward knowledge. In the dialogues Socrates is frequently presented as conversing with others, and questioning them in such a way that they are pushed back step by step until they find that they are contradicting themselves. When a man finds himself contradicting what he has just asserted to be true, it is easy for him to recognize his ignorance, and to desist from obstinate argument. This approach, the "Socratic method" which Socrates used so effectively, was developed and refined by his successor, and ultimately formed the foundation on which the structure of Greek logic was constructed.

Socrates' Logic

As we look at the origins of Greek logic we must keep two things in mind. The first is that logic originated within the study of human concerns, and was not an outgrowth of investigation of natural phenomena. In this period the Athenians put man at the center of the universe, and the knowledge and skills they sought were those that would serve human purposes. The second point is that logic was developed to meet a need which became apparent when people argued among themselves. It was not an inspiration or a revelation, but a tool fashioned to meet a recognized need. In the developing democracy of Athens a man's success or failure frequently hinged upon his ability to convince or persuade his fellow citizens to adopt his approach to problems; and Athenians soon learned that eloquence without logic was not enough to insure success.

Socrates laid down some elementary rules for the conduct of argument and discussion, and these rules became the rudiments of logic. His first rule was that the object of an argument cannot be changed while the argument proceeds; the parties to a discussion must agree on the object of the argument, refuse to change it once it is agreed upon, and be consistent in their conduct of the argument. An argument must be about something that can be defined. If, for example two men are discussing the question "What is justice?" they must agree that justice will be the object of their discussion right to the end, if, that is, they hope to get anywhere. This rule that the object of the argument must be constant and consistent is fundamental.

Socrates' second rule was that definitions must be universal. In argument it is not enough that the object be consistent; it is also necessary that the definition of the object must be universal, that it must include every object that could possibly fall within its scope. When, for example, people discuss morality, they must agree that morality includes courage, thrift, industry, and so on. No party to the argument can take the liberty of defining morality solely in terms of courage, or solely in terms of thrift. These concepts have elements in common, and elements which differ, but it is only their common elements that justify including both under the more embracing concept of morality. This common element is the reality of morality, and characterizes every other concept which is also embraced under this heading. If there were not this common reality, one person might talk about a kind mother's protection of her child, and another about the courage of a soldier on the battlefield; and without the common ground provided by common elements of meaning, their argument would lead nowhere.

The third rule is that the object of the argument must be the same, so that a problem can be formulated. If I assert that snow is white, and you reply that ink is black, we cannot have any real argument, since we have no common object and no agreement or common understanding. Each of us can talk all day, and even though we do not contradict each other, our talking does not constitute a discussion or an argument.

To sum the matter up, the purpose of Socratic logic is to determine common, consistent, and immutable meanings. When justice is being discussed it is enough to get the common, persistent, and immutable meanings which are responsible for the inclusion of a range of objects within the meaning of the subject under discussion. Or when we fully grasp the universal concept of beauty, it is no problem for us to apply it to the appreciation of a poem or a painting. When one knows what beauty is, he recognizes it wherever it occurs.

Socrates extended the logical method we have been discussing and used it in interpreting the social and political situation of his day. He noted that Athenians were plagued with uncertainty, and that they were self-seeking. He deplored the absence of a guide for moral conduct, and the circumstance that men seemed to be driven aimlessly by their rapidly shifting desires and impulses. He could discern no pervading ethic, and concluded that this lack was responsible for the widespread disorder which prevailed in Athens.

Socrates saw people acting at the mercy of momentary emotion and whim; he sensed a lack of any consensus about what constituted right and wrong. He saw people at loggerheads with each other, and even contradicting themselves. Evidences of intellectual and moral skepticism abounded everywhere.

This situation seemed to Socrates to call for some permanent universal principle which could serve as a guide for and as a guarantee against corruptibility of human conduct. He tried his best to persuade the Athenians to set aside their day-by-day concerns and concentrate their efforts on the search for this truth, pointing out to them the while that once they had discovered and established such a principle, their daily affairs would be all the more profitable. But people failed to understand him, and finally they condemned him to death, as people in other ages have often done to teachers whose doctrines they could not comprehend.

When people did question Socrates about the means by which a permanent and universal principle could be determined, he answered that it was possible only by beginning with individual objects and events. Each such thing could be compared with others, and elements common to them could be discovered. Socrates was talking about what we have come to call induction, the process by which we induce widely applicable principles from consideration of a succession of individual facts. Once the principle is induced, we can apply it to define other particulars which fall under the same category—the process that we call logical definition. The inductive method of discovering general principles, and the use of the principles to define further particulars, which Socrates evolved in his search for practical guides for human conduct, have also turned out to be fundamental in the development of science, even though science, as such, was of small concern to him.

The Platonic "Real"

After Socrates' death in 399 B.C., a number of his disciples attained preeminence as philosophers, and several of them founded schools of philosophy. The most famous of these successors was Plato, who associated with Socrates as his disciple for seven or eight years before his death, and who outlived his mentor by fifty-two years, dying in 347 B.C.

Much of Plato's ethical theory derives from Socrates. He gave general assent to the Socratic doctrine that "knowledge is virtue," in that his position was that although knowledge cannot be directly equated with virtue, nevertheless the determination of moral principles depends upon knowledge.

Although Plato accepted many of the teachings of his master, Socrates, he also differed with him in important respects. For one thing, Plato had (as Socrates had not) a great interest in natural philosophy; for another, mathematics was basic to much of his philosophical thinking. He combined these interests with a deep appreciation of the work of Greek philosophers of earlier periods, and incorporated some of their ideas, in modified form, into his own philosophical system.

Some knowledge of the social and political situation in which Plato operated is essential background for our consideration of his philosophical position. After the Athenians repelled the Persian invasion, the state prospered and intellectual and artistic development flourished. In fact, prosperity was so pronounced that the Athenians abandoned their traditional commitment to austerity, and many of them pampered themselves in luxury. They did not realize how soft they had become until they suffered defeat at the hands of Sparta in the Peloponnesian Wars. Plenty was replaced by poverty; the poor repeatedly rebelled, and were as often suppressed. Never had the social and political picture been so confused and disordered. No thoughtful man could ignore the pandemonium, or fail to be moved by the distess of his fellow-citizens.

It was entirely natural that Plato should concern himself to find explanations for the sad state of affairs which he observed, and to seek for principles which could be applied toward effective remedy for the ills of his society. You will recall that we noted earlier that Socrates attributed social disequilibrium to ignorance, and taught that only the search for knowledge could bring society out of chaos.

But Socrates did not delve into the actual origins of disorganization and social collapse, while Plato did. His explanation was that while social disorder did result from ignorance, ignorance itself was the consequence of people having mistaken a shadow-world for the world of reality. If people are to mitigate their distress, he said, it is needful that they abandon their attachment to the world of appearances, and enter into the world of the real. As long as people insist on taking the false for the real, on confusing appearance with reality, Plato said, their society will remain chaotic. Individual preferences and dislikes change; they come into being and cease to be; they appear to be real, but they are only copies of reality; and when people persist in regarding as real that which is, in truth, only shadow, trouble is inescapable.

The instability of sense-perception is readily demonstrable. When the light is strong, the color of an object may appear to be bright; when the light is weak, the color becomes dull; when there is no light, no color is discernible. A house in the distance may be no more than a dot in the landscape, but near at hand it may loom large enough to crowd everything else from view. Some foods taste bitter to a sick man, but sweet to a healthy one. We can multiply indefinitely examples of the unreliability of sense-perception.

And what is true of perception is also true of man's thought processes. Every age has exhibited its own patterns of thinking; and, in fact, each man's thinking is somewhat different from that of his neighbor. For that matter, a man's thinking at one moment may be wholly inconsistent with the way he thinks at another time. And since a man's knowledge—that is, what he knows—is in so large part a function of the patterns of thinking which characterize the age in which he lives, there is at least some ground for the assertion that true and certain knowledge does not exist in this world.

The Platonic "Idea"

Inasmuch as the world is in constant flux, and since appearances provide no warrant for certainty, the supposed knowledge which derives from natural phenomena which are only the shadows of reality cannot be an effective guide for human conduct. With thought always changing, always in flux, and with each man thinking at one time in a way inconsistent with his thinking at another, public opinion cannot be other than erratic, and social unity is an impossible goal. Disputes among individuals and squabbles between parties are natural and expected consequences of dependence on the world of shadows. The only way in which we can hope to escape distress and to achieve unity of outlook and judgment is to transcend this endless flow of phenomena and enter into the world of immutable reality. Then and only then will unity of thought result in consistency of conduct; and only on the basis of such consistency can a stable social order, free of contadictions, be established.

Solution of the problems which beset mankind then requires that man transcend the world of appearances, and gain entrance into the world of reality. And since this immutable and harmonious world of reality can never be perceived by the senses, the only approach to it must be the step by step process of reason; and the cultivation of reason is the end of education. Men must study philosophy, for it is philosophy alone which will enable them to approach, a step at a time, the world of reality.

The method which must be employed in man's efforts to affect entrance into the world of reality is the induction of Socratic logic. Among any number of particular objects, a common element can be identified by use of this inductive method. Socrates himself had limited his own use of this method to the field of ethics, employing it to explore such concepts as justice, beauty, nobility, and the like; but Plato made much broader application of it. Socrates had counselled "Know thyself"; but Plato argued that it was not sufficient—not even possible, for that matter—to know a self which was always changing and inconsistent. True knowledge, he cautioned, cannot derive from this erratic self, but can come only when man succeeds in transcending his "individual self" and become part of the "universal self," through which he then understands the "real self." "I" as one person am only one particular within the universal; I—or any other person—am one shadowy, fleeting and mutable expression of the universal man, who is the permanent and immutable pattern of all mankind. I am a single sample, but my nature is grounded in the universal of which it is a particular. I am different from my father and grandfather; my children are different from me; nevertheless all of us are manifestations of the eternal and unchanging man who alone is real.

Thus we have seen three sorts of relationship between universal man and the individual human being, between the reality of mankind and the phenomenon of the single person. First, universal man is a reality, eternal and immutable, and not perceptible to the senses, while the individual person is a shadow of this reality, somewhat as the reflection in a mirror is only the appearance of the person. In the second place, the universal man is fundamental and general, not only the true model of which each person is an imperfect representation, but at the same time the fundamental source from which the individual person derives. And in the third place, universal man is the final end which the individual person strives to realize. This is why we say that the development of a person is development in the direction of universal man, who exists as reality.

To this immutable and eternal reality Plato gave the name "Idea." This word, used in its Platonic sense, is quite different from our everyday use of the term; as Plato used it, "Idea" represented the reality of the universe, a reality which is absolute and immutable. As we have seen, Plato taught that man can transcend the world of sense-perception and enter into the world of reality only through mastery of philosophy. He recognized that man had to begin with sense-perception, but then by reason he could move upward step by step toward reality, or the world of the Idea.

One example which Plato used was beauty. Man begins by perceiving the beauty of a human body, proceeds to the point at which he can think of beauty of figure without necessarily referring to any particular figure; from here he can ascend further to an appreciation of the beauty of language, the beauty of thought, the beauty of morality, until in the end he can comprehend the reality of beauty itself. This reality is immutable, ineffable, and imperceptible; it is ultimate.

The purpose of education is to help people find their way from the world of sense perception into the world of reality, and thus to enable them to achieve the highest purpose of life. But by what means can one enter into the·world of the real? By definition it cannot be done through sense perception; we can, therefore depend only on reason. Reality results from intuition, not from perception. But when a man, through the cultivation of reason, enters into the world of the real, he may not merely accept his good fortune and contemplate his achievement in quiet happiness. He must return to the world of appearances and bring back into it the insights he has acquired and apply these to the shadows among which his fellows move, and work to reconstruct them into closer approximations of the real which it has been his privilege to encounter.

Other philosophers have given separate treatment to three factors which Plato combined. The first of these is the mysterious and inexplicable progress from the concrete sense experience to the ineffable ideal which is the only real. The second factor is inductive logic by which men derive universal principles from consideration of particular objects and events. And the third factor is the application of universal concepts in the reconstruction of the sense world in the direction of the ideal. Here, in a nutshell, we have the essentials of Plato's philosophy.

Plato's Epistemology

Plato's famous Allegory of the Cave provides us with a vivid exemplification of the essential character of his epistemology, or theory of knowledge. In this allegory he depicts men chained deep within a cavern, so situated that all that they can see are the shadows cast on the wall of the cave by the dim light that comes from behind them. The objects of the real world are behind them, outside the cave, but of these they can know nothing other than what is reflected by the flickering shadows on the cavern wall before their eyes.

Plato then describes what happens when some of these men are freed from their shackles and permitted to leave the cave. When they first encounter the realities of which they had hitherto seen only the shadows, they are blinded by the glare. They are able, at first, to contemplate these realities only as they are reflected in a pan of water or a mirror of polished metal. Subsequently they become able to examine real objects in the dim starlight, and then in the moonlight. Eventually, however, they can look at them in the full light of day, and discern the difference between reality and the shadows it casts on the wall of the cave. Their outlook on the world is broadened incalculably beyond that of their fellows who remain manacled in the cave.

If the men who have encountered reality return to the cave and try to explain to those who are still chained with the light behind them, what they had seen in the world outside the cave, they will not be understood—in fact they will be accused of talking nonsense. Having seen nothing but the shadows which give a distorted reflection of reality, those who have remained in the cave are incapable of crediting the experience of the men who have ventured out into the light of day.

The people who are manacled in the cave represent the majority of mankind. The shadows they behold represent sense perceptions, illusions which only faintly reflect reality. Those who have escaped into the sunshine which reveals reality represent philosophers who have been privileged to discover and contemplate the real world. The process which these philosophers undergo, glimpsing reality at first only as reflected in water or mirrors, and then ultimately being able to grasp it directly in full light, is the process of education.

We can see two implications in Plato's Allegory of the Cave. The first is that a philosopher's view of the world differs from that of ordinary men, because he has transcended the world of appearance and entered into the world of reality. The second is that it is not possible for the philosopher to communicate to ordinary men his experience with the real world, because there is nothing in their experience that can enable them to comprehend what the philosopher may try to tell them. Often they ridicule him; sometimes they blame him for their own misfortunes, as was the case when the Athenians condemned Socrates to death.

Plato delineated three levels of knowledge. First, he said, there is the knowledge gained through sense perception. Such knowledge is relative and variable, since the operation and acuity of the sense organs through which it comes vary with the conditions of the body.

For example, one's impression of a given object is different when he is hungry and cold from what it is when he is well-fed and warm; when he is ill from what it is when he is well. Since sense perception varies according to time and situation, it is undependable. Like the shadows in the Allegory of the Cave, it is at best only a crude approximation of reality, and cannot be regarded as either true or definite.

Even though this is the case, there is an element of curiosity in man's mind which directs his attention to contradictions in the world of experience and which motivates him to seek explanations which will bring him closer to the truth. This is why man can, and wants to, reason. Let us take a very simple example: when we look at our hand, we can see that the ring finger is shorter than the middle finger, while it is longer than the little finger. Is this, then, a contradiction, that one object can be both longer and shorter at the same time? There is no difficulty here for the human mind. What happens when a man resolves this apparent contradiction about the length of his fingers is a ridiculously simple example of the sort of mental activity in which he engages as he seeks for fixed and permanent units which he can use to measure everything, and by means of which he can make more and more accurate approximations of the real nature of things in his world.

Plato insisted that man, if he is to grasp the essential nature of things, must have fixed standards. He pointed out that numbers— one, ten, a hundred, a thousand—in arithmetic, and figures—the square, the circle, the triangle—are a logical extension of Platonic doctrine.

When we referred to Plato's Allegory of the Cave, we noted that those released from their chains and privileged to encounter the world of the real were obligated to return to the cave and undertake to apply what they had learned to the amelioration of the condition of those who remained in chains. Plato insisted that noble philosophers, who will always be few in number, must always assume this same responsibility. They may not remain forever in serene contemplation of the world of the real, but must return to the world of ordinary people, and do what they can to bring the perceptions and behavior of these people into closer approximation to the real. They must help their fellow men to substitute the rationality of the real world for the confusions which characterize the world of phenomena. They must help men to discover principles which can bring order out of confusion, to understand the origins of their troubles, and to reconstruct their society.

Plato wrote a book, *The Republic*, in which he set forth his concept of a Utopian state. In Plato's Republic, the legislators are philosophers, because he believed that only highly intelligent men who have a grasp of the real meaning of the world are competent to assume the responsibility of legislating, and of serving the best interests of their society. A fundamental difficulty, however, lay in the fact that it is possible to have a good state only when the lawmakers are wise, but wise legislators are the product of the good state. Each is cause and effect of the other, at the same time. Recognizing this dilemma, Plato argued that the primary responsibility of the state is educating its people to strive for noble objectives and to grasp the real meaning of human life. Because he had no faith that this could be done in the Athens of his day, Plato depicted an ideal and fictitious Republic which would be free of the imperfections and corruption of the state in which he actually lived.

Plato's educational philosophy was really one aspect of his political philosophy. Since only highly intelligent people should be rulers, the aim of education must be that of locating and cultivating persons with great potentiality. Plato was unequivocal in his advocacy of aristocratic politics, and forthright in his recognition of class distinctions. He did not believe that all men are born equal. It is important to note, however, that the class distinctions which Plato advocated were altogether different from those which prevailed in Greece at the time. Instead of having social status based on inherited position or on property, as was the case at the time, Plato advocated sorting men into classes which would be based on their intelligence.

But how are differences in intelligence to be determined? Plato's answer to this question was all children and youth should be exposed to the same education, which would be designed to develop potential intelligence to the fullest possible extent. Those who possessed small potential would fall by the wayside, while those more liberally endowed would continue their progress toward wisdom. The capacity for profiting from education would be the standard by which social class would be determined.

Plato assumed that the vast majority of people were limited in their potential, and hence unable to profit from education. Once such people had reached the limits of their capacity, they should become workers and artisans, men without noble intelligence, whose efforts would be directed toward the production of material goods. This class, which would constitute the largest segment of the population, should, according to Plato, have no voice in government. In fact, Plato deprecated the idea of democracy, and averred that participation in government by the masses would induce a levelling-down process, and preclude the development of a good state. Because the masses are governed by emotion and desire, because they are crude and easily swayed and prone to violence, their participation in government would lead to disorder and irrationality.

Plato's scheme for division of labor has a certain plausibility about it. The great mass of people can concentrate their efforts on physical labor, on producing the material goods needed by their society, take care of their own immediate needs, and leave the management of their society to their betters. But society must provide education for those of great intelligence, to the end that they may become philosophers and devote themselves to the governance of the state and the guidance of the people by enactment of perfect legislation. Such people should be freed from the need to labor, from the necessity of producing the material goods essential to the satisfaction of their desires.

As we consider Plato's position, there is one fact that we must not overlook. Regardless of what the situation seemed to Plato to be, we know now that it simply is not true that those people who compose what he called "the humble mass" are incapable of being educated. If it were true that these people have no capacity for learning, Plato's theory might be acceptable. But since we have evidence that the majority of "the humble mass" do have capacity for education, that they can be taught, that it is possible for them to continue to develop themselves, to increase their knowledge, to cultivate their tastes and improve their personalities, we have no choice but to reject and repudiate this particular theory of Plato.

Plato's Politics

When we discussed Plato's ethical theory earlier in this series of lectures, we noted Plato's position that human conduct must be regulated by knowledge of the real world rather than on impressions garnered from the world of appearances. For Plato this knowledge of the real is a *sine qua non* of the good life, and the state is the institution which makes it possible for men to cultivate this knowledge. The state must provide education designed to discover each person's potential and to develop his capacities; and this process must result in the optimum division of labor which is the hallmark of a properly organized society.

We also noted Plato's conviction that the majority of people would early reach the limits of their capacity for education, would be incapable of acquiring knowledge and unable to cultivate reason; and his dictum that such persons should be assigned to the status of laborers and artisans. They would supply their own and others' material needs, and be ruled by men of greater intelligence than they were. The skills of leadership and the arts of rule were presumed to be utterly beyond the ken of such men.

The next class above the workers and artisans would be (as the workers were not) citizens—guardians and administrators, men who would protect the state and conduct its routine functions. Such people would have demonstrated a greater capacity for education than the great mass of workers; they would have some appreciation of accurate knowledge and of noble ideals; they could (but only with the aid of concrete examples) show comprehension of philosophical concepts. They could, for example, follow mathematical demonstrations and proofs, given sufficiently detailed diagrams and explanations, but abstract laws and principles, set forth without figures and symbols, would be beyond their grasp. They could know what is, but not understand why it is. This inability to grasp pure principle renders them unfit to legislate, and should exclude them from the highest offices in the state. Still, they would be capable of accurate concepts; they would be ready to obey their superiors, and able to discharge the duties assigned to them. The guardian could display real bravery in defense of his state; the administrator could carry out his duties with dedication and efficiency; and any citizen, no matter what his calling, would know that he should obey the law.

We have remarked upon Plato's aversion to democracy, and his conviction that confusion and disorder would result if the masses were permitted to participate in politics. But he would also exclude this second class, the citizens, from any concern with politics. Plato had as strong doubts about government by oligarchy as he did about government by majority. He feared that if a minority, such as the guardians, should ever come into control of the state, they would be motivated by their craving for fame, in much the same way that members of the masses would be motivated to seek their own advantage rather than the welfare of the state. Plato conceded that the desire for fame is of a higher order than self-seeking; that people so motivated would not be victims of their own appetites; and that such men would show finer character structure than members of the masses would be likely to show. Still, since their love of fame would cause them to seek fame at any cost, they could not be expected to keep the welfare of the state uppermost in their minds, and therefore should not be entrusted with the task of ruling the state.

Plato's highest class would consist of the very small number of those who truly loved wisdom, the philosophers. Such men would not seek their own advantage; nor would they be swayed by a desire to become famous. They would understand the real meaning of life, and have a grasp of the principles according to which the world operates. They would know the meaning of justice, and could be impartial. They could pursue truth without reference to any benefit or advantage which might accrue to them. As philosophers, they are the men who should assume the responsibility of legislating.

These, then, are two major points in Plato's philosophy. First, education and the state are closely interrelated—a good state depends on good education, and good education is possible only in a good state. It is only when the state is good that good talents can be developed; and it is only when good talents are developed that the state can be good. The second point is that education has a selective as well as a developmental function. It is the business of education to determine who shall spend the remainder of his life in which class. Education, to do this, must be accessible to everyone; and it must determine who has the capability of profiting from further education, and whose capacities are so limited that he must be assigned to a menial position in life.

The foregoing description of Plato's philosophy calls for comments from us in the light of contemporary knowledge. While Plato did advocate generally accessible education, his class system, of which education was to be an agent, is far too rigid. He assigned people to three classes, with no provision for moving from one up into another. We recognize today that each person is different from all others, both mentally and physically; but we are no longer willing to assign a person to a permanently inferior position because of a specific lack of academic capacity. On the contrary, we insist that education must undertake to meet a person's individual needs, and to develop to the fullest possible measure whatever potentials the individual may possess. Plato's rigid scheme of social classes ignored the significance of individuality as we have come to appreciate it.

Plato's political philosophy, like his philosophy of education, over-emphasizes the whole at the expense of the individual. Plato envisioned a large-scale plan, in which all components would be connected with each other in a pattern dictated by the design of the over all plan. He appears to have regarded the individual as merely part of a larger whole, never as someone who existed in his own right. Individual variations are relegated to insignificance once a person has been assigned to his "proper" group, and each person is seen solely as a member of his group, no longer as an individual person. Today we would say that Plato's plan was on *too* large a scale. We cannot accept a scheme in which the individual exists *only* as a unit of an embracing whole.

Let us note that it was not in the masses alone that Plato denied the importance of individuality. Even philosophers, members of the highest of Plato's classes, were looked upon as though they were cut from a single pattern. You will recall that in the Allegory of the Cave, Plato insisted that every person who left the cave and encountered the world of reality must return to the cave and try to communicate his experience to those still chained. Plato places identical obligations on all philosophers—all must return to the world of ordinary men and contribute toward the reconstruction of society.

This aspect of Plato's philosophy gave rise to the theory of common ownership of all things. This particular theory has been widely misunderstood. Some people have cited Plato's statements about the common ownership of wives, for example, as indicating that he would have every woman accessible to every man; his remarks about the common ownership of property as meaning that there could be no such thing as private ownership. This is not, of course, what Plato meant. When he spoke of "public ownership," he was referring to his belief that all property was owned subject to the control of the state, and that the individual owner was restricted in his use of disposition of his property by considerations of the general welfare. This, of course, is quite different from what we mean when we use the term "public ownership" in our everyday speech.

Plato's ethical theory derives directly from his political theory. He looked upon the individual as a microscopic reflection of his society. For him, the relationship between society and the individual was something like the relationship between a word printed in capital letters (*e.g.*, POLITICS) and the same word printed in lower case letters (*e.g.*, politics). When we recognize the word printed in capitals, we automatically recognize the word printed in lower case. By the same token, when we want to understand an individual, all we need to do is to gain a clear understanding of the state and the sociey of which he is a member, and we will then know who and what he is.

Human nature and questions of morality are treated by Plato under three headings. But our time is up for today; we will have to speak of these tomorrow.

From Plato to Aristotle

When we were discussing Plato's ethical theory yesterday, our time ran out just as I mentioned that he treated questions of human nature and morality under three headings or categories.

The first of these categories is that of appetites or animal desires. These are common to all men; but whereas members of other classes subordinate them to other considerations, they are the chief controlling factor in the conduct of the great masses of laborers and artisans. Members of this class, according to Plato, seek chiefly to satisfy their appetites and animal desires. This fact necessitates the imposition of moral restrictions, which serve to channel, and to a degree, to control conduct aimed at the satisfaction of desire. When such restrictions are wisely imposed, and are therefore effective, they obviate the possibility of immoral conduct within the masses. The moral counterpart of appetites or desires is moderation.

The second of these categories is high spirit, which is characteristic of the guardians, and of citizens in general. Members of this group subordinate appetite and desire, and look beyond their individual wants and needs. This circumstance conduces to a higher and finer character structure than can be found in the masses, whose interests are concentrated on the satisfaction of immediate needs and appetites. Members of the second class of society seek for good repute or fame, and eschew personal advantage, responding to higher motivations. The moral counterpart of high spirit is courage.

The third category is wisdom, which characterizes philosophers. Its moral counterpart is love of wisdom, or philosophy itself.

Justice is the result of the proper combination of restriction, courage, and wisdom. A society in which these three ordained classes of people can live together without friction or conflict, and in which each class performs its proper functions willingly, is a society characterized by justice. The same rule applies to the individual person— when he can appropriately adjust these three aspects of his character, we say that he is a man of justice, or a just man. In Plato's philosophy, justice is the epitome of morality. When Plato wrote of "the whole man" he had reference to the proper adjustment among these three characteristics; and he made justice the symbol of this wholeness. Every man must sacrifice for the welfare of the whole society. This is what Plato meant when he insisted that "the part must be under the restriction of the large-scale plan."

As we conclude our consideration of Plato, we must call attention to the fact that all the Greek philosophers who preceeded him had one-sided interests, and that their philosophies were therefore limited in scope. Plato was the first of the "universal philosophers," the first whose interests ranged over the whole spectrum of the concerns of men, and the first whose writings attracted hosts of readers. It has become customary to classify Plato's interests under the following headings: first, his mystical and religious interests which transcended the world of appearances; second, his interest in dialectic, through which he explored, with accurate language, the relationship of major concepts with their inner meanings; third, his scientific interests; fourth, his social and political theory; and fifth, his interest in ethical theory and social reconstruction. In Plato's hands the combination of these five interests became a harmonious work of art. In the centuries since his death, he has maintained his preeminence as a philosopher. No man in the western world can lay valid claim to being a philosopher without having read Plato's books, whether or not he accepts or disagrees with Plato's position. There is an enduring allure in Plato's philosophizing.

Having said this, let us go on to Aristotle, the most famous of Plato's disciples. While Aristotle's philosophy was undoubtedly influenced by that of his mentor, there are significant differences in many regards. It is customary to refer to Aristotle's philosophy as being encyclopedic, inasmuch as it deals in systematic fashion with all fields of learning. In contrast we can think of Plato as a "poetic" philosopher whose work is infused with deep emotion and great vitality. Or, to skip to another sort of analogy, we may think of Aristotle's work as a great cupboard of many drawers, in which all knowledge is systematically arranged, while Plato's philosophy reminds one of a magnificent painting. A British wit once remarked that every child that is born is destined to be either a Platonist or an Aristotelian. He had reference, of course, to the fact that people are born with different temperaments, some being intense and intuitive, as Plato was, others being detached and systematic, as Aristotle was. When we take account of this factor of temperament, it is easier for us to understand some of the fundamental differences between these great philosophers.

There are three major points at which Aristotle's philosophy is different from that of his teacher, Plato. For one thing, Aristotle accused Plato of having been unreasonable in his dichotomizing permanent and universal reality on the one hand, and the individual facts of experience on the other. Aristotle taught that the universal must be inherent in the individual event; there could be no such reality as mankind, he said, without the existence of individual men; no concept or "idea" of the perfect triangle apart from the existence of triangles and man's experience with them. For him, the universal idea and the individual object were two aspects of the same reality. This is not to say that Aristotle dispensed with the concept of universal reality; for him the concept was necessary, but he denied the possibility of its existence apart from individual objects. This is probably the most fundamental of the differences between Aristotle and Plato.

In the second place, Aristotle was a methodical person who devoted his attention to experience, and who was constantly engaged in scientific investigation. He was concerned with the distinctiveness of each individual object as well as with the common elements that enabled him to classify them into groups. Aristotle was Plato's inferior in power of imagination, and he never approached Plato's ability to deal with transcendental concepts. Somewhat prosaic by comparison, he never achieved Plato's poetic and emotional expression; nor did he concern himself with future possibilities as Plato had done. When one reads Aristotle he finds the work systematic and informative, but without emotional tone. But when we read Plato we respond with feeling, and recognizing that Plato's thought has inexhaustible implications, we read him over and over again.

The third difference was that Aristotle, with his deep interest in science, was fundamentally a realist. With detached objectivity he investigated the real nature of all things that came in to his experience. For him, the greatest happiness was to grasp the essential nature of things, and the effort to achieve this grasp he regarded as man's noblest enterprise. In this he differed from Plato, who had been much concerned with human affairs, preoccupied with ethical questions, and intent upon finding ways to apply permanent and universal principles in the reconstruction of society. Where Plato had been idealistic and progressive, Aristotle was realistic and conservative. Centuries later the conservative elements in medieval Europe appealed to the authority of Aristotle, while in ensuing periods men of progressive bent derived inspiration from Plato.

While differences in temperament between Plato and Aristotle were in some measure responsible for the differences in their philosophies, other factors also had their influence, notably the social and political milieus in which the two men lived. Aristotle, who was born in 386 B.C. and died in 322 B.C., lived at a time when Athens and other leading Greek city states were in decline. The period was one of political subjugation to Macedonia, as well as of social disorganization and unrest. Things had not been perfect in Plato's time, but the situation was nowhere nearly as bad as it was in Aristotle's time. Plato had wanted to reform and reconstruct the society in which he lived; Aristotle was a dispassionate spectator of his times, recording and analyzing the events which he witnessed for the information of later generations.

Aristotle's "Potentiality" and "Actuality"

In our last lecture we noted that Aristotle took issue with Plato because of the latter's insistence on separating the individual fact from the general principle. We also noted that Aristotle did not dispense with concept of the general principle, but taught that the general principle could not be considered apart from the individual fact in which it inhered. In order to deal with this problem Aristotle developed the concepts of "potentiality" and "actuality," concepts which proved fruitful also in dealing with the problem of the one and the many, the problem of being and becoming, as well as other problems with which earlier Greek philosophers had wrestled. The idea of the relationship between potentiality and actuality was a natural outgrowth of Aristotle's background and interests. As the son of a doctor he was well acquainted with the human body and its functioning; and as a student of botany, zoology, and anatomy, he had accumulated a vast store of knowledge which fit neatly into the framework of his idea. The development of natural creatures from a stage of potentiality into actuality supplied him with illuminating illustrations of his theory, and helped him communicate it to his students.

Aristotle taught that every living thing grows up through many steps. The acorn has the potentiality of becoming an oak tree; the chicken develops from the egg through a step-by-step procedure; a man develops from a fertilized ovum in a similar step-by-step process. Just as the acorn has the potentiality of becoming an oak tree, the egg has the potentiality of becoming a chicken, the ovum has the potentiality of becoming a man. Under proper conditions each potentiality is realized in a gradual process until it reaches full actuality.

The process of actualization is from the internal to the external, from the imperfect to perfection. In Aristotle's view, all immature things are imperfect expressions of perfect form. The acorn is the imperfect expression of the oak tree; the sapling is the imperfect expression of the full-grown tree; the egg is the imperfect expression of the chicken; the child is the imperfect expression of the man.

The fixed final purpose for which each object exists is perfect form, and all changes are controlled by this purpose and directed toward perfect form. The oak is the final purpose of the acorn, and therefore the acorn cannot develop into an elm; nor can the hen's egg become a pigeon. All changes are governed by final purpose—the actualization of the potentiality inherent in the object. Change itself is evidence of continuing imperfection; actualized form is perfect and therefore permanent. But change, even though imperfect, can have a degree of dignity, and this degree is determined by the purpose which controls and directs the change. The growth of living creatures, for example, has as its purpose the actualization of the potentiality inherent in the immature form, and thus possesses a high degree of dignity. But the dust blown about by the wind flies without purpose, and its motion lacks the dignity of change.

This same construct is applicable to the problem of the one and the many. The permanent form is the one; the stages of change are the many. Even though oak trees differ in size and height, they all have something in common, and it is this common element that constitutes the universal oak. Among men, some are barbarians, others are civilized; some are foreigners, others are Greeks, but all of them have as a common possession the characteristics of humanity, the nature of universal man. The universal oak and the universal man are permanent forms, representing species, which are unchanging. The individual oak and the individual man, examples of their species, may continue to change, but the species do not change. This is Aristotle's solution to the ancient problem of the one and the many.

Aristotle explicated not only the problem of the one and the many and the problem of being and becoming, but all other problems of change by means of his concept of potentiality and actuality. For example, he noted that fire by its nature is light, and must move upward beyond the earth into the sky with the sun, the moon and the stars; a stone is by nature heavy, and must move downward. The ascent of the flame and the descent of the stone are thus actualizations of their natures. Aristotle made the same application to the problem of mind and matter. For him, matter is imperfect expression; it is the potential mind which is spirit, the highest form, the final purpose. All change is toward this spirit as final purpose—not just in individual creatures, but the whole of nature. Man is the highest actualization of nature, and reason the highest actualization of man. Everything in the world changes in the direction of reason, but each comes to rest short of the goal when it reaches the limit of its potentiality. Of all creation, only man can achieve the final purpose of reason.

Aristotle saw matter in terms of potentiality, and observed that it was passive. Wood can be used to make a table or a chair, but the wood itself is passive. While it has the potentiality of becoming something, the actualization of this potentiality results only when man's mind is brought into the picture. Mind is the ability to actualize the potentiality of things. All changes in the universe come about as results of the combination of active mind and passive matter. Only God is pure mind, wholly independent of matter.

Aristotle reduced the study of natural phenomena to four basic problems, and taught that if we can solve these four problems, other questions are easily answered. He took as an example a portrait-statue. His first question was, "What is it made of?" If the material is marble, the fact that the statue exists is evidence that the marble had the potentiality of becoming a statue. The second question is, "Who made it?" Obviously a sculptor. The third question is, "What is the nature of its form?" Again, obviously, its form is that of a portrait-statue. The fourth question is, "What is the portrait-statue for; what was the purpose of making it?" It might be, for example, a statue to commemorate Socrates.

Of these questions the fourth is the most important one, because when we understand the purpose of the statue, we can also understand its nature. The sculptor could not have made a portrait of Socrates without a purpose in mind; the marble could not have become a statue until the purpose of the sculptor was brought to bear upon it. Thus the solution of the fourth problem provides answers to the other three.

The framework of Aristotle's philosophy was based on the science of his time. Out of this science he developed his idealism, and concluded that all of nature, both animate and inanimate, undergoes constant change in the direction of an ideal purpose, with the ultimate or final purpose being reason. First there is passive matter alone; then the action of mind upon matter; and eventually the full actualization of potential, and the achievement of the highest purpose.

Since Aristotle died more than three centuries before Jesus was born, and could not, therefore, have been a Christian, it is a matter of some interest that his philosophy was so enthusiastically adopted by the medieval church. We can only conclude that his scientific demonstration that reason is the essential nature of man and the ultimate purpose of all things afforded churchmen a ready tool with which to develop and strengthen their position. At any rate, the Catholic Church formulated its official theology within the framework of Aristotelian philosophy, identified God with Aristotle's concept of the Prime Mover, and interpreted its concept of the salvation of the soul in terms of achieving Aristotle's final purpose. In fact, the whole structure of Aristotle's philosophy was peculiarly congenial to Christian dogma, and this is undoubtedly the chief reason that his work has had such lasting influence on Western thought.

Aristotle's "Individual" and "Species"

In yesterday's lecture we mentioned Aristotle's treatment of the individual and the species. The individual creature comes into being and then ceases to be, often quite unpredictably; but the species of which it is a representative is permanent and unchanging. For example, the individual oak tree may grow old and die, or undergo other change, but the species of oak is eternal. Aristotle believed that since individual creatures undergo unpredictable change, they cannot be the basis of science. Science, for Aristotle, was a matter of universal principles, and not to be applied to individual objects or events. Hence science must deal with species, because a species resents the characteristics that are common to all the individual creatures which belong to it; a species is permanent and unchanging.

Aristotle saw the universe as being composed of innumerable species, each with its own nature, and each with its own degree of dignity. The inanimate earth, which has the least potentiality also has the lowest dignity, while God, who is mind, or reality, possesses the highest degree of dignity. There are unnumbered degrees of dignity between the highest and the lowest. We can return to our oak for an illustration of this system of the dignity of things: the species, oak, stands above the individual oak; creation stands above the species of oak, and God stands above creation. This was Aristotle's "natural system," a classification downward from the highest to the lowest.

Not only did each species, in Aristotle's scheme, have a different degree of dignity, but one species could not be changed for or into another. A creature belonging to species A cannot be made a member of species B. The oak will produce oak trees throughout eternity, but an oak will never produce an elm. Aristotle's insistence that science be concerned primarily with classifications, and that it must ignore disparate facts is the antithesis of modern philosophy of science. Some of Aristotle's present-day disciples are compounding the mistake he made so many centuries ago.

Aristotle's classificatory science and his theory about the relative dignity of species have been markedly influential on Western culture and thought. When barbarians from northern Europe sacked Rome, they adopted the external manifestations of Roman culture, but they did not encourage learning. In the early centuries of the Christian era, at least as far as Western Europe was concerned, such knowledge as men did have was unsystematized. When, in the eighth and ninth centuries, European scholars were seeking for means by which to systematize and extend knowledge, they rediscovered the works of Aristotle, and eagerly adopted what they understood to be his teachings. From the eleventh to the sixteenth century, a period of some six hundred years, Aristotle was as influential in the West as Confucius was in China.

While there has been some relative decrease in Aristotle's influence since the sixteenth century, it is to this day a tremendous factor in Western culture, particularly since the official doctrines of the Roman Catholic Church are cast in an Aristotelian mold, and study of Aristotle's work is mandatory for all the clergy, from the pope down to the parish priest.

Beginning in the sixteenth century experimental science developed rapidly, and many of the scientific discoveries contradicted assertions which Aristotle had made, and which, under the influence of the Church, had become official doctrine. Experimental science was a challenge to dogmatic theology, and the conflict became so intense that people spoke of the warfare between religion and science.

There are three major regards in which experimental science is at marked variance with Aristotelian philosophy. The first of these is that science finds that Aristotle's concept of the relative dignity of things is untenable. Experimental science is possible only when each fact is judged on its own merits, and not according to "a degree of dignity" which has been accorded to the species to which it belongs.

The second divergence is that Aristotle focussed his attention on the fixed object while it was at rest, and formulated his theories with reference to the idea that all change was in the direction of perfect form and under the guidance of final cause, while experimental science focusses attention on changing interrelationships and on energy in its many manifestations.

The third difference lies in Aristotle's preoccupation with universal concepts, while experimental science focusses on the individual object and phenomenon, using classification as a means of dealing with individual objects, not as an end in itself.

Aristotle in the Modern World

Just sixty years ago, Charles Robert Darwin published his *Origin of the Species* in which he advanced the thesis that all species of plants and animals had developed from earlier, simpler forms. This was the very antithesis of Aristotle's theory of the immutability of the species. Men of Aristotelian persuasion attacked Darwin's position and tried to refute it, while others defended Darwin with equal passion. The warfare between these opposing camps reached incredible heights of bitterness and mutual recrimination, the echoes of which have not yet died completely away.

A comparison with Confucius at this point may be instructive. We know that Confucius limited his concern to politics and ethics; but if he had incorporated a theory of science into his philosophy, as Aristotle did, he might have had a greater influence. Then if someone had come along and disproved the scientific theories of Confucius, and had thus automatically called into question the validity of his ethical and political theory, we can imagine how bitter the conflict between Confucius' supporters and his detractors might have been! But this struggle, which we can only imagine for China, was a harsh actuality in Europe when modern science did challenge Aristotle's theories.

With Aristotelianism as deeply ingrained as it was in sixteenth century Europe, it is not to be wondered at that experimental science was confronted with obstacles to its development. In a way, though, this was to the ultimate advantage of science. Scientists were put on their mettle; the greater the opposition they met, the more convincingly they had to demonstrate and present their discoveries; and the more they persisted in the face of difficulties, the more people came to prize science and to recognize it as a necessity.

Only fairly recently has China had any significant degree of contact with the modern Western world, so the conflict between traditional and contemporary philosophers has not been widespread or sharp, although it has not been completely avoided. Traditional Chinese thought was never organized and systematized to the degree that Aristotelianism had achieved in Europe, so that it could not react to contemporary innovations with the same ferocity that sixteenth century Europeans attacked the new experimental science. And it may be that this very fact, namely that there was no organized opposition to the introduction of experimental science into China, that accounts for the failure of the Chinese people to value science and to recognize its importance to life. The people of China appear to accept science as a field of knowledge; they recognize that it can help their country to prosper; but they are not yet aware of the many and significant ways in which science can influence man's spiritual life.

There is not time for me to say much about Aristotle's ethics and his political philosophy, but I will mention two points briefly. We have noted Aristotle's preoccupation with species, and his lack of concern with the individual. This same pattern prevails in his political philosophy, in which he focusses upon the state, and all but ignores the individual. He is much more concerned with social organizations, and with law and order, than he is with individual creative ability and the freedom of individual choice. This view, of course, is totally inconsistent with our own concept of democracy.

The second point I want to mention is that in his ethics, Aristotle taught that man differs from other animals because of his nature. And what is this nature? Man's real nature is reason, and the development of reason is the ultimate purpose of mankind. Perfect reason can be equated with pure knowledge—knowlege that is free from material considerations and human desire, knowledge that is pure contemplation and thought.

The other day when we were talking about Plato, we noted his insistence that the philosopher must not only discover the world of the real, but that he must also apply what he has discovered toward the improvement of life in the everyday world. After beholding the sunlight, the philosopher must return to the cave. Plato was saying that we must not only have ideals, but that we must put them into practice. Aristotle differed from his teacher on this, as on other points. For him the activity of contemplation was the ultimate good of life. He did not require that the philosopher return to the world of ordinary men, or make any application of whatever he achieved in his practice of contemplation.

In Europe the medieval church adapted two of Aristotle's ideas and incorporated them into its doctrine. Where Aristotle had made the state prior to the individual in importance, the church assumed for itself the position of prime importance, and taught that man must be dependent upon it for his welfare. And where Aristotle had characterized contemplation as the ultimate good of life, the church substituted otherworldliness, so that entry into heaven became the final purpose of human life.

However, to do justice to Aristotle, we should make it clear that the Aristotelianism that was so restrictive of thought and so inimical to the development of experimental science was a far cry from Aristotle's philosophy, and was the result of a monumental misunderstanding and misinterpretation of this philosophy. Aristotle's thinking itself was extremely broad and deep. He was the first great systematic thinker in history, and still one of the greatest. But the warped versions of his ideas which became ingrained in medieval European thought exerted a vicious and evil influence, and became an obstacle to intellectual and cultural development for hundeds of years.

The Chinese people tend to think that freedom of thought has existed in Western society for a long time, while oriental society has labored under the restrictions of traditional patterns of thought for millennia. As a matter of actual fact, however, western thought was shackled with a perverted Aristotelianism and dogmatic theology until quite recently. Human thinking cannot be emancipated without struggle; new modes of thinking must challenge the old, and be ready to contend with them. The one difference between you in the East and us in the West is that our emancipation from traditional outlooks and patterns of thinking came a century or so before yours did.